Praise for John Michael

John Michael Greer writes with unsurpassed clarity about the predicaments of energy and economy mankind faces. And he does it with a wonderfully kind, genial, and wise spirit.

—James Howard Kunstler, author, *The Long Emergency* and the *World Made by Hand* novels

The enormous virtue of John Michael Greer's work is that his wisdom is never conventional, but profound and imaginative.

—Sharon Astyk, author, *Depletion and Abundance* and *Independence Days*, www.SharonAstyk.com

When we find ourselves falling off the lofty peak of infinite progress, our civilization's mythology predisposes our imaginations to bypass reality altogether, and to roll straight for the equally profound abyss of the Apocalypse. Greer breaks this spell, and instead offers us a view on our deindustrial future that is both carefully reasoned and grounded in spirituality.

—Dmitry Orlov, author, *Reinventing Collapse* and *The Five Stages of Collapse*

Greer's work is nothing short of brilliant.

—Richard Heinberg, Senior Fellow, Post-Carbon Institute, and author, *The Party's Over* and *The End of Growth*

Greer … offers us not only an excellent read, but tangible tools for navigating the transition.

—Carolyn Baker, author, *Speaking Truth to Power*, www.CarolynBaker.net

DECLINE AND FALL

DECLINE
AND FALL

THE END OF EMPIRE
AND THE FUTURE
OF DEMOCRACY IN
21ST CENTURY AMERICA

JOHN MICHAEL GREER

new society
PUBLISHERS

Cover design by Diane McIntosh.
Cover image © Fotolia (brueckenweb)
Printed in Canada. First printing March 2014.

New Society Publishers acknowledges the financial support of
the Government of Canada through the Canada Book Fund (CBF)
for our publishing activities.

To order directly from the publishers, please call toll-free (North America)
1-800-567-6772, or order online at www.newsociety.com

Any other inquiries can be directed by mail to: ·

New Society Publishers
P.O. Box 189, Gabriola Island, BC V0R 1X0, Canada
(250) 247-9737

LIBRARY AND ARCHIVES CANADA CATALOGUING IN PUBLICATION

Greer, John Michael, author
Decline and fall : the end of empire and the future of
democracy in 21st century America / John Michael Greer.

Includes bibliographical references and index.
Issued in print and electronic formats.
ISBN 978-0-86571-764-0 (pbk.).— ISBN 978-1-55092-557-9 (ebook)

1. United States—Politics and government—21st century—
Forecasting.   2. United States—Economic conditions—21st century—
Forecasting.   3. United States—Social conditions—21st century—
Forecasting.   4. United States—Civilization—21st century—Forecasting.
5. Democracy—United States—Forecasting.   I. Title.

E893.G74 2014   973.93   C2013-907381-7
                                                          C2013-907409-0

New Society Publishers' mission is to publish books that contribute in fundamental
ways to building an ecologically sustainable and just society, and to do so with the
least possible impact on the environment, in a manner that models this vision. We
are committed to doing this not just through education, but through action. The
interior pages of our bound books are printed on Forest Stewardship Council®
registered acid-free paper that is **100% post-consumer recycled** (100% old growth
forest-free), processed chlorine-free, and printed with vegetable-based, low-VOC
inks, with covers produced using FSC®-registered stock. New Society also works to
reduce its carbon footprint, and purchases carbon offsets based on an annual audit
to ensure a carbon neutral footprint. For further information, or to browse our
full list of books and purchase securely, visit our website at: www.newsociety.com

Contents

PROLOGUE: UNDERSTANDING EMPIRE

T HE DECLINE AND IMMINENT FALL of America's global empire is the most important geopolitical fact in today's world. It is also the least discussed. Politicians, generals, diplomats, and intelligence analysts around the world are already wrestling with the immense challenges posed by America's accelerating downfall, and trying to position themselves and their countries to prosper—or at least to survive—in the impending chaos of a post-American world. Outside the corridors of power, by contrast, few people anywhere seem to be aware of the tsunami of change that is about to break over their heads.

That needs to change. This book is an attempt to start a conversation that needs to happen, especially, but not only, in America—a conversation about the end of American empire and what will come after it.

In order to make sense of the impact that the fall of America's empire is going to have on all our lives in the decades ahead, it is crucial to understand what empires are, what makes them tick, and what makes them collapse. To do that, however, it will be necessary to bundle up an assortment of unhelpful assumptions and misunderstandings of history and chuck them into the compost.

We can start with the verbal habit of using empire—or more exactly, the capitalized abstraction Empire—as what S. I. Hayakawa used to call a "snarl word":[1] a content-free verbal noise that's used to express feelings of hatred. The language of politics these days consists largely of snarl words. When people on the leftward end of the political spectrum say "fascist," or "Empire," for example, more often than not these words mean exactly what "socialist" or "liberal" mean to people on the right—that is, they express the emotional state of the speaker rather than anything relevant about the object under discussion. Behind this common habit is one of the more disturbing trends in contemporary political life: setting aside ordinary disagreement in favor of seething rage against a demonized Other on whom all the world's problems can conveniently be blamed.

The need to sidestep this habit makes it urgent to get past the currently popular custom of using terms like "Empire" as snarl words, and recover their actual meaning as descriptions of specific forms of human political, economic, and social interaction. Getting rid of that initial capital letter, arbitrary as it seems, is one step in the right direction. The younger President Bush's administration was able to disguise a stack of dubious motives and justify a misguided rush to war by converting the tangled reality of Muslim resentment and radical militancy into the capitalized abstraction of Terror. In a similar fashion, many people on the other side of the political spectrum have covered equally dubious motives and justified equally unproductive actions by converting the tangled realities of influence, authority, and privilege in modern industrial states into the capitalized abstraction of Empire. The so-called Global War on Terror, of course, turned out to be an expensive flop, and much of what passes for "fighting Empire," though a good deal less costly in blood and money, has been no more productive.

In this book, then, I will be discussing empires, not Empire, and as soon as some initial questions of definition are taken care of, I will be discussing specific empires—the one the United States currently maintains, primarily, but also the British Empire that preceded it, and several others that cast useful light on the American empire's past, present, and future. One striking detail, of course, sets today's American empire apart from most of its predecessors: the curious fact that the only people these days willing to admit in public that the United States has an empire are almost always those who denounce it.

That's a very rare thing in the history of empires. As recently as the late nineteenth century, the world's empires proudly claimed that title, and those who argued that the United States should hurry up and get an empire of its own saw no need to cover that ambition with euphemisms. The popular rhetoric of that era celebrated the huge European empires of the day—especially that of Britain, which covered a quarter of the planet's land surface and had effective control over all its oceans—and insisted that since imperial rule brought peace and the benefits of European civilization to the rest of the world, it was a good thing for all concerned.

This same case has been made in recent years by a handful of conservative intellectuals, notably the historian Niall Ferguson,[2] and a certain number of facts can be cited in its support. Periods when one imperial power dominates any given system of nations tend to be periods of relative peace and stability, while periods that lack such a centralized power tend to be racked by wars and turmoil. Imperial Britain's century of world dominion from 1815 to 1914, for example, featured fewer wars—in Europe, at least—than any comparable period up to that time, and American dominion since 1945 has imposed an even more rigid peace on that fractious continent.

Outside Europe, to be sure, the imperial rule of Britain was a good deal less peaceful, and that of the United States has not been much better. Furthermore, peace, stability, and a Victorian ideal of good government for the natives are not necessarily the only benefits by which to measure. By this I don't mean to bring up such intangibles as freedom and self-determination, though of course they also have a place in any meaningful moral calculus. The issue I have in mind is one of cold hard economics.

A broader view of history may be useful here. The first explorers to venture outwards from Europe into the wider world encountered civilizations that were far wealthier than anything back home. After returning to Italy from the Far East in 1295, Marco Polo was mocked as "Marco Millions" for stories of China's vast riches, which later travelers found to be largely accurate. When the Portuguese explorer Vasco da Gama made the first European voyage around the southern tip of Africa and on to India in 1497, he and his crew were stunned by the extraordinary prosperity of the Indian society they encountered. When Hernán Cortes reached the Aztec capitol of Tenochtitlán in 1519, similarly, it was easily among the most populous cities on the planet—current estimates range from 200,000 to 300,000 within the city alone, and another million in the urban region surrounding it—as well as one of the richest.

A few centuries later, at the zenith of Europe's age of empire, China, India, and Mexico ranked among the world's poorest nations, while England, which had been a soggy backwater on the fringes of Europe known mostly for codfish and wool, was one of its richest. In 1600, for example, India accounted for an estimated 24 percent of the world's gross domestic product, while all of Britain managed around 3 percent.[3] Three centuries later India was among the most poverty-stricken nations on Earth, while England had become the center of the global economy.

Plenty of reasons have been advanced for this astonishing reversal, but there are times when the obvious explanation is also the correct one, and this is one of those. To make the point more clearly, consider that the 5 percent of humanity that lives in the United States of America uses around a quarter of the world's energy and roughly a third of its raw materials and industrial product. This disproportionate share of the world's wealth doesn't come to us because the rest of the world doesn't want such things, or because the United States manufactures some good or provides some service so desirable to the rest of the world that other nations vie with each other to buy it from us. Quite the contrary; the United States produced very little during much of its empire's most prosperous period, and the rest of the world's population is by and large just as interested in energy, raw materials, and industrial product as Americans are.

It's considered distinctly impolite to suggest that the real reason behind the disparity is related to the fact that the United States has more than five hundred military bases on other nations' territory, and spends on its armed forces every year roughly the same amount as the military budgets of every other nation on Earth put together. Here again, though, the obvious explanation is the correct one. Between 1945 and 2008, the United States was the world's dominant imperial power, filling the same role in the global political system that Britain filled during its own age of empire, and while that imperial arrangement had plenty of benefits, by and large they flowed in one direction only.

With this in mind, we can move to a meaningful definition of empire. An empire is an arrangement among nations, backed and usually imposed by military force, which extracts wealth from a periphery of subject nations and concentrates it in the imperial core. Put more simply, an empire is a wealth pump, a device to enrich one nation at the expense of others. The mechanism of the pump varies from empire to empire and from age to age; the straightforward exaction of tribute that did the job for ancient Egypt, and had another vogue in the time of imperial Spain, has been replaced in most of the more recent empires by somewhat less blatant though equally effective systems of unbalanced exchange. While the mechanism varies, though, the underlying principle does not.

None of this would have raised any eyebrows at all in a discussion of the mechanics of empire, in America or elsewhere, during the late nineteenth century. Such discussions took place, in the mass media of the time as well as in the corridors of power, and it was widely understood that the point to having an empire was precisely that it made your nation rich. That's why the United States, after a series of bitter public debates that will be discussed in a later chapter, committed itself to the path of empire in the 1890s, and it's why every nation in western Europe either had or desperately wanted an overseas empire—even Belgium had its own little vest pocket empire in Africa, and exploited it ruthlessly.[4]

The near-total domination of the world by European empires in the eighteenth and nineteenth centuries, in conjunction with the popular racism of the time—Kipling's pompous blather about "the white man's burden"[5] was embarrassingly typical for its era— has given rise in some circles to the notion that there's something uniquely European or, more precisely, uniquely white about empire. In reality, of course, the peoples of Europe and the European diaspora were by and large Johnny-come-latelies to the business of empire.

Ancient Egypt, as already mentioned, was as creative in this as in so many other of the arts of civilization, and had a thriving empire that extended far south along the Nile and north along the Mediterranean coast. The great arc of city-states that extended from modern Turkey through the Tigris and Euphrates valleys and the mountains and plateaus further east to the Indus Valley gave rise to dozens of empires at a time when Europe was a patchwork of illiterate tribal societies whose inhabitants still thought bronze was high tech. China had its own ancient and highly successful empire, and half a dozen other east Asian nations copied the Chinese model and pursued their own dreams of imperial expansion and enrichment. Sub-Saharan Africa had at least a dozen great empires, while the Aztecs were only the latest in a long history of Native American empires as splendid and predatory as anything the Old World had to offer. Empire is one of the most common patterns by which nations relate to one another, and emerges spontaneously whenever one nation has a sufficient preponderance of power to exploit another.

Empires have thus been around for a long time. The evidence of history suggests that they show up promptly once agriculture becomes stable and sophisticated enough to support urban centers, and go away only when urban life also breaks down. Anyone interested in tracking the rise and fall of empires thus has anything up to five thousand years of fairly detailed information from the Old World, and well over three thousand years from the New—plenty of data, one might think, for a coherent picture to emerge.

Unfortunately one major difficulty stands in the way of such a picture: empires attract doubletalk the way a dead rat attracts flies. Some of the doubletalk comes from rival power centers, outside the empire du jour or within it, that hope to excuse their own ambitions by painting that empire in the least complimentary colors that can be found, but an even larger amount gets produced by empires themselves—or, more exactly, by the tame intellectuals that empires produce and employ in numbers as large as the imperial economy can support. Between the doubletalk meant to make any given empire seem much worse than its rivals, and the doubletalk meant to make the same empire seem much better than its rivals, accurate understanding is an early casualty.

At the beginning of this chapter, I mentioned a few examples of the first class of doubletalk. Examples of the second are just as easy to come by, but one that's particularly relevant here is that shibboleth of contemporary economics, free trade. That term has become so thickly encrusted with handwaving and deliberate disinformation that it probably needs to be defined here. As I'm using it, it means a system of international exchange that prohibits governments from taxing or prohibiting the movement of goods, services, or money across borders.

Pick up an introductory textbook of economics, though, and your chances of finding an objective assessment of free trade are very low indeed. Instead, what you'll find between the covers is a ringing endorsement of free trade, usually phrased in the most crudely propagandistic of terms. Most likely it will rehash the arguments originally made by British economist David Ricardo in the early 19th century to prove that free trade inevitably encourages every nation to develop whatever industries are best suited to its circumstances, and so produces more prosperity for everybody.[6] Those arguments will usually be spiced up with whatever more recent additions appeal to the theoretical tastes of the textbook's author or authors, and will plop the whole discussion into a historical narrative that insists that once upon a time, there were silly people who didn't like free trade, but now we all know better.

What inevitably gets omitted from the textbook is any discussion, based on actual historical examples, of the way that free trade works out in practice That would be awkward, because in the real world, throughout history, free trade consistently hasn't done what Ricardo's rhetoric and today's economics textbooks claim it will do. Instead, it amplifies the advantages of wealthy nations and the disadvantages of poorer ones, concentrating capital and income in the hands of those who already have plenty of both while squeezing out potential rivals and forcing wages down across the board. This is why every nation in history that's ever developed a significant industrial sector to its economy has done so by rejecting the ideology of free trade, and building its industries behind a protective wall of tariffs, trade barriers, and capital controls, while those nations that have listened to the advice of the tame economists of the British and American empires have one and all remained mired in poverty and dependence as long as they did so.

There's a rich irony here, because not much more than a century ago, a healthy skepticism toward the claims of free trade ideology used to be standard in the United States. At that time, Britain filled the role in the world system that the United States fills today, complete with the global empire, the gargantuan military with annual budget to match, and the endless drumbeat of brushfire wars across what would one day be called the Third World. British economists were accordingly the world's loudest proponents of free trade, while the United States filled the role of rising industrial power that China fills today, complete with sky-high trade barriers that protected its growing industries and a distinctly cavalier attitude toward intellectual property laws.

When it comes to free trade and its alternatives, that level of understanding is nowhere near so common these days, at least in the United States. I've long suspected that businessmen and officials in Beijing have a very precise understanding of what free trade actually means, though it would hardly be to their advantage just now to talk about that with any degree of candor. On this side of the Pacific, by contrast, even those who speak most enthusiastically about relocalization and the end of corporate globalism apparently haven't noticed how effectively tariffs, trade barriers, and capital controls foster domestic industries and rebuild national economies—or perhaps it's that too many of them aren't willing to consider paying the kind of prices for their iPods and Xboxes that would follow the enactment of a reasonable tariff: the prices, in other words, that would be required if we had the trade barriers that built the American economy and could build it again, and if American workers were paid American wages to provide American consumers with their goods and services.

Free trade is simply one of the mechanisms of empire in the age of industrialism, one part of the wealth pump that concentrated the wealth of the globe in Britain during the years of its imperial dominion and does the same thing for the benefit of the United States today. Choose any other mechanism of empire, from the web of military treaties that lock allies and subject nations into a condition of dependence on the imperial center, through the immense benefits that accrue to whatever nation issues the currency in which international trade is carried out, to the way that the charitable organizations of the imperial center— missionary churches in Queen Victoria's time, for example, or humanitarian non-governmental organizations in ours—further the agenda of empire with such weary predictability. In every case, you'll find a haze of doubletalk surrounding a straightforward exercise of imperial domination. It requires a keen eye to look past the rhetoric and pay attention to the direction the benefits flow.

Follow the flow of wealth and you understand empire. That's true in a general and a more specific sense, and both of these have their uses. In the general sense, paying attention to shifts in wealth between the imperial core and the nations subject to it is an essential antidote to the sort of nonsense, popular among the tame intellectuals previously mentioned and their audiences in the imperial core, that imagines empire as a sort of social welfare program for conquered nations. Whether it's some old pukka sahib talking about how the British Empire brought railroads and good government to India, or his American neoconservative equivalent talking about how the United States ought to export the blessings of democracy and the free market to the Middle East, it's codswallop, and the easiest way to see that it's codswallop is to notice that the price paid for those exports normally amounts to the systematic impoverishment of the subject nation.

In the specific sense, flows of wealth can be used to trace out the structure of empire, which is a more complex matter than the basic outline discussed so far might make it seem. It's entirely possible that long ago, when empires were new, there might have been one or two that consisted, on the level of nations, of a single imperial nation and a circle of subject nations; and on the level of populations, of a single ruling class and an undifferentiated mass of oppressed subjects. Nowadays, by contrast, an imperial system normally involves at least four distinct categories of nations, and an even more complex set of population divisions.

On the level of nations, the imperial nation is in a category of its own. Around it is the second layer, an inner circle of allied nations, who support the empire in exchange for a share of the spoils. The third category consists of subject nations, the cash cows that the empire milks, and in due time will milk dry. Finally, around the periphery, are enemy nations that oppose the empire in peace and war. In theory, at least, this last category shouldn't be necessary, but it may not be accidental that when an empire loses one enemy, the usual response is to go shopping for another.

On the level of populations, the sort of crudely manipulative rhetoric that divides an elite 1 percent from an oppressed 99 percent is a formidable barrier to understanding. An empire that tried to manage its affairs along those lines would fall in weeks. From ancient Rome to modern Washington, DC, "divide and conquer" has always been the basic strategy of empire, and the classic way to do that in modern times is to hand out shares of wealth and privilege unequally to different sectors of the population. The British Empire turned this into an art form, using arbitrary privileges and exclusions of various kinds to keep ethnic groups in each subject nation so irritated at one another that they never got around to uniting against the British. From the simmering rivalry between India and Pakistan, through the troubles of Northern Ireland, to the bitter mutual hatreds of Israelis and Arabs in what used to be British Palestine, the ethnic hatreds whipped up deliberately for the sake of Britain's imperial advantage remain a live issue today.

These same divisions can be traced out within the imperial nation as well, and readily make hash out of any attempt to sort things out along the simplistic "us and them" lines favored by so many political activists these days. In contemporary America, for example, different sectors of the population are subject to the same sort of privileges and exclusions that defined so much of life in British India. If you're an American citizen, the average annual income of your parents is a more exact predictor of your own income than any other factor, but your gender, your skin color, the location on the urban-rural spectrum of the neighborhood where you grew up, and a great many other arbitrary factors have far more to say about your prospects in life than America's egalitarian ideology would suggest.

Still, there's more going on here than simple manipulation from the top down. Within an imperial system, different nations and population groups are always competing against one another for a larger share of the wealth and privilege that empires make available. That happens on the scale of nations, for example, when a subject nation in a strategic location becomes an ally, or when an ally—as America did in 1945—supplants the former imperial center and takes the empire for its own. It also happens on the scale of populations, and on smaller scales still.

The ruling class of any nation, for example, consists of a loose alliance of power centers, held together by the pressures of mutual advantage, but constantly pursuing their own divergent interests and eagerly trying to claim a larger share of power and wealth at the expense of the other power centers. There are always families, factions, and social groups clawing their way up into the ruling class from the levels immediately below it, and others losing their grip on power and slipping down the pyramid. Outside the ruling class is an even more complex constellation of groups who support the power centers within the ruling class, who expect to receive wealth and privileges in return for their support, and who rise and fall in their own intricate rhythm. Proceed step by step down the pyramid, and you'll find the same complexities in place all the way down to the bottom, where a flurry of ethnic, cultural, and social groups compete with one another over whose oppression ought to get the most attention from middle-class liberals.

On the level of nations or that of populations, in other words, it's neither possible nor useful to divide the structure of empire into the simplistic categories of oppressor and oppressed, ruler and ruled. Many nations in any imperial system fall between the summit and the base of the pyramid, and are thereby permitted to pump wealth out of nations lower down on the condition that they forward part of the take further up. The vast majority of people in the imperial nation and its allies, and even some of those in the most heavily exploited subject nations, receive a share of wealth and privilege in exchange for their cooperation in maintaining the imperial system, compete constantly for a bigger share, and generally limit their criticisms of the imperial system to those aspects of it that profit somebody else. That's why empires have proven to be so enduring a human social form; the basic toolkit of empire includes an ample assortment of ways to buy the loyalty, or at least the passive acquiescence, of all those potential power centers that might otherwise try to destabilize the imperial system and bring the empire crashing down.

Yet empires do come crashing down, of course. The fact that the form has proven to be enduring has not given a comparable endurance to any individual empire. Britons during Victoria's reign liked to boast that the sun never set on the British Empire. (That may have been, as the Irish liked to suggest, because God Himself wouldn't trust an Englishman in the dark.) Still, the sun did set on that empire in due time, and once the sunset started, it proceeded with remarkable speed. Children who were just old enough to remember the celebration of Victoria's diamond jubilee in 1897, when the empire was not far from its zenith, had not yet reached retirement age when the last tattered scraps of that empire went whistling down the wind.

It sometimes happens that the fall of the last major empire in any given civilization is also the fall of that civilization, and a certain amount of confusion has come about because of this. The fall of Rome, for example, was the end of an empire, but it was also the end of a civilization that was flourishing long before the city of Rome was founded—a civilization that had seen plenty of empires come and go by the time Rome rose past regional-power status to dominate the Mediterranean world. The example of Rome's decline and fall, though, became so central to later attempts to understand the cycles of history that most such attempts in the modern Western world equated empire and civilization, and the fall of the one with that of the other.

That's the principal blind spot in the writings of Oswald Spengler and Arnold Toynbee, the two great theorists of historical cycles the modern Western world has produced.[7] Spengler and Toynbee each argued that the natural endpoint of what Spengler called a culture and Toynbee a civilization was a single sprawling empire—a Universal State, in Toynbee's phrase—in which every previous movement of the culture or civilization that preceded it reached its completion, fossilization, and death. A barely concealed political subtext guided both authors; Spengler, formulating his theory before and during the First World War, believed that the German Empire would become the nucleus around which Faustian (that is, Western) culture would coalesce into the rigor mortis of civilization; Toynbee, who began his *A Study of History* in the 1920s and saw its last volumes in print in 1954, believed that an Anglo-American alliance would become that nucleus. In each case, national aspirations clearly undergirded scholarly predictions.

Yet it bears remembering that a Universal State along Roman lines is only one of the options. Plenty of successful civilizations— the ancient Mayans are one example of many—never came under the rule of a single imperial power at all. Others, such as the civilization of ancient Mesopotamia, had empires succeeding one another every century or two all through the latter part of their histories, so that no one empire put its stamp on the civilization the way that Rome did on the ancient Mediterranean world. Other civilizations had their own ways of dealing with the phenomenon of empire, and so a distinction needs to be made between the fall of empires and that of civilizations.

I've argued at length elsewhere that what drives the decline and fall of societies is a process that I've termed catabolic collapse.[8] This unfolds from an inevitable mismatch between the maintenance costs of capital—that is, how much economic activity has to be put into maintaining all the things that societies create and collect—and the resource base needed to meet the maintenance costs of capital. Since capital tends to increase steadily over time, but resources are always subject to natural limits, every society sooner or later finds itself with more capital than it can maintain, and that tips it into a maintenance crisis: basically, a loss of capital, usually made worse by conflict over who gets to keep how much of their existing shares.

Empires suffer from the ordinary form of catabolic collapse, just like any other form of human social organization complex enough to accumulate capital. Yet they have their own specific version of the phenomenon, and it's generally this specific form that brings them down. To understand how empires collapse, two things have to be kept in mind. The first is the core concept of catabolic collapse just mentioned—the mismatch between maintenance costs and available resources. The second is the definition of empire introduced above—that an empire is a wealth pump, a system of economic arrangements backed by military force that extracts wealth from subject nations and concentrates it in the imperial core.

Imperial rhetoric down through the centuries normally includes the claim that the imperial power takes only a modest fraction of the annual production of wealth from its subject nations, and provides services such as peace, good government, and trade relations that more than make up for the cost. As already noted, this is hogwash; it's popular hogwash among those who profit from empire, but it's hogwash nonetheless. Historically speaking, the longer an empire lasts, the poorer its subject nations normally get, and the harder the empire's tame intellectuals have to work to invent explanations for that impoverishment that don't include the reasons that matter. Consider the vast amount of rhetorical energy expended by English intellectuals in the 19th century, for example, to find reasons for Ireland's grinding poverty other than England's systematic expropriation of every scrap of Irish wealth that wasn't firmly nailed down.

This sort of arrangement has predictable effects on capital and maintenance costs. The buildup of capital in the imperial center goes into overdrive, churning out the monumental architecture, the collections of art and antiquities, the extravagant lifestyles, and the soaring costs of living that have been constant features of life in an imperial capital since imperial capitals were invented. The costs of building and maintaining all this accumulation, not to mention the considerable maintenance costs of empire itself—the infrastructure of empire counts as capital, and generally very expensive capital at that—are exported to the subject nations by whatever set of mechanisms the empire uses to pump wealth inward to the center. Over the short to middle term, this is an extremely profitable system, since it allows the imperial center to wallow in wealth while all the costs of that wealth are borne elsewhere.

It's over the middle to long term that the problems with this neat arrangement show up. The most important of these difficulties is that the production of wealth in any society depends on a feedback loop in which a portion of each year's production becomes part of the capital needed to produce wealth in future years, and another portion of each year's production—a substantial one—goes to meet the maintenance costs of existing productive capital.

In theory, an empire could keep its exactions at a level which would leave this feedback loop unimpaired. In practice, no empire ever does so, which is one of the two primary reasons why the subject nations of an empire become more impoverished over time. (Plain old-fashioned looting of subject nations by their imperial rulers is the other.) As the subject nation's ability to produce and maintain productive capital decreases, so does its capacity to produce wealth, and that cuts into the ability of the empire to make its subject nations cover its own maintenance costs. A wealth pump is great, in other words, until it pumps the reservoir dry.

The wealth of subject nations, in other words, is a nonrenewable resource for empires, and empires thus face the same sort of declining returns on investment as any other industry dependent on nonrenewable resources. It's thus predictable that the most frequent response to declining returns is an exact analogue of the "drill, baby, drill" mentality so common in today's petroleum-dependent nations. The drive to expand at all costs that dominates the foreign policy of so many empires is thus neither accidental nor a symptom of the limitless moral evil with which empires are so often credited by their foes. For an empire that's already drained its subject nations to the point that the wealth pump is sputtering, a policy of "invade, baby, invade" is a matter of economic necessity, and often of national survival.

The difficulty faced by such a policy, of course, is the same one that always ends up clobbering extractive economies dependent on nonrenewable resources: the simple and immovable fact that the world is finite. That's what did in the Roman Empire, for example.[9] Since it rose and fell in an age less addicted to euphemisms than ours, Rome's approach to extracting wealth from subject nations was straightforward. Once a nation was conquered by Rome, it was systematically looted of movable wealth by the conquerors, while local elites were allowed to buy their survival by serving as collection agents for tribute. Next, the land was confiscated a chunk at a time so it could be handed out as retirement bonuses to legionaries who had served their twenty year terms of service. Then some pretext was found for exterminating the local elites and installing a Roman governor. Thereafter, the heirs of the legionaries were forced out or bought out, and the land sold to investors in Rome, who turned it into vast corporate farms worked by slaves.

Each of those transformations brought a pulse of wealth back home to Rome, but the income from conquered provinces tended to decline over time, and once it reached the final stage, the end was in sight. Hand over farmland to absentee investors who treat it purely as a source of short term profit, and whether you live in ancient Rome or modern America, the results you're going to get include inadequate long-term investment, declining soil fertility, and eventual abandonment. To keep the wealth pump running, the empire had to grow, and grow it did, until finally it included every nation that belonged to the ancient Mediterranean economic and cultural sphere, from the tin mines of Britain to the rich farms of the upper Nile.

That's when things began to go wrong, because the drive to expand was still there but the opportunities for expansion were not. Attempts to expand northward into Scotland, Germany, and the Balkans ran headlong into two awkward facts: first, the locals didn't have enough wealth to make an invasion pay for itself, and second, the locals had the kind of tribal societies that fostered Darwinian selection among their young men via incessant warfare, and quickly found that a nice brisk game of "Raid the Romans" made a pleasant addition to the ordinary round of cattle raids and blood feuds.

Expansion to the south was closed off by the Sahara Desert, while to the east, the Parthian Empire had the awkward habit of annihilating Roman armies sent to conquer it. Thus Roman imperial expansion broke down; attempts to keep the wealth pump running anyway stripped the provinces of their productive capital and pushed the Roman economic system into a death spiral. The imperial government stumbled from one fiscal and military crisis to another, until finally the Dark Ages closed in.

The same process can be traced throughout the history of empires. England's rule over India, once the jewel in the crown of the British Empire, is an example already considered. In the last years of British India, it was a common complaint in the English media that India no longer paid her own way. Until a few decades earlier, India had paid a great deal more than her own way; income to the British government from Queen Victoria's Indian possessions had covered a sizable fraction of the costs of the entire British Empire, and colossal private fortunes were made in India so frequently that they gave rise to an entire class of *nouveaux-riches* Englishmen, the so-called Nabobs.

It took the British Empire, all in all, less than two centuries to run India's economy into the ground and turn what had been one of the world's richest and most productive countries into one of its poorest. Attempts to expand the British Empire into new territory were ongoing all through the 19th and very early 20th centuries, but ran up against difficulties like those that stymied Rome's parallel efforts most of two millennia before. Those areas that could be conquered, such as eastern Africa, didn't yield enough plunder to make the process sufficiently lucrative; where conquest would have been hugely profitable, such as China, British imperial ambitions ran up against stiff competition from other empires, and had to settle for a fraction of the take. Neither option provided enough income to keep the British Empire from unraveling.

The short-lived Soviet empire in Eastern Europe provides another example. In the wake of the Second World War, Russian soldiers installed Marxist puppet governments in every nation they overran, and the Soviet government proceeded to impose wildly unbalanced "trade agreements" that amounted to the wholesale looting of eastern Europe for Russian benefit. Much of the Soviet Union's rapid recovery from wartime devastation and its rise to near-parity with the United States can be assigned to that very lucrative policy of pillage. Once the supply of plunder ran short, so did the Soviet economy's capacity to function. Efforts to expand into new territory ran into the usual difficulties, and when the price of oil crashed in the mid-1980s, depriving the Soviet system of much of the hard currency that kept it afloat, collapse followed promptly.

The United States, as I hope to show, is being driven by the same forces along the same trajectory toward imperial bankruptcy and collapse. Like the empires just described, and many others as well, it has become economically and politically dependent on a set of unbalanced relationships that extract wealth from much of the world and concentrate it here at home. The specific form taken by those relationships, however, unfolds from the unusually complex history of America's empire, and the equally complex history of the language we use to talk about empires and other political arrangements in today's world.

PART ONE

THE COURSE OF EMPIRE

1
ORIGINS OF AMERICAN EMPIRE

UNTIL THE EIGHTEENTH CENTURY, in the Western world as elsewhere around the planet, the core language of political rhetoric came from religion. From monarchs who based their claims to legitimacy on theories of the divine right of kings, straight across the spectrum to revolutionaries who borrowed the rhetoric of Old Testament prophets to call for the slaughter of the rich, political argument drew its terms primarily from theology's vision of an eternal order imperfectly reflected in the material cosmos. Conservatives argued that the existing structure of society more or less mirrored God's order, or would do so if liberals would only shut up and behave. Liberals argued that the existing structure of society was moving toward a more perfect reflection of God's order, and would get there more quickly if conservatives would only stop dragging their heels. Radicals on both ends of the spectrum argued that the existing structure of society was in utter conflict with God's order, and had to be terminated with extreme prejudice (along with liberals and conservatives) so that a new and perfect world could come into being.

The displacement of religion by secular ideologies in the eighteenth and nineteenth centuries left all three of these basic political viewpoints in place, but levered them neatly off their theological foundations, leaving their adherents scrambling to find new justifications. The standard response, then as now, was to force history to play theology's role. Whenever a political question comes up for debate, as a result, it's a safe bet to assume that all sides will immediately drag in canned historical narratives that have been stretched and lopped to fit a theological opposition between good and evil, so that they can tar their opponents by associating them with history's villains (to the contemporary American right, socialists; to the contemporary American left, fascists) and wrap themselves in the mantle of history's good guys.

Thus it's rare to see any public discussion of historical events these days that doesn't fixate on distinguishing the good guys from the bad guys. On the rare occasions when this is attempted, the first reaction of a great many listeners or readers is to figure out how to cram what's been said back into that same simplistic moral dualism. While there's a point to applying ethical philosophy to history, there are whole worlds of understanding that can't be reached so long as the only topic of discussion is who was right and who was wrong. The moral dimensions of American empire, therefore, will be left to my readers to judge for themselves.

Still, as already noted, these difficulties of language are only one of the obstacles to clarity in discussing the rise and fall of American empire. Another comes out of the unusually complex history of American empire, and that in turn unfolds from the fact that the United States of America may be a single political unit but it has never been a single culture or, really, a single country. The fault lines that have split America repeatedly for more than three centuries can be traced back to the European settlement of the continent's eastern seaboard. We will start there.

When the first waves of colonists from western and central Europe arrived on the Atlantic shores of North America in the 17th century, none of them seem to have realized that they were the beneficiaries of a cataclysm. Around the periphery of the Old

World, the European voyages of discovery found crowded nations with no spare territory for migrants, but the Americas and
Australasia seemed all but empty. The native peoples of all three
continents have reasonably enough objected to this description—
after all, they were there—but the perception of empty space wasn't
simply propaganda. It reflected the aftermath of the most appalling
demographic disaster in recorded history.[1]

The accident of plate tectonics that opened oceanic barriers
between the Old and New Worlds had an impact on disease that
wasn't well understood until quite recently. Most of the world's
serious human pathogens came to our species from domestic live-
stock, and nearly all of that happened in the Old World, because
Eurasia and Africa happened to have many more species suitable
for domestication than the New World did. One at a time, over the
tens of millennia between the closing of the Bering land bridge
and the voyages of Columbus, pathogens found their way from
animal vectors into the human population, epidemics swept the
Old World, and the survivors gradually acquired resistance. Those
pathogens didn't cross the ocean to the New World until the first
European ships made the crossing, but when they did, they hit
the native people of the Americas all at once. Within a century of
1492, as a result, native populations collapsed to 10 percent or less
of their pre-contact levels.

The scale of the die-off can be measured by a simple fact still
rarely mentioned outside of the specialist literature: in 1500, the
Amazon jungle as we now know it did not exist.[2] At that time,
and for many centuries before, the Amazon basin was a thickly
settled agricultural region full of sizeable cities and towns. The
first Spanish explorers to travel down the Amazon described it in
these terms, which were dismissed as fables by later writers who
knew only the "green hell" of the post-collapse Amazon. Only
in the last two decades or so have sophisticated archeological
studies shown that the conquistadors were right and their critics
wrong.

The same collapse swept the eastern seaboard of North America, where settled farming villages were established by 2000 BCE, and complex agricultural societies with rich political, cultural, and religious traditions thrived for many centuries before 1492. (A thousand years before the founding of Jamestown, the level of cultural sophistication among the Chesapeake Bay tribes was higher than that found at the same time among the inhabitants of England in the dark ages.)[3] After a century of die-off, the survivors were scattered across a mostly vacant landscape. That was the situation that the first waves of European colonists encountered. They told themselves they were settling in a wilderness, but they were quite wrong: they were arriving in a land that had been settled and farmed for countless generations before their time, and they benefited immensely from the legacies of the peoples whose surviving descendants they elbowed out of the way. The resulting assumption that every future frontier would be just as hospitable as the one they originally seized was to become a fertile source of misunderstanding and misjudgment for centuries thereafter.

Compared to cramped and crowded Europe, the eastern seaboard of North America seemed unimaginably vast—the distance between the two early colonies at Jamestown and Plymouth is greater than the entire length of England from the cliffs of Dover to the border with Scotland—and the sheer impact of space, together with sharp differences in climate and even sharper differences in the people who came to settle, drove the newly founded colonies in radically different directions. In what would become New England, English religious minorities made up much of the first wave of arrivals, and the society they built replicated 17th century English rural society as closely as the new environment would permit.

The resulting patterns of rural settlement proved impossible to transplant further into the country, which is why rural New England remains something of a world unto itself, but it was no accident that the Industrial Revolution got started in New England not much later than it did in the English Midlands. The same cultural forms that drove industrialization at home did much the same thing in the transplanted society, and the industrial society that emerged out of the transformation spread westwards as the country did.

Far to the south, in the band of settlement that started at Jamestown, matters were different. The settlers in what became the tidewater South weren't religious minorities fleeing discrimination, by and large; they were employees of English magnates, and they simply wanted, like their masters, to make as much money as possible. From Chesapeake Bay south, the climate was suited to growing tobacco, which like most drugs was a hugely lucrative cash crop; after a few generations, cotton joined tobacco, and the basic pattern of antebellum Southern life was set. Sprawling plantations worked first by indentured servants shipped over from Britain and Ireland, and then by slaves shipped over from Africa, became the defining human ecology along the southern half of the coast, and spread inland wherever climate and topography allowed.

Between New England and the tidewater South lay a poorly defined intermediate zone, a scattering of small colonies—New Jersey, Delaware, Maryland—and two very large ones, Pennsylvania and New York. Maryland and Delaware were mostly tidewater and might have gone the Southern path, while Pennsylvania, New York, and New Jersey weren't and might have gone the New England path, but Pennsylvania and Maryland enacted religious liberty statutes early on and welcomed all comers, so the middle zone got dealt a couple of wild cards that ended up transforming the entire colonial enterprise.

Those unexpected factors consisted of a torrent of religious and political refugees from central Europe, who fled the aftermath of the Thirty Years War, and a flood of economic and political refugees from northern Ireland, who fled England's tightening grip on her first and most thoroughly plundered imperial colony. West of Chesapeake Bay lay the Potomac valley, one of the few easy routes into the mountains, and it's likely that somewhere up that way—by the nature of the thing, nobody will ever know when or where—German and Scots-Irish traditions blended with scraps of a dozen other ethnic heritages to create the first draft of American frontier culture. Think log cabins and long rifles, homespun cloth and home-brewed liquor, a fierce habit of local independence and an equally fierce disdain for the cultures of the coast, and all the rest: that's where it came from, and it spread westward along a wide front from the Great Lakes to the middle South.

All this ought to be part of any basic course in American history, though as often as not it gets lost in the teach-to-the-soundbites frenzy that passes for education in America these days. What doesn't get in even in those rare schools that teach history worth the name, though, is that these three nascent American cultures— call them New England, Tidewater, and Frontier cultures, if you like—also define three modes of expansion, two imperial and one much less so.

The first mode is the New England industrial model, which spread west to the Great Lakes early on and trickled gradually southward from there. It's one of the shibboleths of modern thought that industrial systems create wealth, but as Alf Hornborg pointed out usefully some years ago in *The Power of the Machine*,[4] they are at least as important as a means of concentrating wealth. In an industrial system, the income that would have gone to a large number of small proprietors and skilled craftspeople in a nonindustrial society goes instead to the very small minority with the money and political connections to build and run factories, control access to raw materials and energy resources, and the like.

An industrial economy thus functions as an internal empire, running a wealth pump of its own to extract wealth from the majority for the benefit of factory owners and stockholders. This is why every nation on Earth that has ever built an industrial economy within a free market system ended up polarized between vast fortunes on the one hand and a relatively impoverished working class on the other. That's the New England model, as well as the English model, and it drives a very specific kind of imperial expansion, in which sources of raw materials, on the one hand, and markets where industrial products can be exported, on the other, are the central targets of empire.

The second mode is the Southern plantation model, which spread due west from the tidewater country. The plantation model was a straightforward export economy in the orbit of the rising British industrial system. Cotton from Southern plantations was eagerly sought by the textile mills of the English Midlands, and the political economy of the cotton belt morphed into a pattern that ought to be profoundly familiar to Americans today, though it's generally not: it's the pattern found today in Third World nations under American or European domination, in which raw materials for industry overseas are produced under harsh conditions by a vast and impoverished labor force, while a small upper class is well rewarded for keeping the system running smoothly. That's the Tidewater model, and it drives a very different mode of imperial expansion, in which arable land and cheap labor are the central targets of empire.

The frontier model is something else again. It also had a powerful expansionist dynamic, but it was egalitarian rather than hierarchical, and didn't provide anybody with a convenient place to hook up a wealth pump. What frontier culture craved from expansion was simply real estate, where people could build a cabin, break the sod, plant crops, and make a life for themselves. Over time, as the model ripened and values shifted, it gave rise to a vision of American expansion in which an entire continent would be seeded first with frontier homesteads, then with prosperous farms and nascent towns, and replicate political and economic democracy straight across to the Pacific. What would happen once that limit was reached was a question very few Americans asked themselves. Before that point, though, these three cultures had to sort out their relative strength and influence on the new American nation.

The three settlement patterns that unfolded from the competing New England, Tidewater, and frontier cultures were anything but fixed. By the time they had finished taking shape, they were already blurring into one another at the edges, and responding in various ways to the new influences brought by further waves of immigration. Still, the patterns are worth watching, because they played a significant role in shaping the modes of expansion that would define its age of empire in a later century.

The New England pattern, as already mentioned, had two sides with profoundly different possibilities for expansion. While many people from rural New England moved westward with the frontier, nearly all of them abandoned the settlement patterns of their home for the freer, more flexible frontier way of doing things; the village greens, town meetings and Puritan attitudes of the New England countryside sparked few imitations elsewhere. The waterwheels and shipyards of New England's nascent mill towns and cities turned out to be a more enduring contribution, driving the first wave of an industrial revolution parallel to the one that had transformed England not long before.

The Frontier pattern also had a twofold form, though the dividing line there was different. The classic Frontier society of independent subsistence farmers emerged at a time when the inland reaches of the middle colonies had no transportation links to the coast except a few muddy trails, and remained viable only when distance or geographical barriers replicated this condition. Elsewhere, as roads, canals, and (eventually) railroads began to wind their way westward, inland farmers discovered that there was ample money to be made by shipping grain eastwards for local use and export, and plenty of ways to spend that money on manufactured goods shipped west in exchange. That's why the Appalachians, for example, which remain a challenge to transportation even today, kept the old frontier pattern long after the frontier itself had vanished out of sight over the western horizon, while upstate New York turned into a prosperous mix of farms and mill towns as soon as the Erie Canal and a network of feeder roads opened it up to efficient freight transport.

In the Ohio River basin, the first of America's many Wild Wests, the industrial system from New England hybridized with the export-oriented reworking of frontier culture to create a new and extremely successful human ecology. Along a network of navigable rivers and canals spilling north to the Great Lakes, towns sprang up. Most of those that had good sites for waterwheels—the prime mover of industry in the days before coal—transformed themselves into industrial cities as soon as population permitted. The spaces in between the towns were given over to small farms, most of them family-owned and operated, which produced nearly all the food needed locally and also raised grains and other bulk products for sale. It turned out to be very easy to extend this hybrid system further west across the northern and central Mississippi basin, and the idea that it could and should be extended straight across the continent took on a nearly religious intensity as the 19th century unfolded.

The two parts of the hybrid—the rising mill towns and industrial centers on the one hand and the agricultural hinterlands on the other—had conflicting interests of great importance, but until 1865 both sides had a very good reason to find grounds for compromise. That reason, of course, was the radically different human ecology on the other side of the Mason-Dixon Line.

The plantation economy of the Tidewater region, like the economies further north, adapted to changing conditions as westward expansion proceeded. Unlike New England's rural economy, it could expand. Across the southern half of the new nation, wherever climate and geography made it profitable to put large acreages into cash crop monocultures, plantations spread west. They had to spread, too, because the plantation economy had a critical weakness: like all cash crop monocultures, from Roman *latifundia* to the latest agribusiness models, Southern plantations stripped fertility from the soil.

The equation is a simple one: growing one crop repeatedly on the same acreage uses up the nutrient base of the soil, and in a farming economy dominated by cash, a farm that invests the money necessary to restore soil fertility will always be less profitable, at least in the short term, than a farm on new soil that concentrates on cutting costs and maximizing profit.

That specific equation is one form of a much more general rule: As providers of raw materials for industry in another nation, the plantations of the South were the business end of a wealth pump. The Southern states may not have been directly ruled by Britain but, economically speaking, they were as much a part of the British Empire as Canada or India. The Southern upper class, like upper classes in Third World nations today, benefited substantially from their role as guardians of the pump's intake pipe, but the fertility stripped from Southern soils to provide cheap cotton for Lancashire mills still represented wealth pumped out of the Southern states for the benefit of Britain. New lands thus had to be brought into the system continually to keep the pump fed without beggaring those who fed it.

The expansion of the plantation system brought it into a complex relationship with the frontier society that moved westward ahead of it. Regions that were unsuited to plantation farming in the South, like regions that were difficult for transportation technologies in the North, became enclaves of the old frontier pattern. Where these were large enough, they became enclaves of support for the Union once the Civil War broke out—the northwestern third of Virginia, which broke away to become the state of West Virginia, and the eastern hill country of Tennessee were strategically important examples. Elsewhere, as plantations spread, the frontier society was absorbed into the plantation system.

Some Southern frontier folk rose to the top—Jefferson Davis, a US senator before he became the president of the Confederacy, was born in a log cabin in rural Kentucky in 1808, when it was still well out on the frontier, less than a hundred miles from the log cabin where Abraham Lincoln was born eight months later.

South of the Mason-Dixon Line, most of the others became the poor white not-quite-underclass of the rural South, and provided the Confederacy with the bulk of its soldiers in the Civil War, just as their equivalents further north made up a very large fraction of Union soldiers when war came.

The competing agendas of Northern and Southern human ecologies made that war inevitable. The plantation society had to expand in order to survive. The mixed farming society further north was not quite so dependent on expansion, but desired it intensely, and population pressure from a booming birthrate and a steady flood of immigrants backed up that desire with potent economic pressures. While the Mississippi valley was free for the taking, both systems could expand without coming into conflict, but by the late 1840s people on either side were looking westward to the Pacific, still distant but too close for comfort. That's when the national debate over the shape of America's human ecology—framed south of the Mason-Dixon Line as a debate about local autonomy, and north of it as a debate over slavery—began to spin out of control.

There were plenty of other issues involved, to be sure.[5] Across the board, on almost every point of national policy that touched on economics, the measures that would support the plantation economy of the South were diametrically opposed to the measures that would support the industrial and farming economies of the North.

Trade policy is one good example: to the North, trade barriers and protective tariffs to shelter rising industries from competition by the industrial behemoth of Britain were simple common sense; to the South, free trade was essential so that British markets would remain open to Southern cotton. The endless debates over federal funding for canals and other internal improvements are another: investments that were essential to the expansion of the Northern economy were useless to the plantation system. That's why it was the North that wove a web of canals and railroads from the Hudson River to the upper Mississippi, while the South built few railways and fewer canals, and relied instead on shallow-draft riverboats that were adequate for getting cotton to market but for very little else. The resulting lack of transport infrastructure would cost the South terribly once war came.

Still, the issue that couldn't be resolved short of war was the future shape of America's territorial expansion. That's why Southern leaders, for all their belief in the virtues of local autonomy, bitterly opposed any compromise that would give the people of each newly settled territory the right to decide whether or not slavery would exist within that territory. That's why the South backed the annexation of Texas and the war with Mexico so fervently in 1844 and 1845, and why many Southerners in the decades before the Civil War supported the Order of the Golden Circle, a society that advocated the outright military conquest of Mexico, Central America, northern South America and the islands of the Caribbean, so that the plantation economy would have ample room to expand. Meanwhile, north of the cotton belt, younger sons of frontier farmers looked hungrily westwards at the Great Plains and imagined farms of their own, if only slavery could be kept out—and that, in turn, is what made "Bleeding Kansas" the scene of a decade of terrorism and guerrilla war between pro- and antislavery factions, and lit the fuse that finally went off at Fort Sumter.

By the time the war ended at Appomattox Court House four lean and bloody years later, four points had been settled for the foreseeable future. The first was that victory in the wars of the next century would be determined by which side had a bigger industrial base, a larger population, and a greater willingness to chuck the traditional rules of war and treat enemy civilians as a military target. The second point was that if wealth was going to be pumped out of the South, as of course it was, it was going to benefit the United States—more precisely, the industrial states of the North— rather than England or any other foreign power.

The third point was that the United States had become a major military power, capable of fighting and funding both sides of one of the 19th century's biggest wars on land and sea, and potentially capable of intervening in the affairs of Europe if it came to that. Every major European power had military attachés prowling the battlefields of the Civil War, and this was partly because that uncomfortable reality was beginning to dawn on politicians in Europe's capitals. Partly, though, it was because the technological advances of the 19th century had as dramatic an impact on the battlefield as elsewhere, and the Civil War provided a disquieting glimpse of how repeating rifles, improved cannons, ironclad ships, and rail transport could transform warfare. Most of them drew exactly the wrong conclusions—a point we'll discuss in some detail later—but the fact that the attachés were there points up the extent to which America, a backwater in world affairs fifty years previously, had become much less so by 1860.

The fourth point, though, was the most crucial for the theme we're exploring here. The end of the war was also the end of the debate over the mode of America's continental expansion. The plantation economy wasn't abolished—textile mills in the North depended on Southern cotton just as much as mills in the English Midlands did—but the door was slammed on its hopes of expansion as a series of Homestead Acts threw open the Great Plains to the family-farm model of the Northern economy. Questions of public policy that had been central to prewar debates—trade policy, internal improvements, and the rest—were settled for the rest of the century to the North's satisfaction. The wealth pump kicked back into gear without the safety valve of new lands, and the South's relative prosperity in the prewar era gave way to a regional depression that didn't end until after the Second World War. Meanwhile, protected by tariffs and trade barriers, supported by federal investments in railroads and the like, and buoyed by the wealth pump, the Northern economy boomed.

The settlement of the rest of the continent followed promptly, and it followed the Northern pattern. The military technologies that had broken the South were turned on those First Nations that still defended their tribal territories, with even more devastating effect. European military attachés were still prowling around during the Indian Wars—the United States was a continuing object of interest to all the major European powers from the Civil War on. They wrote admiringly that the Plains tribes were the finest light cavalry in all of history, but repeating rifles, Gatling guns, and a systematic campaign of extermination directed against the buffalo that provided the bulk of their food made the native peoples' defeat inevitable. As the tribes were driven onto tiny, barren reservations, white settlers streamed onto their land, laying out the same pattern of towns and farms that had succeeded so well further east. It would not succeed as well on the plains, and further west it would not succeed at all, but the first signs of its failure went unnoticed for many decades.

Still, in the age of the railroad, the West simply wasn't that big any longer, and the shores of the Pacific put a hard limit in the way of further territorial expansion. During the heady days of the 1840s, when it was still possible to forget the cost of war, American politicians seriously debated the invasion and conquest of all of Mexico—they settled for half—and during the Oregon Territory controversy of the same decade, a substantial faction had demanded the seizure of the southern half of Canada's four westernmost provinces, even if it meant war with Britain.

Cooler heads prevailed in each of these debates, and by the last decades of the 19th century, nobody was seriously suggesting either option: Britain by then had far and away the world's most powerful and technologically advanced military, and the idea of absorbing the rest of Mexico into an expanded United States ran headlong into a pervasive racism that would not have tolerated the idea of millions of Mexicans suddenly becoming American citizens. The modes of expansion that defined 19th century America thus ended before the century did, and that hard fact ultimately launched America into its age of overseas empire.

THE STRUGGLE OVER EMPIRE

THE STRUGGLE BETWEEN Northern and Southern models of human ecology in nineteenth-century America determined more than the shape of American continental expansion. The South followed what was becoming the standard pattern in the non-European world during that century, focusing on the production of commodities that were traded on global markets and using the profits to pay for manufactured goods from European factories. That's what the South did with cotton, tobacco, and a variety of lesser cash crops, and it's also what British North America, as Canada was then called, was doing at that same time with grain, lumber, fish, and the like.

Had the South kept the dominant position it originally held in American national politics, and arranged the nation's trade policy to its own satisfaction, that's what would have happened between the Mason-Dixon Line and the Canadian border, too. Without the protection of tariffs and trade barriers, the North's newborn industrial system would have been flattened by competition from Britain's far more lavishly capitalized factories and mercantile firms. The products of America's farms, mines, and logging camps would have had to be traded for hard currency to pay for manufactured products from overseas. That would have locked the United States into the same state of economic dependency as the nations of Latin America, where British banks and businesses—backed as necessary by the firepower of the Royal Navy—maintained the unequal patterns of exchange by which Britain prospered at the rest of the world's expense.[1]

That possibility vanished once the rising spiral of conflict between North and South exploded into war. Southern opposition to trade barriers was no longer an issue once Southern congressmen packed their bags and went home in 1860. With that difficulty out of the way, Northern industries got the trade barriers they needed, and the requirements of the war poured millions of dollars—a lot of money back then—into Northern factories. The North's total victory put the seal on the process, and not incidentally put paid to any lingering thoughts of regime change in America that might have been aired in private among Europe's upper classes. Reports sent back to European capitals from the military attaches mentioned earlier made it uncomfortably clear that the United States was capable of exercising military power on a scale that European nations could no longer ignore.

If the powers of Europe needed any reminder of these issues, it came in 1867, when the short-lived French puppet regime in Mexico was terminated with extreme prejudice.[2] That's one of those bits of history remembered by nobody north of the Rio Grande and everybody south of it, and it deserves discussion here for reasons that will quickly become apparent to those readers who have been watching the current situation in Europe. The short version is that banks in Britain, Spain and France loaned large sums of money to the government of Mexico, which then fell on hard times—there was a civil war involved, the *Guerra de la Reforma*, which is a bit further than Greece or Spain have gotten yet—and had to suspend payment on its debts. The British, Spanish and French governments responded by pressuring the Mexican government to pay up; this being the nineteenth century instead of the twenty-first, that pressure took the form of military intervention.

The British and Spanish forces were willing to settle for cash, but the French emperor Napoleon III had a wider agenda and launched a full-scale invasion. After more than a year of heavy fighting, the French army controlled enough of the country to install a friend of Napoleon's, an Austrian prince named Maximilian, as Emperor of Mexico. That's one of several good reasons the Union forces threw so much effort into seizing the Mississippi valley in the first part of the Civil War: Napoleon III was known to be sympathetic to the Southern cause, and so any land route by which he could get money and arms to the main Confederate armies and population centers had to be sealed off.

As soon as the Civil War ended, toppling Maximilian's government became a top priority for the United States government. Money and arms poured south across the Rio Grande to support guerrillas loyal to Mexican president Benito Juarez, while the French came under heavy American pressure to withdraw their forces from Mexico. Napoleon III pulled his troops out in 1866, and a year later Maximilian got marched out in front of a Mexican firing squad. That was the last time any European power attempted to expand its holdings in the New World.

North of the Rio Grande, though, the potential for further conflict was hard to miss. It's a commonplace principle of history that the aftermath of a war normally includes quarreling among the victors. All of the disagreements they had to keep at bay while there was still an enemy to defeat typically come boiling up once that obstacle is removed. That's what happened across the North in the wake of the Civil War, as the loose alliance between industrial and agrarian interests began to splinter about the time the last of the confetti from the victory celebrations got swept up. Alongside the ordinary sources of economic and political disagreement was a hard fact better understood then than now: the farm states of the Midwest were unwilling to accept the unequal patterns of exchange that the industrial states of the East required.

To make sense of this, it's necessary to take a second look at the way industrial production functions as a system of wealth concentration. To build and maintain an industrial system takes vast amounts of capital, since factories don't come cheap. All that capital has to be extracted from the rest of the economy, placed in the hands of a few magnates and kept there, in order for an industrial economy to come into being and sustain itself.

That's why, in a market economy, the technological dimension of industrialism is always paired with the economic and social dimension of industrialism. Put another way, the replacement of human labor with machines always comes with the creation of unequal patterns of exchange that concentrate wealth in the hands of factory owners at the expense of workers, farmers, and pretty much everybody else. The exact mechanisms used to impose and maintain those unequal exchanges vary from case to case, but some such mechanism has to be there, because an economy that allows the wealth produced by an industrial system to spread out evenly through the population pretty quickly becomes an economy that no longer has the concentrated capital an industrial system needs to survive.

That's the problem the United States faced in the latter third of the 19th century. The rising industrial economy of what would eventually become the Rust Belt demanded spectacular concentrations of capital, but attempts to extract that capital from the farm states ran into hard limits early on. The epic struggle between the railroad barons and the Grange movement—an early agricultural advocacy group founded in 1867—over shipping rates for farm commodities made it uncomfortably clear to the industrialists that if they pushed the farm belt too far, the backlash could cost them much more than they wanted to pay.[3] During the Reconstruction era, the defeated South could have what was left of its wealth fed into the business end of the industrial wealth pump, but that only worked for so long. When it stopped working, in the 1870s, the result was what normally happens when the industrial wealth pump runs short of fuel: depression.

They called it the Long Depression, though you'll have a hard time finding references to that term in most economic texts these days. The first warning came with a spectacular stock market crash in 1873. The US economy faltered, struggled, then plunged into full-scale deflation in 1876 and 1877. There were plenty of ups and downs, and some relatively calm years in the 1880s, but a good many economic measures stayed on the wrong side of the scale until better times finally arrived in 1896.

There's one good reason and at least three bad ones that you won't hear much discussion of the Long Depression in today's troubled economic time. The good reason is that most of today's economic theories came into being in response to a later crisis— the Great Depression of the 1930s—and the desire to avoid a repeat of the ghastly consequences of that latter collapse has inspired a certain amount of tunnel vision on the part of economic historians. The bad ones? Well, that's a little more complex.

Many of my readers will have encountered pundits who insist that economic crises happen because modern currencies aren't based on a gold standard, or because central bankers always mismanage the economy, or both.[4] That's a popular belief just now, but it's nonsense, and it only takes a glance at American economic history between the Civil War and the founding of the Federal Reserve in 1912 to prove once and for all that it's nonsense. The Panic of 1873, the Long Depression, the Panic of 1893, the Depression of 1900–1904, the Panic of 1907, and several lesser economic disasters all happened in an era when the US dollar was on the strictest of gold standards and the United States didn't have a central bank. That's bad reason number one: once you acknowledge the Long Depression, most of the rhetoric backing a very popular set of economic notions is revealed as self-interested handwaving.

More broadly, across nearly all of the squabbling theological sects of modern economic thought, Adam Smith's belief in the invisible hand remains glued in place. Smith insisted that a free market economy is innately self-regulating, as though controlled by an invisible hand, and tends to maximize everybody's prosperity so long as it's left to its own devices.[5] Exactly how much leeway should be left to the invisible hand is a matter of much disagreement among economists. There's a broad spectrum from the Keynesians, who want government to cushion the market's wilder vagaries, to the Austrian school, which insists that whatever the market does is by definition right, but you'll have a hard time finding anybody in the economic mainstream willing to consider the possibility that the market, left entirely to itself, might dive into a depression twenty-three years long. That's bad reason number two: once you acknowledge the Long Depression, it becomes very hard to ignore the fact that an economy left to its own devices can dole out decades of misery to everybody.

Then there's bad reason number three, which is that the cause of intractable problems like the Long Depression was well understood at the time, but nobody wants to talk about it now. That unwillingness, in turn, reflects the way that a concept once very widespread in economics—the concept of overproduction—came to be associated with a single economic school or, even more precisely, with a single economist, Karl Marx. Overproduction is one, though only one, of the elements Marx wove into his system of economic ideas, and generations of Marxist theorists and publicists used it as a reason why capitalist economies must eventually collapse. Capitalist theorists and publicists thus automatically shy away from the subject of overproduction, and the Long Depression makes it excruciatingly hard for that subject to be evaded for long.

For all that, overproduction is easy to understand, and it offers a crucial insight into how industrial economies work—or, more precisely, how they stop working. An industrial system, as we've discussed already, is a wealth pump that extracts wealth from the many and concentrates it in the hands of the few, to provide the capital concentrations needed to build and maintain the industrial system itself. The way this usually works in practice is that whatever the people on the losing end have to exchange—whether it's the labor of a workforce, the raw materials of a foreign country, or what have you—is given an artificially low value, while the products of the industrial system have an artificially high value. Thus, the people on the losing end get a pittance for their labor, their crops, and so on, while high prices for industrial products keep the factory owners rich.

The problem comes when the people who are getting next to nothing for their labor, crops, and so on are also the people who are supposed to buy those expensive industrial products. As the people on the losing end of the exchange get poorer, their ability to buy industrial products goes down, and unsold products pile up in warehouses. The result is a dilemma of no small scale: if the factory owners cut prices to move product, they risk dispersing the concentration of capital they need to keep the system going. If they cut production and lay off workers, they decrease the number of people able to buy their products even further. There are other options, but all of them add up to serious trouble for the industrial wealth pump.

That's overproduction. In the Long Depression, as in the Great Depression, it was an everyday reality, driving severe deflation and high unemployment, and we'd still be talking about it today if Marx hadn't been turned into an intellectual figurehead for one side in the bare-knuckle brawl over global power that dominated the second half of the twentieth century. There's much to be said for talking about it again, since it's becoming an everyday reality in America as we speak, but it also needs to be factored into any understanding of the rise of America's global empire, because the decision to go into the empire business in a big way was driven, in large part, by the overproduction crises that pounded the American economy in the late nineteenth century.

Read the literature of empire from the Victorian period and the connection is impossible to miss. Why did industrial nations want imperial colonies? The reason given in book after book and speech after speech at the time is that the industrial nations needed markets. Free trade rhetoric, then as now, insisted that all an industrial nation had to do was to build a better mousetrap and the world would beat a path to its door, but then as now, that's not how things worked. The markets that mattered were the ones where a single industrial nation could exclude competitors and impose the unequal exchange of cheap labor and raw materials for expensive manufactured products that would keep the wealth pump churning away.

That was the option that faced America as it approached the beginning of the twentieth century. It says something for the influence of ideals in American public life that this option wasn't chosen without a fight.[6] The debate over an American empire was fought out in the halls of Congress, in the letters pages of hundreds of newspapers, in public meetings, and any number of other venues. Important politicians of both major parties opposed imperial expansion with every resource and procedural trick they could muster, and scores of cultural figures—Mark Twain among them— filled the popular magazines of the time with essays, stories, and poems challenging the imperial agenda.

In the end, though, they lost. To a majority of Americans, the economic case for empire outweighed the moral and political arguments against it. By 1898, the pro-Empire faction had become strong enough that it could push the country into action. The annexation of Hawai'i and the Spanish-American War that year crossed the line and redefined America as an imperial power, launching it along a trajectory that would very quickly draw it into conflicts that generations of Americans had done their best to avoid. The logic that drove those conflicts was set out in advance in one of the forgotten classics of American historical literature.

It's a curious feature of American history that many of its turning points are best summed up by books. In the years just before the American Revolution, Thomas Paine's *Common Sense* was the book, focusing colonial grievances until they were ready to burst into flame. In the years before the Civil War, it was Harriet Beecher Stowe's novel *Uncle Tom's Cabin*; that's the book that made the North redefine a national dialogue over a range of regional differences as a moral debate over slavery, pure and simple, and so pushed both halves of the country into positions from which they couldn't back down short of war.

Both of those books stayed famous long after the issues they influenced were settled. Back when American children actually learned about American history in school, most people knew the titles—though you won't find many people of any recent generation who read either one. The book that played a similar role in launching America on its career as a global empire didn't get the same kind of treatment. Unless you know a fair amount about military history, you've probably never heard of it. Its title is *The Influence of Sea Power upon History*, and its author was Alfred Thayer Mahan.

Mahan was an officer in the US Navy; he'd seen combat duty in the Civil War, and remained in the service during the postwar decades when the country's naval forces were basically tied up at the dock and allowed to rot. In the 1880s, while serving at the Naval War College, he became a leading figure among the intellectuals—a small minority at that point—who hoped to shake the United States out of its focus on internal concerns and transform it into an imperial power. He was among the most original of American military strategists as well as a capable writer, and he had an ace in the hole that neither he nor anybody else knew about when his book saw print in 1890: his good friend and fellow lecturer at the Naval War College, a New York politician and passionate imperialist named Theodore Roosevelt, would become president of the United States just over a decade later by way of an assassin's bullet.

Mahan argued, first of all, for the importance of maritime trade to a national economy, partly because sea transport was (and is) cheaper than land transport, and partly because most international trade had to go by sea; second, for the necessity of a strong navy to protect shipping routes and defend national economic interests overseas; and third, for the need to establish permanent naval bases at a distance from the nation's own shores, along important trade routes, so that naval forces could be refueled and supported, and so that a naval blockade could be effectively countered. Mahan here was thinking about his own experiences with the Union blockade of the Confederacy during the Civil War. He backed up all these points with detailed case studies from history, but his aim wasn't limited to understanding the past; he was proposing a plan of action for the United States for the near future.

In 1890, the United States had spent a quarter century following exactly the opposite advice. The Union victory in the Civil War handed control of the nation's economic policy to industrial and agrarian interests that wanted high tariffs and trade barriers to protect domestic industry. As those took effect, other nations followed suit by raising tariffs and barriers against goods from the United States, and America distanced itself from the global economy of the late 19th century. Straight through the Long Depression of 1873 to 1896, economic self-sufficiency was one of the core elements of national policy; the idea was that American farms and factories should produce the goods and services Americans needed and wanted, so that the United States could avoid the state of permanent dependency that British-supported policies of free trade, backed by the superlative size and power of the British Navy, was imposing on so many other countries at that time.

Mahan's advocacy of naval expansion came at a crucial time, when the wealth pump of America's industrial system was struggling to keep from consuming itself, and a growing number of Americans were beginning to look enviously at Europe's global empires. The huge success of *The Influence of Sea Power upon History*—it was an international bestseller, was translated into more than a dozen languages, and became required reading for politicians and naval officers around the world—had a massive role in reformulating the debate around imperialism. Armed with

Mahan's logic, the proponents of an American empire could redefine the pursuit of global power in terms of the nation's safety and
prosperity. By the mid-1890s, the obsolete Civil War-era ships that
made up what there was of the Navy a decade earlier were rapidly
being replaced by a new fleet on the cutting edge of naval technology. All that the nation needed was an opportunity to put the new
fleet to use and begin carving out an American empire.

That last step came in 1898, with the Spanish-American war.
Those of my readers who think that the neoconservatives of recent years marked a radical departure from America's previous
behavior in the world should take the time to read a book or two
on this now-forgotten conflict. Spain at that time was the weakest
of the European colonial powers, with only a handful of possessions remaining from her once-vast empire—a few islands in the
Caribbean, notably Cuba and Puerto Rico, and the Philippines
were among the most important. The project of seizing Cuba from
Spain had been a popular subject of discussion in the South in
the years before the Civil War, when finding new acreage for the
plantation system had been a central theme of regional politics.
Mahan's book argued forcefully that the United States needed at
least one large naval base somewhere in the islands to the south
of the US mainland, and the hope that new territorial possessions
might become captive markets for American industry gave new
incentive to the old plan.

The Philippines were the target of similar logic. In the pre-trade
barrier era before the Civil War, the United States had begun to establish a presence along the western shores of the Pacific, sending
a fleet to wring trade concessions from Japan in 1854 and making
substantial inroads into the lucrative markets in China. The Civil
War and the years of relative isolation that followed put paid to
that, but regaining a place along the shores of eastern Asia was
a high priority for the pro-empire party. The possibility of a US
naval base in the Philippines was a tempting one, and added to the
incentives for a war with Spain.

All that was needed was a provocation. That was provided, first, by propaganda campaigns in the American mass media accusing the Spanish government in Cuba of atrocities against the Cuban population, and second, by an explosion aboard the USS *Maine*, one of the Navy's new battleships, which was making a port call in Havana. The cause of the explosion has never been satisfactorily determined, but the American press instantly blamed it on a Spanish mine. The flames thus fanned, the rallying cry "Remember the Maine!" took hold as popular support for conflict grew.

Congress, which in those days still fulfilled its constitutional role by setting policies that presidents were expected to carry out, duly declared war. US naval forces were already in position, and sailed at once. Ten weeks later, Cuba and Puerto Rico were conquered, two Spanish fleets had been crushed in separate battles nearly half the world apart, and the United States had its overseas naval bases and its empire.

The American president at that time, William McKinley, was not among the cheering majority. He was no opponent of American expansion—it was during his presidency that the United States annexed Hawai'i and what is now American Samoa—but service in the Union infantry in the Civil War gave him a more realistic attitude toward war, and he did what he could, with the limited power that presidents had in those days, to stop the rush to war with Spain. He won reelection easily in 1900, but the next year he was assassinated by, yes, a lone gunman. His vice president was none other than Theodore Roosevelt, who proceeded to turn Mahan's strategic principles into national policy. It's an interesting commentary on the difference between that era and ours that nobody, as far as I know, has ever proposed a conspiracy theory to account for McKinley's death.

The dawn of American empire had effects reaching well beyond the handful of territories the United States seized and held in McKinley's day. The same Congress that declared war against Spain had passed a resolution forbidding the annexation of Cuba—this was partly to win support for the war from the anti-empire faction in Congress, partly a bit of pork-barrel protectionism for the American sugar and tobacco industries—and that limit forced the proponents of empire to take a hard look at other options. The system that resulted was one that remains standard throughout the American empire to this day. Cuba got a new constitution and an officially independent government, but the United States reserved the right to interfere in Cuban affairs at will, got a permanent lease on a naval base at Guantánamo Bay, and turned the Cuban economy into a wholly owned subsidiary of American commercial interests. The result fed the wealth pump of empire, but cost the United States much less than an ordinary colonial government would have.

It also proved easy to export. In 1903, by means of a stage-managed revolution backed by US ships and Marines, the United States manufactured the new nation of Panama out of a chunk of northern Colombia, and established a Cuba-style government there under American oversight to maintain control over a planned canal uniting the Pacific Ocean with the Caribbean Sea. Other Latin American countries fell under US control in the years that followed, and had their resources fed into the increasingly busy wealth pump of American empire. Standards of living across Latin America duly began their long downward slide, while the United States boomed.

Meanwhile, as one of the last major acts of his presidency, Roosevelt launched what would be the definitive announcement that America had arrived on the world stage: the voyage of the "Great White Fleet." In December 1907, sixteen battleships and their support vessels—their hulls painted stark white, the Navy's peacetime paint scheme just then—sailed out of East Coast harbors to begin a voyage around the world, stopping at ports along the way. By the time they returned to Hampton Roads in February 1909, governments around the world had been forced to deal with the fact that a new power had entered the global political order.

All of this—Mahan's theories, the Spanish-American war and its aftermath, the growth of a US empire in Latin America, and the military implications of America's huge naval buildup and sudden attainment of global reach—was discussed at great length in books and periodicals at the time. What very few people noticed, because the intellectual tools needed to make sense of it hadn't been developed yet, was that the United States was developing what amounted to a second empire, parallel to the one just described, during these same years. Where the imperial expansion we've just examined established an empire across space, this second empire was an empire across time. Like the move to global empire, this empire of time built on an earlier but more limited method of feeding the wealth pump, and turned a large but otherwise ordinary nation into a world power.

This "empire of time," of course, consisted of the American fossil fuel industries. Where an empire extracts wealth from other countries for the benefit of an imperial nation, fossil fuel exploitation extracts wealth in the form of very cheap thermal energy from the distant past for the benefit of one or more nations in the present. The parallels are remarkably precise. An empire is profitable for an imperial nation because that nation's citizens don't have to produce the wealth that comes from foreign colonies and subject nations; they simply have to take it, either by force or by unbalanced systems of exchange backed by the threat of force. In the same way, fossil fuel extraction is so profitable because nobody nowadays has to invest their own labor and resources to grow and harvest prehistoric trees or extinct sea life, or to concentrate the resulting biomass into coal, oil, and natural gas. Equally, as we've seen already, empires go under when the wealth pump drives colonies and subject nations into poverty, just as fossil fuels become problematic when sustained extraction depletes them. In both cases, it's a matter of drawing down a nonrenewable resource, and that leads to trouble.

Nobody seems to know for sure when European settlers in the New World first mined coal, but the anthracite coal fields of eastern Pennsylvania were already being developed by the time of the Revolution, and the coming of the industrial revolution made coal an important commodity. Like the real estate that fueled America's westward expansion, coal was abundant, widely distributed, and of even more widely varying value; it was more than adequate to fuel the growth of a national economy, but not enough by itself to open the door to world power. It took the second empire of time—the one embodied in petroleum—to do that, just as the concentrated wealth that could be had from overseas empire made it possible for the United States to transform itself into a global force.

There's another fascinating parallel between America's overseas empire of space and its second empire of time. That second empire had its beginnings in 1859, with the drilling of America's first oil well in western Pennsylvania, right about the time that the United States was taking its first tentative steps toward intervention in Asia. For decades thereafter, though, petroleum was used mostly as a source of lamp oil. It took a flurry of inventions in the 1880s and 1890s—just as the push for empire was taking shape in the United States—to turn petroleum from a useful commodity to a source of nearly limitless mechanical power. It was in the wake of that transformation that the two empires fused, and the United States transformed itself into a superpower.

3

AMERICA AT ZENITH

IT IS A SOURCE of continuing irony that so many people on the leftward end of American politics today act as though America's current empire is unique in the history of the world, either in scale, malevolence, or some combination of the two. In any form, this notion is impressively absurd, and it presupposes an equally impressive ignorance of history. Still, I've come to think that there may be an unexpected factor behind that bit of historical blindness—the complete inability of most Americans today to take Britain seriously.

Americans these days, by and large, think of Britain in much the same terms that the British think of Luxembourg: a darling little country, quaint and colorful, of interest mostly as a destination for tourists—oh, and they're stuck in a strategic position, poor dears, so we had to send the troops over there a few times, didn't we? If the technology existed to project the average American's notions about Britain onto a screen, you'd see a giddy collage of Big Ben, Beefeaters, Mary Poppins, Monty Python, half-timbered houses, ivy-covered castles inhabited by ivy-covered aristocrats, Her Majesty the Queen imitating everybody's grandmama as she waves to the crowd, and a mishmash of misremembered history in which King Arthur, Robin Hood, the other Queen Elizabeth, and maybe a blushing war bride or two, all jostle one another against the backdrop of a green, pleasant, and very small land.

Mind you, America functions as the same sort of projection screen for fantasies in the British imagination. Most of a decade ago, while visiting England, my wife and I stopped at a supermarket in St. Albans to pick up travel food. Out in front was one of those rides for small children that give parents something to use as a bribe for good behavior inside the store, the sort that rumble and lurch around without actually going anywhere. The vehicle that did the rumbling and lurching was a little plastic convertible with the roof down, and in front of it, to fuel the riders' imaginations, was a flat panel with a landscape meant to represent America: on one side, a desert fitted out with some badly rendered saguaro cactus and a cow skull; on the other, a city consisting entirely of skyscrapers; straight ahead, a sweep of cowboy-infested plain with mountains in the distance, and a long straight road that vanished into infinity. It was a fascinating glimpse at the other side of a complex cultural relationship.

No doubt it doesn't help Britons understand America much to have images of that latter kind stuck in memory. I'm guessing this because of the corrosive effects of American imagery of Britain, not merely on Americans' understanding of Britain but on their understanding of the last three centuries of world history and of the nature of modern empire. As long as my American readers think of Britain as a cute little country, all this is out of reach.

It's out of reach because, until quite recently, Britain was not a cute little country. It was an arrogant, ruthless, rapacious global hyperpower with the world's largest and most technically sophisticated military machine and the largest empire in human history. Around a quarter of the world's land surface, and roughly the same fraction of the human race, was ruled outright from London, and anyone in that empire who objected to this state of affairs too loudly could expect to have their attitude adjusted by the business end of a Maxim machine gun. The world's maritime transportation routes—then as now, the primary arteries of global trade—existed subject to the whim of the Royal Navy. When patriotic Britons belted out "Rule, Britannia! Britannia rules the waves," they were stating the single most important fact of 19th and early 20th century economics and geopolitics.

It has become fashionable in recent years, among a certain faction of historians, to paint the British Empire as a global force for good and a model for all the things to which more recent empires, such as the United States, ought to aspire. In reality, though, the British Empire exercised its power with a breathtaking amorality. Consider the Opium Wars, in 1839–42 and 1856–60.[1] Britain bombarded civilian targets along the Chinese coasts and followed this up with a full-scale invasion, not once but twice, to force the Chinese government to reverse its decision to ban the import of opium and try to control what was then a pervasive and hugely destructive drug problem in China. To the British, the fact that British merchants could make plenty of money at China's expense by selling opium to Chinese addicts was enough to justify what, even by today's loose standards, was an unusually blatant abuse of power. That's not a part of British history discussed much these days; nor, for that matter, is it usually remembered that concentration camps were used by the British, with great enthusiasm and a substantial death toll, during the Boer War of 1899 to 1902.[2]

Now of course it's only fair to say that this is how all the European empires of the 19th century behaved. Britain had far and away the biggest empire, but its behavior was no worse than most and notably better than some. It's equally fair to note that as the age of European empire peaked and began its decline, the first two non-European nations that began to establish significant empires—the United States and Japan—didn't behave any better. Empire is a brutal business, and the notion that moral considerations ought to guide the behavior of the great powers is usually a talking point declining empires wield as a means of criticizing the rising powers that will eventually supplant them. This last point, however, is getting well ahead of our story.

When the United States began taking its first uneasy steps down the road to empire in the closing decade of the 19th century, modern notions of cute little England were nowhere to be found in the American consciousness. To a great many Americans, in fact, Britain was by definition the national enemy. The American national anthem commemorates the defense of an American fort against a British bombardment, and the Revolutionary War and the War of 1812 played a much larger role in the nation's collective imagination than they do today. On a more immediately pragmatic level, a great many Americans worried about their nation's northern border, and brooded over the possibility that the hostile superpower that ruled the other side of that border might someday send an invasion force south to reclaim its former colonies. As late as the 1930s, the standard scenario for the US Army's annual exercises each summer was defense against a British invasion from Canada.

I don't know if meaningful polls were ever done, but these Anglophobic attitudes were probably shared by a majority of Americans in the 1890s. There was also an Anglophile minority. Attitudes toward Britain served as a reliable litmus test in America's enduring cultural divide between the impoverished, patriotic, Christian hinterlands and the wealthy, internationalist, skeptical coastal cities: one side celebrated the Fourth of July with a noticeable animus toward the redcoats and their Union Jack, and talked earnestly about the evils of free trade and the plight of the Irish, while the other kept up with the latest British literary and intellectual news, copied London fashions, and faked an English accent when they thought they could get away with it.

Behind these vagaries lay a serious question. As the United States took control of its first handful of overseas colonies, naval bases, and treaty ports, it was venturing into a world that was dominated by British fleets and, more broadly, by British political and economic power. By the 1890s, the major powers had already begun to sort themselves out loosely into pro- and anti-British factions. It was by no means certain who would end up on which side; until the Anglo-French Entente of 1904, informed opinion considered France as likely to end up Britain's enemy as her ally. The question that faced America's people and politicians in the years between 1890 and 1917 was whether to ally with Britain or with the younger powers, notably Germany, that were pretty clearly headed toward a confrontation with the British Empire.

It could have gone either way. In 1895, Britain and America very nearly ended up at war over the border between British Guiana and Venezuela.[3] The Venezuelan government, at that time an ally of the United States, appealed to President Grover Cleveland to pressure Britain into arbitration. The Cleveland administration did exactly that, in belligerent language; British Prime Minister Lord Salisbury responded dismissively, while public opinion on both sides of the Atlantic yelled for war. It took the sudden outbreak of a new crisis in South Africa—the Jameson Raid, one of the foreshocks of the Boer War—to provide enough of a distraction for passions to moderate and cooler heads to prevail.

Still, it's significant that Cleveland, who was ready to challenge Britain even if it meant war, was also the last effective opponent of American empire to be elected president. McKinley, elected in 1896, personally opposed imperial expansion but lacked the strength to counter the rising popularity of the pro-empire faction. McKinley's assassination in 1901 handed the presidency to Theodore Roosevelt, a passionate imperialist and an equally passionate Anglophile, as well as a personal friend and disciple of naval strategist Alfred Thayer Mahan. From 1901 until 1912, the presidency was in the hands of enthusiastic imperialists, and until 1920, of Anglophiles; during this same period, America and Britain settled their remaining differences and moved gradually into an informal alliance that the First World War would make official.

A significant number of people in both countries, for that matter, envisioned something much closer than alliance. In "The Adventure of the Noble Bachelor," a Sherlock Holmes story published in 1892, Arthur Conan Doyle had his famous detective say, "I am one of those who believe that the folly of a monarch and the blundering of a minister in far gone years will not prevent our children from being some day citizens of the same world-wide country under a flag which shall be a quartering of the Union Jack with the Stars and Stripes."[4]

Doyle was far from the only intellectual on either side of the Atlantic to raise that prospect. Americans on the Anglophile end of the national spectrum, as often as not, felt they had more in common with the British than with the culture of America's Anglophobe majority, and dreamed of a union of the nations that would put them on a par with the upper crust of the world's greatest empire.

Britons, for their part, had good reason to want the United States on their country's side. Those in Britain who dismissed the United States as irrelevant in international politics received a series of abrupt awakenings in the half-century following 1860. During that period the Civil War demonstrated America's ability to fight an extended land war on a continental scale, the explosive growth of US industry and technology put Britain's industrial dominance at risk, and the remarkably swift production of a world-class navy after 1890 made it impossible not to notice that the United States was rapidly approaching the same ability to project force worldwide that the British Navy considered its private property. British politicians thus made conciliating the United States a central element of policy from 1890 onward, a decision that almost certainly saved Britain from defeat once war came.

What very few people grasped in the years before the First World War was just how brittle the British Empire had become, and how badly it would turn out to need help from across the Atlantic. The root of the trouble was that perennial bane of empires:

the long-term impact of the wealth pump on the subject nations that were being fed into its intake. The torrent of wealth that Britain extracted from its global empire left its subject nations starved of capital, and this put a limit on how long the wealth could keep on flowing. At the same time, the rise of Germany had forced Britain into a horrifically expensive arms race, especially at sea, where rapid advances in naval technology gave each generation of warships a shelf life of not much more than a decade before it had to be replaced, at steadily increasing cost. Thus Britain was being squeezed at both ends; income from its imperial possessions was faltering, while the cost of defending those possessions and countering potential rivals was soaring.

Then war came, and Britain found out the hard way that it had invested far too much of its military budget in the wrong things. The mighty British battleship fleet spent most of the war sitting in port, waiting for the smaller German fleet to come out and fight. The German fleet finally did so in 1916, the inconclusive Battle of Jutland followed, and then both fleets returned to port and basically sat out the rest of the war. Meanwhile, British naval forces had to improvise ways to counter the depredations of German submarines, while the struggle on the ground turned into a nightmare of trench warfare for which the British army was utterly unprepared.

Very nearly the only thing that kept the Allies going through the First World War was American aid. Until 1917, that came under a flag of neutrality—public opinion in America was firmly opposed to involvement in the bloodbath in Europe—but US President Woodrow Wilson, a passionate Anglophile, arranged for Britain, France, and Russia to borrow immense sums of money from American banks to pay for food and munitions. When the war reached crisis in 1917—Germany succeeded in that year in knocking Russia out of the war, and was preparing to turn its whole military force against the Western Front—American neutrality went out the window.

Wilson won reelection in 1916 under the slogan "He Kept Us Out Of War," but with Britain on the ropes, he did a 180-degree spin of a kind familiar to more recent observers of American politics. He got a declaration of war from Congress, sent the first of what would eventually be 1.2 million American soldiers into the meat grinder of the Western Front, and backed up that force with a sharply accelerated program of financial and military aid for the remaining Allies. Those steps provided the edge that allowed the battered Allied armies to stand their ground against Germany's final offensive, then turned the tide and ramped up the pressure until Germany was forced to sue for peace.

In the wake of the Allied victory, Wilson launched an ambitious program to create a new world order centered on a permanent Anglo-American alliance and locked into place by a new international organization: the League of Nations. Wilson's rush to war and his attempt to weave the United States into a global system of entangling alliances, though, alienated far too many people back home; Congress decisively rejected US involvement in the League of Nations, and the 1920 presidential election was an overwhelming victory for the Anglophobe majority. For the next twenty years, the United States did its level best to stay out of transatlantic politics, and concentrated instead on establishing its control over Latin America.

The next part of the story can't be understood without a sense of the military realities that drove that process. I apologize in advance to those of my readers who find military history uninteresting, but it has to be included here, partly because of its importance in the fall of the British empire and its replacement with the current American one, and partly because it sets the stage for the approaching fall of the American empire—a process that will inevitably have its own military dimension.

It's too often ignored that an unbroken string of victorious wars is one of the most dangerous things that can happen to a nation. Plenty of things could have clobbered the British Empire, and plenty of things contributed, but a strong case can be made that the blowback from too much success was the thing that finally tipped Britain over the edge into imperial collapse.

That effect could be seen at work all through the nineteenth century, in the steady drumbeat of bungled crises and minor disasters that called forth one hamfisted response after another from Britain's immense military machine, but never quite taught it to rethink its mistakes. A rebellion in India or the Sudan, a war in South Africa or Afghanistan, or whatever else, wherever else, generally began with a series of disastrous reverses for the British side. Usually, though not quite always, this was the doing of the army, the red-coated stepchild of Britain's military establishment, whose officer corps for generations was where England's noble families parked their incompetent younger sons.

So a regiment or an army would get slaughtered, a city or a province end up temporarily under the control of the people who lived there, and the British press would start baying for blood. Parliament would bicker decorously, and then immense military forces would converge on whatever corner of the planet was to be taught a lesson. Meanwhile the British army would work its way down through the list of available commanders, throwing them a few at a time into the crisis, until it finally found one who could figure out the not impossibly difficult puzzle of how to use overwhelming military and technological superiority to win a war. Once the natives were machine-gunned into submission, in turn, the successful general would head home to London and a peerage, the others would be quietly pensioned off, and every lesson that might prevent the next disaster was promptly forgotten. It was all so far away from London, and each generation of officers in training dutifully read Clausewitz and daydreamed of Waterloo and forgot to notice how fast the world was changing around them.

Not even the First World War managed to shake the serene confidence of Britain's imperial elite that what worked in the past would continue to work in the future. That time, it wasn't so far away from London, and the army on the other side wasn't outnumbered, outgunned, and out of its league in technological terms. Germany in 1914 was one of the world's major industrial nations, with a large and extremely competent army. Ironically enough, that army was nearly as hampered by a string of successes as Britain's was, and tried to repeat its 1870 triumph over France without paying attention to the possibility that the French might be expecting that. As it happened, they were, and the German offensive ground to a halt along a ragged line across northern France and Belgium. Parliament bickered decorously, and then Britain tried the usual trick of overwhelming its enemy with the massed forces of its empire – and that's when things went haywire, because throwing massed forces against an entrenched enemy equipped with machine guns and modern artillery simply meant that whole regiments were annihilated to gain a few yards of blood-soaked mud.

Worse, the British army failed to follow its usual practice of cashiering one general after another until it finally found one who could figure out how to win. Instead, the same handful of top commanders kept on using the same tactics straight through the war, even though those tactics consistently failed and cost tens or hundreds of thousands of British lives. The war on the western front turned into a struggle of sheer attrition, which the Allies won only because the United States threw its resources, its wealth, and finally its soldiers into the balance. When the victory celebrations were over and the top British commander retired with the traditional peerage, it was all too easy to forget that without the flood of American aid, Britain might well have lost the war.

As it was, the First World War very nearly bankrupted the British Empire, transforming Britain from the world's largest creditor nation to its largest debtor.[5] The wealth pump had been running too hard for too long, stripping wealth from existing colonies, and the expansion of British economic interests into central Europe couldn't make up the difference because the war had very nearly bled central Europe dry. Ireland's successful war of independence from 1919 to 1921 showed which way the wind was blowing.

England had crushed numerous Irish rebellions down through the centuries, but in the wake of the First World War that was no longer an option. After two years of bitter fighting, British Prime Minister David Lloyd George, scrambling to stave off full Irish independence, used threats of escalating violence to pressure the Irish provisional government into accepting self-rule under nominal British authority. That turned out to be a stopgap, and a weak one at that. Over the next three decades, as Ireland cut its remaining ties with the British Empire, politicians in London merely grumbled and looked away; the resources to do anything else couldn't be spared from other, more urgent needs.

Meanwhile, on the far side of the North Sea, a far more serious challenge was building. Britain's secondhand victory in the First World War spared it the opportunity to learn the lessons the war had to teach; Germany's defeat made those lessons impossible for Germans to ignore, and the Versailles Treaty that ended the war fed far too much of that nation's remaining assets into the wealth pumps of Britain and France, adding the insult of impoverishment to the injury of defeat. (Since Britain and France both ended the war with huge debts to banks in the United States, quite a bit of that wealth flowed promptly across the Atlantic, where it helped put the roar into the Roaring Twenties.) Through the 1920s, when the German army remained bound by the sharp limits imposed at Versailles, young officers whose names would become famous a few years later talked late into the night about how their nation could have won the war, and what kind of an army could win it. When they got the chance to build that army—courtesy of a little man with a Charlie Chaplin mustache, whom the foreign press by and large dismissed as a Mussolini imitator until far too late—a frighteningly different mode of making war began to take shape.

What these officers realized, or partly realized, was that the petroleum-powered internal combustion engine had completely redefined the potential shape of war. Britain had converted its fleet from coal to oil in the years just before the First World War, to be sure, and equipped its armies with tanks, trucks, and aircraft, but the strategic vision that directed all these things remained mired in the nineteenth century. In the minds of military planners in Britain and France, the nature of war remained what it had been for several centuries before then: two opposing armies form up, march toward each other, jockey for position, and then fight a battle, and the army that withdraws from the battlefield first has lost. Rinse and repeat, until the army, the government, or the nation of one side gives way. The new way of war Germany's young officers began to sketch out no longer followed those rules. It's necessary to take an extended look at that difference, partly because the current American way of war is wholly based on the principles those German officers developed, and partly—well, we'll get to that as we proceed.

In Chapter Two I mentioned that the European military attachés who followed the armies and witnessed the battles of the American Civil War almost uniformly learned the wrong lesson from it. That's because they paid attention to the two most famous generals of that war, Ulysses S. Grant and Robert E. Lee, and to the part of the war that was closest to Washington, DC, and the port cities of the eastern seaboard—a rough triangle of eastern Virginia whose points were at Washington, Richmond, and the sea. The battles fought there after Grant took command of the Army of the Potomac were a close first approximation to the useless slaughter on the western front in the First World War, with one crucial difference: they weren't useless. From Grant's and the Union's perspective, those battles made up half of a broader and extremely sophisticated strategy.

Grant is said to have described that strategy in the homely language he preferred: "I'm going to hold the cat down, and Sherman is going to skin him." That was exactly what happened, too.[6] Grant's job was to pin down Lee and the Army of Northern

Virginia, respectively the Confederacy's most brilliant general and its toughest army, so that neither one could be spared for the more vulnerable western front. Meanwhile Grant's opposite number, Gen. William T. Sherman, marched an army from Tennessee through Georgia to the sea, and then north through the Carolinas toward Virginia. His job was to punch a hole straight through the Confederacy's heartland, shatter its economic and agricultural systems, cripple its ability to feed and supply its armies, and make it impossible for the South to keep fighting. That was why Sherman's "bummers" stripped the country bare, leaving behind memories that are still bitter today, and it also explains a detail that rarely gets mentioned in any but the most technical histories of the Civil War: in the course of a months-long campaign that took him straight through the heartland of the Confederacy, Sherman fought only two significant battles.

Grant got the glory and earned it fairly, but Sherman may have been the nineteenth century's most innovative military thinker. When he came face to face with a Confederate army, whenever the strategic situation allowed, he evaded it, slipped past it, got behind it, and threatened its lines of communication and supply, forcing it to retreat in disarray. Long before anyone else, he grasped that it's not necessary to fight a pitched battle to win a war, and that a force that can move fast, get behind its enemy, and target the vulnerable territory behind the lines can cripple the ability of the other side to wage war at all. Most of a century later, that approach to war came to be called "blitzkrieg." Today it remains the core of American military strategy.

Those German officers who talked late into the night in the 1920s may have remembered Sherman, and realized something the other European armies had missed: that what he did with infantry on foot could be done far more effectively with tanks, airplanes, and infantry loaded into trucks. When 1940 came and a re-armed Germany set out to even the score with Britain and France, the strategy the German high command finally chose was for all practical purposes the same one that Grant and Sherman used to shatter the Confederacy. The British and French set out to refight the First World War, moving their armies into northern France to contain an expected German thrust through Belgium. The Germans made that thrust with part of their force, pinning down the Allied armies—holding the cat, in Grant's metaphor. Then, once the Allies were fully engaged, the rest of the German force drove through the rugged Ardennes hills, got behind the Allied lines, and proceeded to skin the cat with aplomb. Less than two months later, France had surrendered, and the British forces had suffered a humiliating defeat, fleeing across the Channel from Dunkirk and leaving their tanks, artillery, and everything else behind.

Around the same time that those young German officers were sitting up late at night and talking strategy, furthermore, another coterie of young officers on the other side of the Eurasian continent was doing much the same thing, with equally dramatic results. Japan didn't have the advantage of a recent defeat to draw on, but the humiliating events of 1854, when American gunboats had forced Japan to open its ports to American merchants and reverse a centuries-old policy of economic localization, left a lasting scar on Japanese memories. Aware that the alternative was subjugation by one of the existing imperial powers, Japan's leaders frantically built up a modern military and the industrial economy that was necessary to give it teeth; a short and successful war with the Russian Empire, in which the Japanese fleet crushed its Russian rivals in two flawlessly executed naval battles, duly followed. The young officers of the Imperial Navy recognized soon after the First World War that the day of the battleship was over, and embraced the possibilities of naval air power at a time when most other nations with navies still thought that aircraft carriers were a waste of time.

My American readers doubtless remember how these preparations affected the United States on December 7, 1941, and the days that followed, but they may not be aware that British forces in the Pacific suffered a series of equally disastrous and humiliating defeats. Once again, the cause was simply that Japan had noticed and embraced the new military possibilities that petroleum and the internal combustion engine made possible, and Britain had not. Fortified naval bases that were essential to British strategy in the Pacific and the Indian Oceans, and were considered invulnerable in London, fell into Japanese hands like ripe fruit. Perhaps the best display of the mismatch, though, was the doomed voyage of the battleship *Prince of Wales* and the cruiser *Repulse*, the two most powerful British naval vessels in the southwestern Pacific, which sailed from Singapore the day after Pearl Harbor to attack a Japanese landing force up the Malay coast. It was a move straight out of Alfred Thayer Mahan, but the Japanese were no longer playing Mahan's game; the ships were promptly spotted and sunk by Japanese torpedo bombers.[7]

The war that followed is usually called the Second World War, but it might more usefully be given a different name: the Gasoline War. That's partly because the stunning initial victories of the two Axis powers that counted came from their grasp of what gasoline engines could do in war. Mussolini's Italy never did figure out the revolution in warfare that petroleum made possible, and so got the stuffing pounded out of it early and often. It's partly, also, because a great deal of the strategy of the war on all sides focused on access to petroleum; the two Allied powers that counted, the United States and the Soviet Union, had immense petroleum reserves, while the Axis had none, and the attempts of the latter to seize oilfields and the former to prevent that from happening shaped much of the war. Finally, it's because victory in that war went to those who were able to bring the most petroleum-based energy to bear on the battlefield. While Germany and Japan could manage that, they remained in the ascendant, but once the United States and Soviet Union applied the same methods using their much more abundant oil supplies, the Axis was doomed.

And the British Empire? It's considered utterly impolite to talk about what happened to it in straightforward terms, but a thought experiment may be useful.

Imagine that the twists and turns of history that brought the United States into two world wars on Britain's side had gone the other way. Perhaps it was the Venezuela crisis of 1895, or one of the other flashpoints in British-American relations that were successfully dodged by statesmen on both sides. It really doesn't matter; the key detail is that in 1914 and thereafter, in this alternate history, the Anglophobes rather than the Anglophiles controlled America's response to the coming of war in Europe, and Britain was left twisting in the wind. Imagine that Germany won in 1918, and that a later German leader—let's suppose it was the young Kaiser Wilhelm III, son of the conqueror of France—went to war in 1939 against a crippled British Empire and forced Britain to surrender. What would have happened then?

The potential war aims of any of Britain's early 20th century rivals are easy enough to imagine or, for that matter, to look up. First, the British Empire would have been dismantled, those portions of it that the conquering nation wanted would have been seized, other parts would have been allowed to go their own way, and a few token colonies would be left under British control where that suited the conqueror's interests. Second, the British government would become a permanent and subordinate ally of the new imperial power. Third, Britain's military would have been reduced to a fraction of its previous size, and the British government would be obligated to provide troops and ships out of the remainder to support the new imperial power when the latter decided on a military adventure. Fourth, Britain would be expected to pay a large sum of money as reparations for the costs of the war. Finally, to guarantee all these things, the British government would have been forced to accept an occupying force in Britain, and permanent military bases would be signed over to the new imperial power in Britain and its remaining colonies. That, by and large, is what happened to defeated nations in the wars of the nineteenth and twentieth centuries.

Now compare that list of imagined consequences to the actual relations between Great Britain and the United States from 1945 to the present. That's the thing that can't be mentioned to this day in polite company: the British Empire ended in the early 1940s when the United States conquered and occupied Britain. It was a bloodless conquest, like the German conquest of Luxembourg, and since the alternative was submitting to Nazi Germany, the British by and large made the best of it. Still, none of Queen Victoria's prime ministers would have tolerated for a moment the thought of foreign troops being garrisoned on British soil, where US military personnel are still garrisoned as I write these words. That's only one of the lasting legacies of the Gasoline War.

More generally, a complex and self-justifying mythology has grown up around the process by which the United States made the transition from regional power to global empire during and after the Second World War. That sort of thing is common enough that it probably belongs on the short list of imperial obsessions—Rome had its imperial myth, as did Spain, Britain, and just about any other empire you care to think of—but the American version of it deserves close attention, because it obscures factors that need to be understood as the American empire hurtles down the curve of its own decline.

The mythology runs more or less like this: in the aftermath of the First World War, America withdrew from the international responsibilities it had briefly taken up during that war, refusing to join the League of Nations and distancing itself from global politics. In the vacuum thus formed, the coming of the Great Depression sent the conflicts that drove the world to war in 1914 spinning out of control again. As Japan invaded China and Germany prepared for war, the United States faced a sharp political conflict between isolationists, who more or less wanted to build a wall around the country and shut the rest of the world out, and those who recognized America's responsibility to the rest of the world. That struggle only came to an end with the Japanese attack on Pearl Harbor; thereafter the American people united to win the war. Once it was won, in turn, they refused to repeat the mistake of 1919, and took up the burden of global leadership that America retains to this day.

Thus the mythology. The reality was considerably more complex.

To begin with, the conflict between isolationists and internationalists was far less simple than the myth proposes. The isolationist Republican administrations of the 1920s saw no conflict at all between their rejection of the League of Nations and their enthusiastic use of the US Marines to impose puppet regimes and keep the wealth pump running at full roar all through Central America and the Caribbean. The isolation that the isolationists sought was simply a matter of distancing the United States from the lethal quarrels of the Old World. Behind their policies stood a vision of the shape of global politics in the post-British era—a vision that divided the world into separate spheres of influence, each under the control of a major power. Latin America, according to this scheme, was the natural prey of the United States, and that's where the isolationists focused their attention in the years between the wars. They weren't the only influential group with that idea; the Japanese government, with its dream of a Greater East Asian Co-Prosperity Sphere that would subject east Asia to Japan's wealth pump, was tracing out exactly such a sphere of influence.

The internationalists, by contrast, were Anglophiles rather than Anglophobes, and they also liked to imagine the American future on a larger scale, one in which Central American banana republics were hardly worth noticing. The dream of a global empire formed by a future US-British union had never really lost its hold in Anglophile circles, while others less enamored of Britain but no less ambitious had begun to imagine a future in which the United States would be the dominant force, Britain a favored but subordinate partner, and the entire planet would feed into the American wealth pump. Their vision of the post-British world was guided by the science or pseudoscience of geopolitics, which argued that the distribution of land masses, oceans, and resources could be read as a blueprint for a world empire.

You'll have to look hard to find information on classical geopolitical theory today, unless you have the unusual luck to live near a university library that doesn't follow the currently fashionable practice of purging its stacks of books that contain insufficiently modern ideas.[8] If you can find books on the subject, though, it's worth doing, for much the same reason that rereading Alfred Thayer Mahan's *The Influence of Sea Power upon History* is worth doing. In both cases, the validity of the theories is a minor issue at best; what makes them important is that influential people believed them, and acted on them. In the case of geopolitics, American foreign policy from Pearl Harbor right up to the present is a good deal easier to understand if you grasp the basics of geopolitics.

In the writings of Halford Mackinder and Karl Haushofer, the two most influential geopoliticians of the first half of the twentieth century, the world can be imagined as a giant bull's-eye, with a central zone surrounded by three (or, rather, two and a half) bands. The central zone is the Heartland or Pivot Area, and includes most of Eurasia, from the eastern European plain straight across to the valley of the Lena River in eastern Siberia. Surrounding this on three sides is the Marginal Crescent, which extends from central Europe across Turkey and the Middle East to India, China, and far eastern Siberia. Next are the Outer Crescents—this is the half a band—which consists of two arcs of islands and peninsulas around the fringes of Eurasia, one extending from Iceland through Britain to western Europe, the other from Japan through the islands and peninsulas of southeast and southern Asia. Furthest out, separated from the rest by oceans or the Sahara Desert, is the Insular Crescent, which consists of both Americas, Africa south of the Sahara, and Australasia.

The geopoliticians argued that this scheme showed the structure of the coming world empire. In the past, they pointed out, the major wars of the modern Western world had pitted a maritime power in the western Outer Crescent against a land power in the western part of the Marginal Crescent. So far, the maritime power (Spain, then Britain) had been able to draw on the resources of the Insular Crescent to contain and defeat the land power. As the basis of the land power shifted further east into the Pivot Area, though, access to the resources of continental Eurasia—not to mention invasion routes into the rich lands of the Marginal Crescent—would more than make up for the resources available to the maritime power, and allow the land power to become a universal empire. Mackinder put it this way in 1904: "The oversetting of the balance of power in favor of the pivot state, resulting in its expansion over the marginal lands of Euro-Asia would permit of the use of vast continental resources for fleet-building, and the empire of the world would then be in sight."[9]

Domination of the Pivot Area, in turn, depends on control of the eastern European plain, and this inspired a thesis of Mackinder's that received a great deal of attention back in the day: "Who rules East Europe commands the Heartland; who rules the Heartland commands the World-Island; who rules the World-Island commands the world."[10] Mackinder was warning a British audience about the risk that a German empire that managed to seize control of Russia could supplant Britain's global dominion; Haushofer, writing a couple of decades later, took Mackinder's fears as a working plan for German world domination. Neither geopolitician seems to have considered the possibility that the Heartland might have imperial designs of its own, or that the Insular Crescent might turn out to be a far more secure base for the next great maritime power than a small island perched uncomfortably close to the shores of western Europe. Still, that's what happened.

It probably bears repeating here that whether classical geopolitics is valid or not is a secondary question for our present purposes. Geopolitics is important here because its ideas had a major influence on the leaders who launched America along the final phase of its rise to empire, and still govern the grand strategy of the American empire as it approaches its end. The Anglophile minority in American politics between the world wars saw geopolitics as a blueprint for world power, and wanted the structure raised on that blueprint to have "Made in America" written on it. That was an unpopular view in the 1920s, but it had wealthy and influential backers, who were well-positioned to act when circumstances began to shift their way.

The first of these shifts was the Great Depression or, more precisely, the feckless response of both American mainstream political parties to the economic collapse that followed the 1929 stock market crash. In the crucial first years after the crash, Democrats and Republicans alike embraced exactly the same policies they are embracing in today's economic troubles, with exactly the same lack of success, and showed exactly the same unwillingness to abandon failed policies in the face of economic disaster. Then as now, the federal government launched a program to bail out big banks and corporations—it was called the Reconstruction Finance Corporation in those days—and pumped dizzying amounts of money into the upper end of the economy in the belief, real or feigned, that the money would work its way down the pyramid, which of course it didn't do. Then as now, politicians used the shibboleth of a balanced budget to demand austerity from everybody but the rich, and cut exactly those programs which could have helped families caught by hard times. Then as now, things got worse while the media insisted that they were getting better, and the mounting evidence that policies weren't working was treated as proof that the same policies had to be pursued even more forcefully.

In many countries, this sort of thinking drove the collapse of democratic governments and the rise of dictators who won absolute power by doing what everyone outside the political establishment knew had to be done. In the United States, that didn't quite happen. What happened instead was that a faction of dissident Democrats and former Republicans managed to seize control of the Democratic Party, which hadn't won a presidential race since 1916, and put Franklin D. Roosevelt into office in 1932. Roosevelt, like the dictators, was willing to do what the masses demanded: use public funds to provide jobs for the jobless, keep families from losing their homes to foreclosure, and reinvest in the nation's dilapidated infrastructure. It didn't end the Depression, but it was successful enough that Roosevelt won reelection in 1936 in one of the greatest landslides in American political history.

What made Roosevelt's ascendancy of historic importance was that he was a passionate Anglophile, and as Europe moved toward war, he and his administration did everything in its power to get America involved. That faced fierce opposition, and not only among isolationists; a great many Americans believed at the time, and not without reason, that the United States had received essentially nothing in exchange for saving Britain and France in the First World War—neither of the latter two countries, for example, had ever gotten around to paying off their war debts to the United States. All through 1940 and 1941, as a result, the Roosevelt administration played a high-stakes game of chicken with Germany and Japan, trying to lure one or both into a declaration of war or an attack on American interests drastic enough to give him the political momentum to counter the isolationists and launch a second American rescue of England. In the meantime, the United States poured money, supplies and arms into the faltering British war effort, stopping just short of active involvement in the fighting until war finally came.

After Pearl Harbor, despite the myth, isolationism didn't simply go away. Saturation propaganda and the arrest and trial of antiwar activists on a variety of charges, most famously the Great Sedition Trial of 1944, was needed to break the back of the peace movement in the United States. Then much the same thing had to be done again on a bigger scale, via a series of Red scares, after Germany and Japan were defeated and the two Allied powers that mattered, the United States and the Soviet Union, started quarreling over the spoils. Still, the internationalists had won once the Soviet Union turned out to be America's last remaining rival, because the isolationists—who were by and large old-fashioned conservatives— loathed Marxism even more than they loathed US involvement in Old World quarrels. The Republican Party, which had gone from the party of empire in the 1890s to the party of isolation in opposition to Wilson, proceeded to reinvent itself yet again as more international than the internationalists when it came to opposing "godless Russia." Meanwhile the occupation forces in Germany and Japan, not to mention those in Britain and a good many of its former colonies, settled down for a long stay.

The official strategy of the United States and its allies, as they consolidated their hold on half the world and looked out uneasily across the borders with the half controlled by Russia and its allies, was described by George F. Kennan in a famous 1947 essay as "containment."[11] What that meant in practice was Mackinder's geopolitical strategy under a different name: the United States established a massive military presence in both eastern and western Outer Crescents, while trying to pry Soviet allies loose and gain influence over neutral nations in the Marginal Crescent, and keeping the Insular Crescent under the control (and subject to the wealth pumps) of the United States and its allies. Salvador Allende and Patrice Lumumba, among many others, paid the price of this latter policy.

Like every imperial system, this one has had its ups and downs. It avoided Britain's successful but costly policy of bringing large regions under direct political control, preferring instead to install compliant local rulers who would keep the wealth pump running in exchange for a small share of the take. It faltered in the 1970s as America's other empire, the empire of time that paid tribute by way of oil wells, reached its peak production and tipped into permanent decline. American leaders then gambled everything in the next decade on a daring strategy of economic warfare.

That gamble paid off spectacularly, wrecking the Soviet Union and fueling the 1990s boom by feeding the nations of eastern Europe into the business end of America's wealth pump, stripping half a dozen nations to the bare walls under the euphemisms of economic reform and a market economy. For a few years it looked as though Russia itself might be fed into the wealth pump in the same way, before an efficient counterstroke by the Putin administration pulled that prize out of American hands. Meanwhile the rise of China hinted that Mackinder's thesis might turn out to be overly Eurocentric, and the north China plain might prove to be just as effective a springboard to the resources of the Heartland as the eastern European plain.

Through all this, the basic structure of American empire has remained essentially the same as it was at the end of the Second World War: a global military presence positioned according to the concepts of classical geopolitics, whether these are relevant or not; a global political system run by local elites propped up by American aid and, when necessary, military force, tasked with keeping the wealth pump going but left mostly to its own devices otherwise; a global economic system that was designed to suck wealth out of the rest of the world and channel it into the United States, but has sprung large and growing leaks in various places and increasingly fails to do its job; and a domestic political system in which a fantastically bloated executive branch headed by an imperial presidency keeps the forms of constitutional government in place, while arrogating to itself most of the functions originally exercised by Congress, and most of the rights originally left to the states and the people. That's where we are today—in the aging, increasingly brittle, effectively bankrupt, but still immensely powerful global empire of the United States of America.

That's the empire that is sinking into its twilight as I write these words, and that faces dismemberment and dissolution in the decades ahead. The global supremacy Theodore Roosevelt and his peers dreamed of achieving has become a reality, and now the price of that supremacy has to be paid. Exactly how that price will be exacted is impossible to know in detail, but it's not hard to see the foreshadowings of decline and fall in the rising spiral of political, economic, and military troubles shaping today's headlines. It is to these that we now turn.

PART TWO

THE WIDENING GYRE

THE FAILURE OF POLITICS

THE DECLINE AND FALL of America's empire involves all the dimensions of collective life, and the whole picture will be easier to grasp if we consider the more important of the resulting trajectories one at a time. We'll start with the obvious one: the political dimension, and the final collapse of what remains of American democracy. The pattern that collapse follows is not new; it was traced out by the oldest democracies on record, those of ancient Greece.

The Greek historian Polybius, who chronicled the conquest of Greece by Rome in the second century BCE, gave a convenient label for the process by which democracies destroy themselves: anacyclosis.[1] He noted that the squabbling city-states of the Greek world tended to cycle through a distinctive sequence of governments—monarchy first, followed by aristocracy, followed by democracy, and then back around again to monarchy. It's a cogent model, especially if you replace "monarchy" with "dictatorship" and "aristocracy" with "junta" to bring the terminology up to current standards.

A short and modernized form of the explanation—anyone interested in the original form should consult the *Histories* of

Polybius—is that in every dictatorship, an inner circle of officials and generals emerges. This inner circle eventually takes advantage of weakness at the top to depose the dictator or, more often, simply waits until he dies and then distributes power so that no one figure has total control; thus a junta is formed. In every country run by a junta, in turn, a wider circle of officials, officers, and influential people emerges; this wider circle eventually takes advantage of weakness at the top to depose the junta, and when this happens, in ancient Greece and the modern world alike, the standard gambit is to install a democratic constitution to win popular support and outflank remaining allies of the deposed junta. In every democracy, finally, competing circles of officials, officers, and influential people emerge; these expand their power until the democratic system freezes into gridlock under the pressure of factionalism or unsolved crisis; the democratic system loses its legitimacy, political collapse follows, and finally the head of the strongest faction seizes power and imposes a dictatorship, beginning the cycle over again.

It can be educational to measure this sequence against recent history and see how well it fits. Russia, for example, has been undergoing a classic round of anacyclosis since the 1917 revolution: dictatorship under Lenin and Stalin, a junta from Khrushchev through Gorbachev, and a democracy—complete with corruption, rigged elections, and the other features democracies lack in theory and always display in practice—since that time. China, similarly, had democracy from 1911 to 1949, a dictatorship under Mao, and has had a junta since then, with stirrings of democracy evident over the last few decades. The United States of America, for that matter, has been around the cycle three times since its founding. The one difference in this last case—and it is a crucial one—is that all three cycles have taken place under the same constitution.

A case could be made that this is the great achievement of modern representative democracy—the development of a system so resilient that it can weather anacyclosis without cracking. The three rounds of anacyclosis we've had in the United States so far have each followed the classic pattern. They've begun under the dominance of a single leader whose overwhelming support from the political class and the population as a whole allowed him to shatter the factional stalemate of the previous phase and impose a radically new order on the nation. After his death, power passes to what amounts to an elected junta, and gradually diffuses outwards in the usual way, until a popular movement to expand civil rights and political participation overturns the authority of the junta. Out of the expansion of political participation, factions rise to power, and eventually bring the mechanism of government to a standstill; crisis follows, and is resolved by the election of another almost-dictator.

In American history the pattern repeats over a period that runs roughly seventy to eighty years. The dictator figures were George Washington, Abraham Lincoln, and Franklin Roosevelt, each of whom overturned existing structures in order to consolidate their power, and did so with scant regard for existing law. Each man's presidency ended an era—we can call them, respectively, Colonial America, Federal America and Gilded-Age America—and began another. The era that began with Roosevelt's presidency, Imperial America, is nearing its end in our time.

The juntas were the old Whigs, the Republicans, and the New Deal Democrats, each of them representatives of a single social class. They were overthrown in turn by Jacksonian populism, the Progressive movement, and the complex social convulsions of the Sixties, each of which spread power across broader sectors of the citizenry. The first cycle ended in stalemate over slavery; the second ended in a comparable stalemate over finding an effective response to the Great Depression; the third—well, that's where we are right now.

There's no shortage of crises sufficient to tip the current system into its final stalemate, and no shortage of people in the political class who show every sign of being willing to give it that final push. What distinguishes this round from its predecessors, it seems to me, is the fashionable contempt for democratic institutions that pervades American public life today. In 1860, that habit was so far from finding a place in the political dialogue that the constitution of the Confederate States of America was largely copied from the one signed at Philadelphia a long lifetime before. In 1932, though a few Americans supported Marxism, fascism, or one of the other popular authoritarianisms of the day, the vast majority who put Roosevelt into the White House four times in a row expected him to maintain at least a rough approximation of constitutional government.

That's much less true this time around. There's not a great deal of public support for overtly authoritarian ideologies—although I expect to see Marxism make a large-scale comeback on the American left in the next few years—but as Oswald Spengler pointed out almost a century ago, in the endgame of democratic societies, it's not the cult of ideology but the cult of personality that's the real danger.[2] A Russian proverb warns that it's never a good idea to let the perfect become the enemy of the good; in our time, as a growing number of Americans insist that America isn't a democracy because it doesn't live up to their fantasies of political entitlement, it's all too possible that a mass movement could coalesce around some charismatic figure who offers to fix everything that's wrong with the country if only we let him get rid of the checks and balances that stand in his way. How many civil liberties would survive the victory of such a movement is not a question I like to contemplate.

Still, there's a further complexity in the way of understanding the predicament of American democracy. The pattern that Polybius outlined, and that American politics has cycled through three times so far, begins with most of the nation's political power concentrated in a single person and follows the diffusion of power to the point that the entire political system settles into a gridlock only a massive crisis can break. Just now, according to that model, we are in the stage of gridlock, and thus of maximum diffusion of power.

This interpretation flies in the face of the standard narrative that surrounds power in America today. Both sides of the political spectrum like to insist that too much power is in the hands of the other side, at least when the other side is in the White House or has a majority in Congress. The further from the mainstream you go, the more strident the voices you'll hear insisting that some small group or other has seized absolute power over the US political system and is running things for their own advantage. The identity of the small group in question varies widely—it's hard to think of anyone who hasn't been accused, at some point in the last half century or so, of being the secret elite that runs everything—but the theory that some small group or other has all the power and is keeping it from everybody else is accepted nearly everywhere. Whether it's Occupy Wall Street talking about the nefarious 1 percent, or the Tea Party talking about the equally nefarious liberal elite, the conviction that power has been concentrated in the wrong hands is ubiquitous in today's America.[3]

It's an appealing notion, especially if you want to find somebody to blame for the current state of affairs in this country, and of course hunting for scapegoats is a popular sport whenever times are hard. Still, there is an alternative description that explains much more about the current state of the American political system. It suggests that the political system is lurching forward like a driverless car along a trajectory set by the outdated policies of an earlier time, and that just now, nobody is behind the wheel at all. Unpopular though this way of thinking about power in America may be, I suggest that it makes more sense of our predicament than the more popular belief in a nation strangled by overwhelmingly centralized power.

It's important to understand what this suggestion means and, more importantly, what it doesn't mean. A great many of those who insist that power in America is in the hands of a small elite offer, as evidence for the claim, the fact that a relatively small number of people get an obscenely large share of national income and wealth, and they're quite correct.[4] The last three decades or so have seen America turn into something close to a Third World kleptocracy, the sort of failed state in which a handful of politically well-connected people plunder the economy for their own benefit. When bank executives vote themselves and their cronies million-dollar bonuses out of government funds while their banks are losing billions of dollars a year, just to name an obvious example, it's impossible to discuss the situation honestly without using words like "looting."

Still, the ability to plunder one corner of a complex system is not the same thing as the ability to control the whole system, and the freedom with which so many people pillage the institutions they're supposed to be managing could as well be understood as a sign that there's no center of power willing or able to defend the core interests of the US empire against death by financial hemorrhage. The only power the executives of, say, Goldman Sachs need is the power to block any effort to stop them from stripping their bank to the bare walls for their personal enrichment, or to cut them off from the access to tax dollars that has made that process so lucrative. That much power they certainly do have, but it's a kind and a degree of power shared by many other influential groups in America just now.

Consider the defense industries that are busy profiting off the F-35 fighter, an immense and impressively corrupt corporate welfare program currently chewing gargantuan holes in the US defense budget and the military budgets of several other nations.[5] Years behind schedule and trillions of dollars over budget, the F-35 is by all independent accounts a dog of a plane, clumsier and more vulnerable than the decades-old fighters it is supposed to replace. The consortium of interests that profit from its manufacture have the power to keep the process chugging along, even as the delays stretch into decades and the cost overruns head toward lunar orbit, and again, that's all the power they need. It's all the more telling that they're able to do so when the F-35 project is directly opposed to crucial US interests. Having the United States and its allies equipped with a substandard fighter, at a time when China and Russia are both busily testing much better planes, risks humiliating defeat in future wars—and yet the program moves steadily forward.

Examples of the same sort of thing can be multiplied endlessly, and they aren't limited to corporations. Cities and counties all over the United States, for example, are being driven into bankruptcy by the cost of public-sector salaries and benefits that politically influential unions have extracted from vulnerable or compliant local politicians. Equally, other countries—China and Israel come to mind—have learned to make use of the diffusion of American power for their own interests. It doesn't matter how blatantly the Chinese manipulate their currency or thumb their noses at intellectual property rights, for example; so long as they keep their lobby in Washington well-funded and well-staffed, they're secure from any meaningful response on the part of the US government. I sometimes think that the only reason the US government is down on Iran is that religious scruples keep the Iranian government from buying immunity the way the Chinese do; they've got the petroleum and therefore the money, and could doubtless have their own influential lobby capable of blocking hostile legislation in Congress, if only they didn't let their ideals get in the way.

What each of these groups exerts is essentially a veto power. They may not be able to get new policies through the jungle of competing interests in Washington—a task that is increasingly hard for anyone to manage at all—but they can prevent policies that are not in their interest from being enacted, and they can defend any policy already in place that benefits them or furthers their ability to loot the system. They have that veto power, in turn, because no one in contemporary America has the power to get anything done without assembling a temporary coalition of competing power centers, each of which has its own agenda and each of which constantly has its hand out for the biggest possible share of the take.

Not every potential power center in American politics functions as a veto group, mind you. A great many groups have become captive constituencies of one of the existing power centers, and lost whatever independent influence they might have had. Compare the way that the Democratic Party has seized control of the environmental movement to the way that the Republicans have played the same trick on gun owners. In both cases, the party can ignore the interests of its captive constituency until elections come around, and then bombard it with propaganda insisting that the other party will do horrible things to, for example, the environment or the Second Amendment if they win the election. The other party duly plays its part in this good-cop/bad-cop routine by making threatening noises about gun rights or environmental issues at intervals. It's an efficient scam, one that keeps environmentalists voting for Democrats and gun owners voting for Republicans even though neither party gives more than lip service to the issues that matter to either group.

To the members of the captive constituencies, in turn, all this simply feeds the belief that there must be somebody in the system who has the power they lack; after all, they keep on voting for the right people, and yet none of their policies ever get enacted! Since very few gun owners ever sit down and drink a couple of beers with environmentalists, there's rarely an opportunity for them to compare notes and notice that neither side is getting what it wants, and that the same confidence game is being played on both. The one place on the political continuum where this sort of comparison does take place is out on the fringes, where the extreme left increasingly bends around to touch the extreme right, and the paranoiac beliefs endemic to the farther shores of American politics turn the whole thing into yet another proof that the Freemasons or the Jews or some other nefarious group runs everything after all.

Just as the ability to plunder one part of a financial system does not equal control over the whole system, though, the ability to manipulate a handful of politically naive pressure groups does not equal the ability to manipulate the whole political system. It's precisely because no one group has an effective monopoly on power that political parties and other power centers have to resort to complicated and expensive gimmickry as they hammer together the temporary coalitions that enable them to cling to whatever power they have and, on increasingly rare occasions, force through some policy or other that favors their interests.

As the system settles ever more deeply into gridlock, in turn, policies put in place in previous decades become increasingly resistant to change. Even those that turned out to have severe flaws will inevitably get support from those who profit from them, and from employees of government bureaucracies whose jobs would go away in the event of a policy change. Machiavelli noted a long time ago that reforms always face an uphill struggle, because those who benefit from the status quo can be counted on to fight fiercely to hold on to what they've got, while those who might benefit from reform have less incentive to fight for gains they know perfectly well they may never see.[6] Factor in the mutual support among power centers who have a shared interest in keeping the status quo fixed in place, and you have a recipe for exactly the sort of stasis the United States sees every seventy or eighty years, as the cycle approaches its end.

How the endgame plays out is a matter of more than academic interest. In 1860 and 1932, a political system frozen in gridlock and incapable of anything like a constructive response to crisis finally hit a crisis that could not be evaded any longer, and the system shattered. In the chaos that resulted, a long-shot candidate with a radical following was able to pull together enough support from the remaining power centers and the people in general to win the White House and force through changes that redefined the political landscape for decades to come. That's a possibility this time around, too, but a possibility is not a certainty, and nowhere is it written in stone that a crisis of the sort we're discussing has to have a happy ending.

The range and scale of the crises facing the United States as it finishes the third lap around the track of anacyclosis, to begin with, pose a far more substantial challenge than the ones that punctuated the cycle in those earlier years. In 1860, the question was which of two incompatible human ecologies would dominate the North American continent; in 1932, it was the simpler though still challenging matter of how to pry the dead fingers of a failed economic ideology off the throat of the nation. This time, the United States faces two immense and parallel difficulties, neither one of which has the sort of straightforward solution that Lincoln and Roosevelt, respectively, had to hand.

The first difficulty is that the global empire established by the United States in the wake of the Second World War is coming apart. The American way of empire—the strategy of leaving the administration of subject countries to puppet governments drawn from local elites—was cheaper than the traditional British approach of subjugation and rule by an imperial viceroy, but it turned out to be more vulnerable to change and less directly profitable to the imperial government: American corporations profited mightily from the wealth pump directed at Latin America, for example, but very little of that money ended up in the coffers of the US treasury, where it could have helped cover the costs of empire.

As the American empire falters, in turn, rival powers expand their own military capacities and apply pressure wherever they can get away with it, short of being drawn into a premature war. The US military has reacted with the same sort of stereotyped response that characterized the latter years of the British Empire, preparing to fight bygone wars with ever more ornate and overpriced technology, while its most likely opponents show every sign of asking the hard questions about basic issues that lead to sudden revolutions in military practice. When this has happened in the past, the results have almost never been good for the established imperial power, and there's no reason to think that things will be noticeably different this time around.

Meanwhile America's "empire of time," its once-immense energy resource base, has been drawn down at breakneck rates for more than a century and a half. Recent handwaving around shale gas reserves has served mostly to pump up the price of drilling company stocks, and enable a certain number of rich men in influential positions to get away with another round of looting; we've all heard the strident claims that the United States will become an energy exporter sometime very soon, but the numbers don't even begin to add up. It's a safe bet that a few years down the road shale gas will have gone the way of ethanol and all the other energy sources that were allegedly going to replace petroleum and keep the industrial age running smoothly ahead.[7] The American economy is utterly dependent on very large quantities of petroleum, as is the American military. Drastic changes, going far beyond the baby steps involved in manufacturing a few electric cars or running a naval vessel or two on biodiesel, would have to get started well in advance if they are to cushion the end of either dependency, and those changes are not taking place.

Lincoln dealt with the long debate over the shape of America's human ecology on the battlefield. Roosevelt jerry-rigged a set of temporary expedients to overcome the mismatch between real wealth and a dysfunctional financial system during the Great Depression. There are no such relatively simple solutions, however, to deal with the consequences of the end of America's current dual empires. It will require massive changes in every aspect of American life, starting with a steep decline in standards of living and the forced abandonment of privileges most Americans think of as theirs by right. That would be an immense crisis at the best of times, and these are not the best of times; our political system has spent the last thirty years trying to evade exactly these issues, while sinking further and further into stasis, and it's our luck that the crisis seems to be arriving just as American politics freeze up completely.

It's not surprising, under these circumstances, that so many Americans have given up on the political process altogether. The question that needs to be asked is why what was once one of the world's most vigorous democracies can't do better, and the answer has a great deal to do with the historical processes by which American democracy emerged and collapsed.

When the United States won its independence from Britain, the constitution that was signed in Philadelphia in 1787 established a form of government that was not, and did not pretend to be, democratic. It was an aristocratic republic, of a type familiar in European political history: the government was elected by ballot, but the right to vote was restricted to those white male citizens who owned a significant amount of property—the amount varied from state to state, like almost everything else in the new republic, but it was high enough that only 10 percent to 15 percent of the population had the right to participate in elections.

What broke the grip of the old colonial aristocracy on the American political system, and launched the nation on a trajectory toward universal adult suffrage, was the rise of the modern political party.[8] In America—the same process took place in Britain and several other countries around the same time—the major figure in that rise was Andrew Jackson, who seized control of one fragment of the disintegrating Democratic-Republican party in 1828, transformed it into the first successful political mass movement in American history, and rode it into the White House. Central to Jackson's strategy was support for state legislation extending the right to vote to all white male citizens; in order to make that support effective, the newly minted Democratic Party had to organize right down to the neighborhood level; in order to make the neighborhood organizations attract potential members, the party had to give them an active role in choosing candidates and policies.

That was the origin of the caucus system, the basic building block of American political parties from then until the late twentieth century. Jackson's rivals quickly embraced the same system, and one of those—the Anti-Masonic Party, which was a major force in national politics in the 1820s and 1830s—built on the Jacksonian template by inventing state and national conventions, which everyone else quickly copied. By the 1840s, the American political party had established itself as an essential part of the way Americans chose their candidates and made their laws.

Here's how it worked. Party caucuses existed in every urban neighborhood, small town, and rural center, and they didn't simply meet once every four years; they met regularly, as often as once a week, to talk politics and keep party members informed of what was going on in local, state, and national affairs. Ambitious young men—after 1920, ambitious young women as well—attended caucus meetings throughout their voting districts, pressing flesh, making connections, and learning the ropes of politics. As election time approached, caucuses went into overdrive, nominating candidates, drafting policy proposals, and electing delegates to city or county conventions, who would support the candidates and the proposals at that level.

The city and county conventions then did much the same thing, sorting through the candidates and proposals from lower down, choosing party candidates for local offices, and electing delegates to the state convention. The same process repeated itself at the state level, sorting out proposals from below, nominating candidates for state offices and Congressional seats, and electing delegates to the national convention, where the presidential candidate was chosen.

I once had the misfortune to be stuck in the Atlanta airport, waiting for a long-delayed flight back to the west coast, while large television screens all over the concourse showed the Republican National Convention in full swing. A series of forgettable talking heads were bellowing at the top of their lungs about the alleged virtues of whatever forgettable candidates the GOP was fielding that year; I suspect the point of all the yelling was to keep the delegates from dozing off, because the proceedings reminded me of nothing so much as a high school pep rally for a team that's already lost its shot at the local playoffs. The candidate had already been selected; ditto the party platform, a collection of bland sound bites that not even the most diehard of the faithful expected anyone to remember the day after the election. All that remained was the sort of tepid rah-rah atmosphere you get when people are going through the motions of something that used to matter, but no one remembers why anymore.

As recently as the 1960s, that kind of atmosphere was unthinkable at a political convention, because what happened there actually made a difference.[9] Since the local caucuses all happened at more or less the same time, as did the local and state conventions, the absurdity of the current nominating process, in which victory in three or four early state primaries can all but cinch the nomination for a candidate long before most party members have any voice in the matter, was not an option. Instead, it was standard for delegates to converge on the national convention to choose among as many as half a dozen serious candidates, and the candidate who proved best at making speeches, managing his public presence, and engaging in no-holds-barred backroom political deals—not bad job training for the presidency, all things considered—usually came out with the nomination.

That was the way the system worked. Was it vulnerable to corruption? You bet. Most large American cities spent many decades under the one-party rule of political machines that funneled public money to an assortment of private pockets, buying and selling votes like so many pork bellies. The bosses of the biggest machines—Chicago's Richard Daley was among the most famous of the recent examples—could play kingmaker on a national scale in a tight election. Party machines more generally were full of able political connivers whose obvious interest in advancing their personal power and wealth noticeably outweighed any concern they might have had for the public good. All these were among the reasons why the caucus and convention system was gutted, stuffed and mounted in the 1960s and 1970s, and primary elections became the standard way to choose candidates.

Compare the older system to the way presidential nominations are handled nowadays, though, and it's not exactly easy to claim that the present process is more representative or less blatantly corrupt than the caucuses and conventions of the past. Where winning a presidential nomination in 1852 or 1952 required solid organizational skills, the backing of a significant fraction of the party's local movers and shakers, excellent public relations, and a good dollop of the amiable ruthlessness that makes for success in the world of political dealmaking, winning a presidential nomination nowadays requires precisely one thing: money. Business interests unquestionably had a seat at the table in the days when caucuses and conventions mattered, but theirs was far from the only such seat, and it happened quite often that a candidate favored by the very rich got elbowed aside by some upstart with populist notions who was just that little bit better at playing the political game.

Crucially, it's worth taking a look at the kind of people who advanced to power through the old system, and comparing them with the kind of people who advance to power through the new. A Kansas City haberdasher like Harry Truman wouldn't be elected to a city council today, but he was one of those ambitious young men I mentioned earlier, and his exceptional skills as a campaigner, organizer, and bare-knuckle political bruiser took him all the way to the White House. The world-class drubbing he dealt out to media favorite Thomas Dewey in the 1948 election was typical of the man. Very few of the significant political leaders of American history between Jackson's time and the beginning of the 1960s could get elected in today's money-driven environment, and the bland nonentities that fill so many elected positions today compare very poorly to those earlier equivalents. If we're going to have a corrupt political system—and we are, since no political system anywhere will ever be more honest than the people it governs—we might as well have one that produces leaders more capable than the airbrushed marionettes who infest the American political scene these days.

Quite a few of the reforms that reshaped American politics in the 20th century had the same effect as the gutting of the caucus and convention system. Two of the Progressive Era's chief reforms—direct election of US senators and nonpartisan elections for city governments—are cases in point. Until 1913, US senators were appointed by state legislatures, were directly answerable to state governments, and thus reliably opposed attempts by the House of Representatives to expand federal power at the expense of the states. Once US senators were elected by popular vote, that check went away, and the backroom political deals that previously put state politicians in the Senate gave way to outright purchase of senators by corporate interests, which could readily provide the money that candidates needed to win elections. In the same way, campaigns to "clean up" cities by abolishing political machines got rid of the machines, but this simply meant that business interests no longer had to bargain with machine politicians for favors; they could simply buy elections and get what they wanted.

Changes along these lines, it deserves to be said, are tolerably common when a nation gets into the empire business. The rise of each of the major European empires, for example, was preceded by bitter struggles between the national government and feudal domains that had existed as quasi-independent states for centuries; only when traditions of local autonomy and decentralization are crushed can a nation concentrate the power and wealth needed for imperial adventures. The distribution of power in the United States under its original constitution made conflicts of this kind inevitable. Still, certain consequences that followed those struggles bid fair to have a massive impact on our future.

The first of those consequences unfolds from the historical detail that the gutting of the caucus and convention system took place alongside the collapse of an entire world of democratically run voluntary organizations, which had provided citizens with most of the training they needed to take an effective role in local politics.[10] In 1920, for example, half of all adult Americans, counting both genders and all ethnic groups, belonged to at least one fraternal order, and these orders—ranging in size from multimillion-member organizations such as the Freemasons and the Odd Fellows down to little local orders with a single lodge and a few dozen members—were nearly all run by the same democratic processes used by caucuses to elect delegates and vote on policies. Nearly all other institutions of American civil society, from gun clubs and historical societies to lending libraries and farmers' cooperatives, ran their affairs in exactly the same way.

Those days are long gone. The vast majority of those institutions went extinct decades ago, abandoned in the course of America's transformation from an active civil society to a passive mass society, and even in the few organizations that remain, it's rare to find anybody who still remembers how to chair a meeting so that all viewpoints get heard, the necessary decisions get made, and everyone still gets home at a reasonable hour. Without that reservoir of basic competence in the skills of democratic politics, any movement toward a revitalization of what's left of America's democratic institutions faces a steep uphill struggle; the implications of this difficulty will be central to a later chapter.

The second consequence is that, by gutting the caucus system, the American political system deprived itself of a crucial source of guidance and feedback. When local caucuses were still debating political issues over mugs of beer and passing recommendations up the line to county, state, and national conventions, canny politicians of both major parties paid attention, since shifts in the political wind could be sensed there more quickly than elsewhere. Canny politicians in the major parties also paid close attention to anything the small parties did that attracted more than the usual number of voters. That meant that serious problems generally got attention from the political system: not always quickly, and not always the kind of attention that helped matters much, but more often than not it kept the United States from sailing blindly into disasters that everybody but the political class saw well in advance.

The current political system doesn't have that advantage. These days, American politics is a closed loop in which the competing pressure groups that make up the political class need not listen to anyone outside of their own narrow world of power brokers, corporate donors, and tame intellectuals. It's a perfect medium for groupthink, efficiently screening out the divergent voices and alternative views a nation needs in order to survive in an uncertain and troubled world.

The third consequence is that the reshaping of American political institutions, thorough as it was, never quite reached all the way down to the level of structure. Many European countries scrapped their old regional provinces entirely in the process of centralizing power, replacing the traditional geography of power with a new structure that deliberately disrupted local ties and loyalties. The United States never managed to break up the states, say, into a couple of hundred administrative districts with boundaries that cut across the old state lines and only such powers as Congress chooses to hand out. Instead, the states retain fully functional governments, clinging jealously to what remains of their old prerogatives, and possessed of rarely exercised powers that could turn out to be decisive in a time of crisis.

Political power's a remarkable thing. Though Mao Zedong was quite correct to point out that it grows out of the barrel of a gun,[11] it has to be transplanted into more fertile soil in short order or it will soon wither and die. A successful political system of any kind quickly establishes, in the minds of the people it rules, a set of beliefs and attitudes that define the political system as the normal, appropriate, and acceptable form of government for that people. That sense of legitimacy is the foundation on which any enduring government must build, for when people see their government as legitimate, no matter how appalling it appears to outsiders, they will far more often than not put up with its excesses and follow its orders.

It probably needs to be said here that legitimacy is not a rational matter and has nothing to do with morality or competence. Great nations throughout history have calmly accepted the legitimacy of governments run by thieves, tyrants, madmen and fools. Still, a government that has long held popular legitimacy can still lose it, and with remarkable speed. Those of my readers who watched the collapse of the Soviet Union and its Warsaw Pact satellites will recall the speed with which the rulers of Communist nations saw the entire apparatus of government dissolve around them as the people they claimed the right to rule stopped cooperating.

Now of course that sudden collapse of legitimacy was long in preparing. Just as a singer or writer who becomes an overnight success normally gets there after many years of hard work, the implosion of a system of government normally follows many years of bad decisions and unheeded warnings, and it's not too hard in retrospect to trace how simmering unrest eventually rose to a full boil. The benefits of hindsight can be misleading, though, because it's actually quite rare for anyone to catch on to what's building in advance. Thus in the last decades of prerevolutionary France, as one tawdry scandal after another dragged the prestige of the monarchy in the mud and laid the foundations for the complete delegitimization of the *ancien régime*, few if any observers seemed to be aware of the looming consequences.

We have seen plenty of equally tawdry scandals in the United States of late, and it's easy to ignore the impact of, let's say, the Obama administration's systematic refusal to bring charges against any of the financiers whose spectacularly blatant acts of fraud helped fuel, and then pop, the housing bubble of a few years back. Had Obama acted otherwise, the Democratic party would likely have come to dominate the American political scene for the next forty years as thoroughly as it did for the four decades or so after 1932; instead, by giving the country a remarkably good idea of what third and fourth terms of George W. Bush would have looked like, the Obama administration has convinced a sizable fraction of Americans that they have nothing to hope for from either party.

It's all too common for the political class of a troubled nation to lose track of the fact that its power depends on the willingness of a great many people outside the political class to do what they're told. In Paris in 1789, in St. Petersburg in 1917, and in a great many other places and times, the people who thought that they held the levers of power and repression discovered to their shock that the only power they actually had was the power to issue orders, and those who were supposed to carry those orders out could, when matters came to a head, decide that their own interests lay elsewhere. In today's America, equally, it's not the crisply dressed executives, politicians, and bureaucrats who officially hold power who have the capacity to enforce that power in a crisis; it's the hundreds of thousands of soldiers, police officers and Homeland Security personnel, who are by and large poorly paid, poorly treated, and poorly equipped, and who have not necessarily been given convincing reasons to support the interests of a political class that most of them privately despise, against the interests of the classes to which they themselves belong.

Such doubts and dissatisfactions can build for a long time before the crisis hits. If history shows anything, it's that trying to time that crisis is very nearly a guarantee of failure. Sooner or later, once the system's legitimacy becomes sufficiently doubtful, some event dramatic enough to seize the collective imagination will trigger the final collapse of legitimacy and the implosion of the system, but what that event will be and when it will come is impossible to know in advance. No one in pre-Revolutionary France seems to have guessed in advance that the calling of the Estates-General in 1789 would set off the final crisis of the monarchy—but then who could have predicted the spur-of-the-moment improvisation that led representatives of the Third Estate to proclaim themselves a National Assembly, or the circumstances that sent a Paris mob running through the streets to storm the Bastille?[12]

What follows the moment of crisis is a little less opaque to anticipation. France in 1789 and Russia in 1917 were both politically centralized nations in which power was primarily exercised from the capital city. Revolutionary politicians and urban mobs in Paris and St. Petersburg respectively thus had an overwhelming impact on the course of events, and radical change there spread rapidly throughout the country, since there were no effective centers of power outside the core. In less centralized countries, control of the capital is less decisive; the seizure of power by Parliament and the London mob in 1641 in England bears close comparison with events in the two later revolutions, but when the rubble of the English Civil War finally stopped bouncing, the system that resulted was much closer to the one that had been in place before 1641 than, say, France after the revolution resembled the *ancien régime*. The survival of familiar modes of government in peripheral centers made it easier for those same modes to be restored once the revolutionary era was over.

That degree of regional independence did not survive in England, but the European pattern of political geography, whereby the capital city of each nation-state normally becomes its political and cultural hub and its largest population center, did not catch on in North America. In the United States and Canada alike, the national capital and the largest population center are two different cities; in both nations, as well as Mexico, large regional divisions— states or provinces—maintain a prickly independence from the central government, and regional cultures remain a potent political force. The United States is the most extreme example of the lot; Washington, DC, is a modest regional center that happens to share space with the offices of a national government, and there is no place in the country where even the largest urban mob could have a decisive impact on the survival of the federal government.

The complex historical processes that brought thirteen diverse colonies under a single federal system, however, left a great deal of power in the hands of the states. Very little of that power is used these days; repeated expansions of the originally very limited powers given to the national government have left most substantive issues in the hands of federal bureaucrats, and left the states little more to do than carry out costly federal mandates at their own expense. Still, the full framework of independent government—executive, legislative, and judicial—remains in place in each state; state governors retain the power to call up every adult citizen to serve in the state militia; and, finally and critically, the states have kept the constitutional power to bring the whole system to a screeching halt.

That power is spelled out in Article V of the US Constitution. If two-thirds of state legislatures call for a constitutional convention to amend the Constitution, the convention will happen; if three-quarters of state legislatures vote to ratify any amendment to the Constitution passed by the convention, that amendment goes into effect. It's that simple. Congress has nothing to say about it; the President has nothing to say about it; the Supreme Court has nothing to say about it; the federal government is, at least in theory, stuck on the sidelines. That power has never been used; the one time it was seriously attempted, in 1913, Congress forestalled the state legislatures by passing a constitutional amendment identical to the one for which the states were agitating, and submitting it to the state legislatures for ratification. The power nonetheless remains in place, a bomb hardwired into the Constitution.

What makes that bomb so explosive is that there are practically no limits to what a constitutional convention can do. The only thing the Constitution specifies is that no amendment can take away a state's equal representation in the Senate. Other than that, as long as two-thirds of the states call for the convention and three-quarters of the states ratify its actions, whatever comes out of it is the supreme law of the land. Everything is up for grabs; it would not be beyond the power of a constitutional convention, for example, to provide a legal means for states to withdraw from the Union, or even to repeal the Constitution and dissolve the Union altogether.

Had the leaders of the Southern states in 1860 been less proud and more pragmatic, it's entirely possible that they could have won their independence and spared themselves the catastrophe of the Civil War by some such measure as this. It's eerily plausible to imagine Senator Jefferson Davis of Mississippi rising in the Senate that year to propose an amendment to provide for the peaceful dissolution of the Union, denouncing the radicals on both sides of the slavery issue who were pushing the nation toward civil war, and offering a peaceful separation of the states as the only workable solution to the problem that had dogged the nation for so long—and it's by no means hard, at a time when most Americans still wanted to avoid war, to imagine such a proposal getting the votes it would need from Congress and the states to take effect.

Any further development of that speculation can be left to fans of alternate history. Under most conditions, of course, no such proposal would ever be seriously made, much less accepted, but 1860 offers a trenchant reminder that under the pressure of irreconcilable conflict, the system of government we have in the United States can freeze up completely and make desperate measures the order of the day. In 1860, the US government lost its legitimacy in a third of the country, and it took the bloodiest conflict in the nation's history to bring back the southern states to a grudging and incomplete obedience. In the crisis of legitimacy that's building in today's America, a rising spiral of conflicts between regions also plays an important role, but this time the federal government can hardly count on the passionate loyalty it got a century and a half ago from the Northeast and the Midwest; in fact, it's hard to think of any corner of the country where distrust and disaffection for the current government haven't put down deep roots already.

If and when the crisis comes, it's anyone's guess what exactly will happen, but the possibility that the states will call on their power to redefine the Constitution—whether they use it to reshape the national government, or to let the country split apart into smaller nations along regional lines—belongs somewhere on the list of potential outcomes. For that matter, it's anyone's guess what will spark such a crisis, if in fact one does come. The triggering event might be political, or economic, or even environmental. Still, if I had to make a guess, I would say that the most likely triggering event will be military. We'll open that immense can of worms in a later chapter.

THE ECONOMIC UNRAVELING

T HE PURSUIT OF EMPIRE does to nations many of the same things that drinking cheap bourbon does to individuals: it produces euphoric feelings at the time and then wallops you the next morning. It's been just over a hundred years now since the United States launched itself on its path to global empire, and the hangover following that century-long bender is waiting in the wings. I suspect one of the reasons the US government is frantically going through the empties in the trash, looking for a bottle that still has a few sips left, is precisely that first dim dawning awareness of just how bad the hangover is going to be.

It's worth taking a few moments to go over some of the more visible signposts of the road down from empire. To begin with, the US economy has been crippled by a century of imperial tribute from overseas. That's what happened to our manufacturing sector; once the rest of the industrial world recovered from the Second World War, manufacturers in an inflated tribute economy couldn't compete with the lower costs of factories in less extravagantly overfunded parts of the world, and America's industrial heartland turned into the Rust Belt. As the impact of the tribute economy spread throughout US society, in turn, it became next to impossible to make a living doing anything productive, and gaming the imperial system in one way or another—banking, investment, government contracts—turned into the country's one consistent growth industry.

That imposed distortions on every aspect of American society that will burden it long after the empire goes away. As productive economic sectors withered, the country's educational system reoriented itself, churning out an ever-expanding range of administrative specialties for corporations and government while shutting down what was once a world-class system of vocational and trade schools. We now have far more office fauna than any sane society needs, and a drastic shortage of people who have any less abstract skill set. For the time being, the United States can afford to offshore jobs, or import people from other countries to do them at substandard wages; as the empire winds down and those familiar bad habits stop being possible, the shortage of Americans with even the most basic practical skills will become a massive economic burden.

Meanwhile the national infrastructure is caught in a downward spiral of malign neglect made inevitable by the cash crunch that always hits empires on the way down. Empire is an expensive habit; the long-term effects of the imperial wealth pump on those nations subjected to its business end mean that the income from imperial arrangements goes down over time, while the impact of the tribute economy at home generally causes the costs of empire to go up over time. The result can be seen on Capitol Hill day by day, as one fantastically expensive weapons system after another sails through Congress with few dissenting votes, while critically important domestic programs are gutted by bipartisan agreement, or bog down in endless bickering. The result, as in previous empires, is a shell of a nation, seemingly strong when observed from outside but hollowing out within, and waiting for the statistically inevitable shove that will launch it on its final skid down the rough slope into history's compost bin.

Two things can be said about that final impact. The first is that America's global empire will fall; the second is that those who rule it will not let it fall without a struggle. The US government and the fractious alliance of power centers that dominate it are clearly unwilling to take Britain's path, and accept the end of empire in exchange for a relatively untraumatic imperial unraveling. To judge by the evidence that's currently available, they will instead cling to the shreds of imperial power, and the wealth and privilege that goes with it, until the last of those shreds are pulled from their cold stiff hands. That's a common boast, but it bears remembering that the moment always comes when those shreds do get pried loose from those pale and rigid fingers.

These two hard facts, the imminence of imperial downfall and the unwillingess of the existing order to accept that imminence, impose certain hard consequences on the decades ahead of us. Some of the most obvious of those consequences are economic. The American standard of living has been buoyed to its current level by an imperial wealth pump that funnels much of the wealth of the world to the United States. There's no shortage of the sort of self-congratulatory nonsense that insists that US prosperity is a product of American ingenuity or what have you, but let us please be real; nothing Americans do—nothing, that is, other than maintaining garrisons in more than 140 countries and bombing the bejesus out of any nation that gets too far out of line—justifies the fact that the five per cent of humanity that can apply for a US passport use a quarter of the planet's energy and a third of its natural resources and industrial product.

As the US empire ends, that vast imbalance will go away forever. It really is as simple as that. In the future now breathing down our necks, Americans will have to get used to living, as our not-so-distant ancestors did, on a much more modest fraction of the world's wealth—and we'll have to do it at a time when the ongoing depletion of fossil fuels and other nonrenewable resources, and the ongoing disruption of the environment, are making ever sharper inroads on the total amount of wealth that's available to distribute in the first place. That means that nearly everything that counts as an ordinary American lifestyle today is going to go away in the decades ahead. It also means that my American readers, not to mention almost everyone else in the United States, are going to be very much poorer in the wake of empire than they are today.

Too many of the plans currently in circulation at the green end of US alternative culture miss this point, and assume that we'll still be able to dispose of wealth on the same scale as we do today. The lifeboat ecovillages beloved by the more apocalyptic element of that subculture, just as much as the solar satellites and county-sized algal biodiesel farms that feature in the daydreams of their cornucopian counterparts, presuppose that such projects can be supplied with the startup capital, the resources, the labor, and all the other requirements they need.

The end of American empire means that these things aren't going to happen. To judge by previous examples, it will take whatever global empire replaces ours some decades to really get the wealth pump running at full speed and flood its own economy with a torrent of unearned wealth. By the time that happens, the decline in global wealth driven by resource depletion and environmental disruption will make the sort of grand projects Americans envisioned in our empire's glory days a fading memory all over the world. Thus we will not get the solar satellites or the algal biodiesel, and if the lifeboat ecovillages appear, they'll resemble St. Benedict's original hovel at Monte Cassino much more than the greenwashed Levittowns so often proposed these days. Instead, as the natural systems that undergird industrial civilization crumble away, industrial societies will lose the capacity to accomplish anything at all beyond bare survival—and eventually that, too, will turn out to be more than they can do.

That's the shape of our economic future, for reasons that closely parallel the fate of every nation that embraces empire and figures out too late just how large of a bill that decision brings with it. Post-imperial America, however, faces a second crisis on top of the usual one, because a similar collision between failing resources and rising costs is winding up America's "empire of time," by way of the broader decline of global conventional petroleum production—the phenomenon known as peak oil.

It's a source of wry amusement, to those of us who have been watching the peaking and decline of oil production for a while now, to see the latest flurry of claims that hydrofractured ("fracked") shale has somehow disproved the rule that the Earth contains a finite supply of petroleum. Enthusiastic claims about the latest oil prospect are hardly new, and indeed they've been central to cornucopian rhetoric since M. King Hubbert pointed out in 1956 that a finite planet can't supply infinite amounts of oil.[1] A decade ago, it was the Caspian Sea oilfields that were being invoked as supposedly conclusive evidence that a peak in global conventional petroleum production wouldn't arrive in our lifetimes. Compare the grand claims made for the Caspian fields back then, and the trickle of production that actually resulted from those fields, and you get a useful reality check on the equally sweeping claims now being made for the Bakken shale. Still, that's not a comparison many people want to make just now.

On the other side of the energy spectrum, the insistence that we can power some equivalent of our present industrial system on sun, wind, and other diffuse renewable sources runs up against equally severe difficulties.[2] It's probably not accidental that this insistence seems to increase in volume with every ethanol refinery or solar panel manufacturer that goes broke, and every study showing that renewable energy can't effectively replace our rapidly depleting fossil fuel supplies. It's also probably not accidental that the rhetoric surrounding the latest fashionable fossil fuel play heats up steadily as production at the world's supergiant fields slides remorselessly down the curve of depletion. The point of such rhetoric isn't to deal with the realities of our situation; it's to pretend that those realities don't exist, so that the party can go on and the hard choices can be postponed just a little longer.

Thus the United States has entered what John Kenneth Galbraith called "the twilight of illusion,"[3] the point at which the end of a historical process would be clearly visible if everybody wasn't so busy finding reasons to look somewhere else. For more than a decade now, those of us who paid attention to peak oil were pointing out that if the peak of global conventional petroleum production arrived before any meaningful steps were taken, the price of oil would rise to previously unimagined heights, crippling the global economy and pushing political systems across the industrial world into a rising spiral of dysfunction and internal conflict.[4] With most grades of oil above $100 a barrel, economies around the world mired in a paper "recovery" worse than most recessions, and the United States and European Union both frozen in political stalemates between regional and cultural blocs with radically irreconcilable agendas, that prophecy has turned out to be pretty much square on the money, but you won't hear many people mention that these days.

Fantasies of technological breakthroughs and sudden collapse have clustered so thickly around the peak oil phenomenon that it can be hard to recognize that the more likely consequences of the peaking of oil production is what we're seeing right now: a long ragged slope of rising energy prices, economic contraction, and political failure, punctuated with a crisis here, a local or regional catastrophe there, a war somewhere else, all against a backdrop of disintegrating infrastructure, declining living standards, decreasing access to healthcare and similar services, and the like. All of this has been happening here in the United States for some years already. A detached observer with an Olympian view of the country would be able to watch things unravel, but the freedom to be a detached observer is granted to very few. At each point on the downward trajectory, those who still have jobs will be struggling to hang onto them, those who have lost their jobs will be struggling to stay fed and clothed and housed, and the crises and catastrophes and wars just mentioned, not to mention the human cost of the broader background of decline, will throw enough smoke in the air to make a clear view of the situation difficult to obtain.

Meanwhile, those who do have the opportunity to get something approaching a clear view of the situation will by and large have every reason to avoid saying a word about what they see. Politicians and the talking heads of the media have nothing to gain from admitting the reality and pace of decline, and it will no doubt be entertaining to watch them scramble for reasons to insist that things are actually getting better and a little patience or a change of government will bring good times back again. There will doubtless be much more of the sort of overt statistical dishonesty that insists, for example, that people who no longer get unemployment benefits are no longer unemployed—that's been standard practice in the United States for decades now.[5]

Behind this handwaving, though, is a real issue that bears directly on the shape of the future before us. The peak of global conventional petroleum production arrived in 2005. The years since then have given us a first glimpse at the future on the far side of peak oil. Conventional petroleum production has declined, and the price of oil has wobbled unsteadily up to levels that mainstream analysts considered impossible a decade ago. Overall production of liquid fuels, however, has remained steady and even risen slightly, as high prices have made it profitable for unconventional petroleum and a range of petroleum substitutes—tar sand extractives, natural gas liquids, biodiesel, ethanol, and the like—to be poured into the world's fuel tanks.

The standard argument that economists have used to dismiss the issue of peak oil was precisely that rising prices would make other energy sources economical, following the normal workings of supply and demand. That process has done a great deal to shape the curve of fuel production, to be sure, but the results have not followed the economists' expectations. As the rate of conventional petroleum production peaked and began its decline, to be sure, prices rose, which made more expensive sources of liquid fuels profitable, and kept total production of liquid fuels not far from where it was when conventional oil peaked in 2005. The wild swings in price since then balanced the ragged decline of conventional petroleum and the equally ragged expansion of substitute fuels by influencing the profitability of any given fuel over time. In its own way, it's an elegant mechanism, however much turmoil and suffering it happens to generate in the real world.

Does this mean that peak oil is no longer an issue? Not by a long shot, because the economic shifts necessary to bring substitute fuels into the fuel supply don't exist in a vacuum. Tar sand extractives, for example, cost more to produce than light sweet crude because pressure-washing tar out of tar sands and converting it to a rough equivalent of crude oil takes much more in the way of energy, resources, and labor than it takes to drill for the same amount of conventional oil. Each year, therefore, as more of the liquid fuels supply is made up by tar sand extractives and other substitute fuels, larger fractions of the annual supply of energy, raw materials, and labor have to be devoted to the process of bringing liquid fuels to market, leaving a smaller portion of each of these things to be divided up among all other economic sectors.

Some of the effects of this process are obvious enough—for example, the spikes in food prices since 2005, as the increasing use of ethanol and biodiesel as liquid fuels diverts grains and vegetable oils from the food supply to use as feedstocks for fuel. Many others are less obvious—for example, as energy prices have risen and energy companies have become Wall Street favorites, many billions of dollars that might otherwise have become capital for other industries have flowed into the energy sector instead. Each of these effects, however, represents a drain on other sectors of the economy, and thus a force for unwelcome changes.

Those changes are a good deal more complex than the ones traced so far, since they involve competition for capital and other resources among different sectors of the economy, a struggle in which political and cultural factors play at least as large a role as economics. Still, one result can be traced in the unexpected decline in petroleum consumption that has taken place in the United States since 2008,[6] which precisely parallels the similar decline that happened between 1975 and 1985 in response to a similar rise in oil prices. A complex array of factors has fed into the decline in oil consumption, but it's probably safe to assume that the increasing impoverishment of most Americans is playing a very large role in it.

Ironically, *The Limits to Growth*—the most accurate and thus, inevitably, the most maligned of the various guides to our unwelcome future offered up during the brief heyday of sustainable thought in the 1970s—sketched out our current situation decades ago. By the simple expedient of lumping resources, industrial production, and other primary factors into a single variable each, the *Limits to Growth* team avoided the fixation on detail that so often blinds people to systems behavior on the broad scale.[7] Within the simplified model that resulted, it became obvious that growth on a finite planet is a self-limiting process. It became just as obvious that the most important of the limits is the simple fact that in any environment with finite resources and a finite capacity to absorb pollution, the costs of growth would eventually rise faster than the benefits, and force the global economy to its knees.

That's what's happening now. It's hard to see at first glance, because the costs of growth are popping up in unexpected places; put too much stress on a chain and it'll break, but the link that breaks isn't necessarily the one closest to the source of stress. The economies of the world's industrial nations depend utterly on a steady supply of liquid fuels, and so a steady supply of liquid fuels they will have, even if every other sector of the economy has to be dumped into the hopper in order to keep the fuel flowing. As every other sector of the economy is dumped into that hopper, in turn, the demand for liquid fuels goes down, because when people who used to be employed by the rest of the economy can no longer afford to spend spring break in Mazatlan, or buy goods that have to be shipped halfway around the planet, or put gas in their cars, their share of petroleum consumption goes unclaimed.

The reallocation of ever larger fractions of capital, resources, and labor to the production of liquid fuels thus represents a subtle drain on most other fields of economic endeavor, driving costs up and profits down across the board. The one exception is the financial sector. Since increasing the amount of paper value produced by purely financial transactions involves no additional capital, resources, or labor, a derivative worth ten million dollars costs no more to produce, in terms of real inputs, than one worth ten thousand, or for that matter ten cents. Thus financial transactions become the only reliable source of profit in a faltering economy, and the explosive expansion of abstract paper wealth masks the contraction of real wealth.

It's quite possible that as we move further past the peak of conventional petroleum production, the consumption of petroleum products will continue to decline, so that when the ability to produce substitute fuels and supply other vital resources declines as well—as it will[8]—the impact of the latter decline will be hard to trace. Ever more elaborate towers of hallucinatory wealth, ably assisted by reams of doctored government statistics, will project the illusion of a thriving economy onto a society in free-fall; the stock market will wobble up and down for a long time to come, booming and crashing on occasion as bubbles come and go. Meanwhile a growing fraction of the population will be forced to drop out of the official economy altogether, and be left to scrape together whatever sort of living they can in some updated equivalent of the Hoovervilles and tarpaper shacks of the 1930s.

No doubt the glossy magazines that make their money by marketing a rose-colored image of the future to today's privileged classes will hail declines in petroleum demand as a sign that some golden age of green technology is at hand, and trot out a flurry

of anecdotes to prove it. All they'll have to do is ignore the hard
figures showing that demand for renewable-energy systems is
dropping too, as people who have no money find solar panels as
unaffordable as barrels of oil. For that matter, the people who are
insisting in today's media that the United States will achieve energy independence by 2050 may just turn out to be right; it's just
that this may happen because the United States will have devolved
into a bankrupt Third World nation in which the majority of the
population lives in abject poverty and petroleum consumption
has dropped to a sixth or less of its current level. The media in
2050 may well be insisting that everything is actually just fine, the
drastic impoverishment of most of the American people is just
the sort of healthy readjustment a capitalist economy needs from
time to time, and we'll be going back to the Moon any day now,
just as soon as we finish reopening the Erie Canal to mule-drawn
barge traffic so that grain can get from the Midwest to the slowly
drowning cities of the East Coast.

It's no longer necessary to speculate, then, about what kind of
future the end of the age of cheap abundant energy will bring to the
industrial world. That package has already been delivered, and the
economic rigor mortis and political gridlock that have tightened
its grip on this and so many other countries in the industrial world
are, depending on your choice of metaphor, either part of the package or part of the packing material, scattered across the landscape
like so much bubble wrap. Now that the future is here, abstract
considerations and daydreaming about might-have-beens need
to take a back seat to the quest to understand what's happening,
and work out coping strategies to deal with it now that it's upon
us. Central to those strategies is a crucial issue that was recently
brought into focus in an intriguing essay by ecological economist
Herman Daly.[9]

In the murky firmament of today's economics, Daly is one
of the few genuinely bright stars. A former World Bank official
as well as a tenured academic, Daly has earned a reputation as

one of the very few economic thinkers to challenge the dogma of perpetual growth, arguing forcefully for a steady state economic system as the only kind capable of functioning sustainably on a finite planet. The essay just cited—entitled "Growth, Debt and the World Bank" —covers quite a bit of ground, but the detail relevant to the present subject appears in the first few paragraphs.

In his training as an economist, Daly was taught, as most budding economists are still taught today, that inadequate capital is the most common barrier to the development of the so-called "developing" (that is, never going to develop) nations. His experience in the World Bank, though, taught him that this was almost always incorrect. The World Bank had plenty of capital to lend; the problem was a shortage of "bankable projects"—projects that, when funded by a World Bank loan, would produce the returns of ten percent a year or so that would be needed to pay off the loan and also contribute to the accumulation of capital within the country.

It takes a familiarity with the last half-dozen decades of economic literature to grasp just how sharply Daly's experience flies in the face of the conventional thinking of our time. Theories of economic development, by and large, assume that every nonindustrial nation will naturally follow the same trajectory of development as today's industrial nations did, building the factories, hiring the workers, providing the services, and in the process generating the same ample profits that made the industrialization of Britain, America, and other nations a self-sustaining process. Now of course Britain, America, and every other nation that succeeded in industrializing did so behind a wall of protective tariffs and predatory trade policies that sheltered industries at home against competition, a detail that gets discussed next to nowhere in the literature on development and was ignored in the World Bank's purblind enthusiasm for free trade. Still, there's more going on here.

In *The Power of the Machine*, as explained earlier, Alf Hornborg pointed out trenchantly that the industrial economy is at least as much a means of wealth concentration as it is of wealth production.

In the early days of the Industrial Revolution, when the hundreds of thousands of independent spinners and weavers who had been the backbone of Britain's textile industry were driven out of business by the mills of the English Midlands, the income that used to be spread among the latter went to a few mill owners and investors instead, with a tiny fraction reserved for the mill workers who tended the new machines at starvation wages. That same pattern expanded past a continental scale as spinners and weavers across much of the world were forced out of work by Britain's immense cloth export industry, and money that might have stayed in circulation in countries around the globe went instead into the pockets of English magnates.

Throughout the history of the industrial age, that was the pattern that drove industrialism: from 18th century Britain to post-World War II Japan, a body of wealthy men in a country with a technological edge and ample supplies of cheap labor could build factories, export products, tilt the world's economy in their favor, and make immense profits. In the language of Daly's essay, industrial development in such a context was a bankable project, capable of producing much more than ten percent returns. What gets misplaced in current thinking about industrial development, though, is that at least two conditions had to be met for that to happen. The first of them, as already mentioned, is exactly the sort of protective trade policies that the World Bank and the current economic consensus generally are unwilling to contemplate, or even to mention.

The second, however, cuts far closer to the heart of our current predicament. The industrial economy as it evolved from the 18th century onward depended utterly on the ability to replace relatively expensive human labor with cheap fossil fuel energy. The mills of the English Midlands mentioned above were able to destroy the livelihoods of hundreds of thousands of independent spinners and weavers because, all things considered, it was far cheaper to build a spinning jenny or a power loom and fuel it with coal than it was to pay for the skilled craftsmen and craftswomen who had done the same work in an earlier day. In economic terms, in other words, industrialism is a system of arbitrage.

Those of my readers who aren't fluent in economic jargon deserve a quick definition of that last term. Arbitrage is the fine art of profiting off the difference in price between the same good in two or more markets. The carry trade, one of the foundations of the global economic system that came apart at the seams in 2008, was a classic example of arbitrage. In the carry trade, financiers borrowed money in Japan, where they could get it at an interest rate of one or two per cent per year, and then lent it at some higher interest rate elsewhere in the world. The difference between interest paid and interest received was pure profit.

What sets industrialism apart from most other arbitrage schemes was that it arbitraged the price difference between different forms of energy. Concentrated heat energy, in the form of burning fossil fuel, was cheap; mechanical energy, in the form of complex movements performed by the hands of spinners and weavers, was expensive. The steam engine turned concentrated heat into mechanical energy, and opened the door to what must have been the most profitable arbitrage operation of all time. The gargantuan profits yielded by this scheme provided the startup capital for further rounds of industrialization and so made possible the immense economic transformations of the industrial age.

That arbitrage, however, depended—as all arbitrage schemes do—on the price difference between the markets in question. In the case of industrialism, the difference was always fated to be temporary, because the low cost of concentrated heat was made possible purely by vast unexploited reserves of fossil fuels that could easily be accessed by human beings. For obvious reasons, the most readily accessible reserves were mined or drilled first, and so as time passed, production costs for fossil fuels—not to mention the many other natural materials needed for industrial projects, and thus necessary for the arbitrage operation to continue—went up, slowly at first, and more dramatically in the last decade or so.

The shortage of bankable projects in the nonindustrial world that Herman Daly noted was arguably an early symptom of that last process. Since nonindustrial nations in the 1990s were held (at gunpoint when necessary) to the dogma of free trade, the first condition for industrialization—a protected domestic market in which new industries could be sheltered from competition—was not an option. At the same time, the systemic imbalances between rich and poor countries meant that human labor simply wasn't that much more expensive than fossil fuel energy.

That was what drove the globalization fad of the 1990s: another round of arbitrage, in which huge profits were reaped off the difference between labor costs in industrial and nonindustrial countries. Very few people seem to have noticed that globalization involved a radical reversal of the movement toward greater automation—that is, the use of fossil fuel energy to replace human labor. When the cost of hiring a sweatshop laborer became less than the cost of paying for an equivalent amount of productive capacity in mechanical form, the arbitrage shifted into reverse; only the steep differentials in wage costs between the Third World and the industrial nations, and a vast amount of very cheap transport fuel, made it possible for the arbitrage to continue.

Still, at this point the same lack of bankable projects has come home to roost. A series of lavish Federal Reserve money printing operations (the current euphemism is "quantitative easing") flooded the banking system in the United States with immense amounts of cheap cash, in an attempt to make up for the equally immense losses the banking system suffered in the aftermath of the 2005–2008 real estate bubble. Pundits insisted that the result would be a flood of new loans to buoy the economy out of its doldrums, but nothing of the kind happened. There are plenty of reasons why it didn't happen, but a core reason was simply that there aren't that many business propositions in the industrial world just now that are in a position to earn enough money to pay back loans.

Among the few businesses that do promise a decent return on investment are the ones involved in fossil fuel extraction, and so companies drilling for oil and natural gas in shale deposits have more capital than they know what to do with. The oil boomtowns in North Dakota and the fracking projects stirring up controversy in various corners of the country are among the results. Elsewhere in the American economy, however, good investments are increasingly scarce. For decades now, profits from the financial industry and speculation have eclipsed profits from the manufacture of goods—before the 2008 crash, it bears remembering, General Motors made far more profit from its financing arm than it did from building cars—and that reshaping of the economy seems to be approaching its logical endpoint, the point at which it's no longer profitable for the industrial economy to make anything at all.

This may turn out to be one of the most crucial downsides of the arrival of peak oil. If the industrial economy, as I've suggested, was basically an arbitrage scheme profiting off the difference in cost between energy from fossil fuels and energy from human laborers, the rising cost of fossil fuels and other inputs needed to run an industrial economy will sooner or later collide with the declining cost of labor in an impoverished and overcrowded society. As we get closer to that point, we may begin to see the entire industrial project unravel, as the profits needed to make industrialism make sense dry up. If that's the unspoken subtext behind the widening spiral of economic dysfunction that seems to be gripping so much of the industrial world today, then what we've seen so far of what peak oil looks like may be a prologue to a series of wrenching economic transformations that will leave few lives untouched.

At the core of these transformations are factors that operate well below the surface. One of the things that makes the predicament of industrial society so difficult for most people to notice, in fact, is that its effects are woven so deeply into the patterns of everyday life. Over the last decade, for example, crude oil prices have more than tripled; over the last decade, behind a froth of speculative booms and busts, the world's industrial economies have lurched deeper into depression. Peak oil researchers have pointed out for years that the former trend would bring about the latter, but long after events proved them right, the connection still remains unnoticed by most people.

To be fair, the way most people and nearly all economists think about economics makes this sort of blindness to the obvious hard to avoid. It's standard these days to treat the circulation of money—the tertiary economy, to use a term from my book *The Wealth of Nature*—as though it's all that matters, and to insist that the cycles of nature and the production of goods and services (the primary and secondary economies) will inevitably do whatever we want them to do, so long as there's enough money. This is why, for instance, you'll hear economists insisting that the soaring price of oil is good for the economy; after all, all the money being spent to buy oil is getting spent in turn on other things, right?

What this ignores, of course, is the fact that the price of oil is going up, in large part, because petroleum and its substitutes are getting steadily more difficult to extract as the easily accessible sources run dry, and so the cost of oil production rises while the amount of oil being produced does not. As a growing fraction of industrial civilization's capacity to produce goods and services has to be diverted into oil extraction in order to maintain something like current production, the amount of that capacity that can be used for anything else decreases accordingly. Notice, though, that this diversion isn't an obvious thing; it happens one transaction at a time, throughout the economy, as laborers, raw materials, capital, and a thousand other things go into oil production instead of some other economic sector.

The essay by Herman Daly cited earlier offers unexpected insight into the consequences. The World Bank, as Daly recounts, tried to make up for the shortage by lowering its standards, and pouring money into projects that counted as bankable only in the same imaginary world where Pets.com stock and subprime mortgage-backed securities are good investments.

A shortage of bankable projects, however, has been a problem for some time now in regions not normally consigned to the Third World. The Rust Belt town where I live, Cumberland, Maryland, is one example. Until 1974 it was a significant industrial center, with two large breweries, a tire factory, a fabric mill, and several smaller concerns. 1974, though, was the year that the consequences of America's first brush with peak oil hit home, and Cumberland was one of the impact zones. A combination of soaring raw material costs, slumping sales, and competition from overseas shuttered every factory in town, and none ever reopened. Cumberland, like the rest of the Rust Belt, suddenly had a shortage of bankable projects, and rock-bottom real estate prices, favorable tax policies, low labor costs, and two colleges nearby to provide workforce training at state expense couldn't lure factory jobs back into the region.

That same experience is being repeated now all over America, and across much of the industrial world as well. Capital shortage isn't an issue—with limitless quantitative easing and a tacit agreement on the part of bank regulators not to raise awkward questions about the actual value of the paper assets owned by banks, there's plenty of money available to lend—but loans aren't being made, and the reason given by bank after bank is that next to nobody who wants to borrow money has a credible plan that will allow them to pay it back. That was exactly what happened to Cumberland; in the changed economic environment after 1974, a factory built here wouldn't have made enough money to pay back the loans that would have been needed to build it, and so the loans weren't made. Increasingly, that seems to be true of the industrial world as a whole.

All this can be described as a widening mismatch between the economy of money and the economy of goods and services—or, to put the matter even more simply, a rising tide of paper wealth chasing a falling tide of actual value. Still, there's another way of looking at it, and it unfolds from the perspectives discussed in previous chapters.

Let's step away for a moment from the game of arbitrary tokens we call "money," and look at the economy as a system for producing goods and services by applying energy to an assortment of raw materials. Until the coming of the industrial revolution, the vast majority of the energy that went into human economic systems went from sunlight to crops to human and animal muscle, which produced and distributed goods and services. The industrial revolution transformed that equation, adding torrents of cheap abundant fossil fuel energy to the annual income from photosynthesis. Only a small fraction of the labor force and other resources had to be diverted from food production to bring this flood of energy into the economic equation, and only a small fraction of fossil fuels had to be cycled back into the fossil fuel extraction process; the rest of the labor force, other resources, and all that additional energy from fossil fuels could be poured into the rest of the economy, producing goods and services in unparalleled amounts.

Physicist Ilya Prigogine has shown by way of intricate equations that the flow of energy through a system increases the complexity of the system.[10] If any further evidence was needed to back up his claims, the history of the world's industrial economies provides it. The three centuries that followed the development of the first functional steam engines saw economic complexity, measured by the creation of new job categories, soar to a level almost unimaginably greater than any previous civilization had achieved. The bonanza of wealth produced by adding fossil fuel energy to the sun's annual contribution spread throughout the industrial economies, and the ways and means by which money sprayed outwards from the pockets of coal magnates and oil barons quickly became institutionalized.

Governments, businesses, and societies ballooned in complexity, creating niches for entire ecosystems of office fauna to do tasks the presidents and tycoons of the nineteenth century had accomplished with a tiny fraction of the personnel; workloads obeyed Parkinson's Law—"work expands so as to fill the time available for its completion"[11]—and everyone found that it was easier to add more staff to get a job done than to get the existing staff to do it themselves. The result, in most industrial societies, is an economy in which only a small fraction of the labor force actually has anything directly to do with the production of goods and services, while the rest are kept busy managing the sprawling social and economic machinery that has come into being to organize, finance, manage, staff, market, advertise, sell, analyze, tax, regulate, review, praise, and denounce the production of goods and services.

What seems to have been lost sight of, though, is that this immense superstructure all rests on the same foundation as any other economy: the use of energy to convert raw materials into goods and services. More to the point, it depends on a certain level of surplus that can be produced in this way, and that depends in turn on being able to add plenty of fossil fuel energy to the economic system without having to divert too large a fraction of the labor force, resource base, and energy supply into the extraction of fossil fuels. Some sense of the difference made by fossil fuels can be measured by comparing the economies of the industrial age to those of societies that, by any other standard, were near the upper end of human social complexity—Tokugawa Japan and Renaissance Italy come to mind. Urban, literate, and highly cultured, each of these societies had the resources to support extraordinary artistic, literary, and intellectual creativity. Still, they did this with economies vastly simpler than anything you'll find in a modern industrial society.

The division of the labor force among economic roles makes a good measure of the difference. In both societies, the largest economic sector, employing around fifty percent of the adult population (nearly all adult women and most elderly people of both sexes), was the household economy, and thus a good half of the total economic value produced in each society came out of the kitchen gardens, spindles, looms, and other economic facilities associated with households. Another thirty percent or so of the population in each society, including most of the adult men, was engaged full time in farming and other forms of direct food production; maybe ten percent of the adult population worked in the skilled trades; and the remaining ten percent or so were divided among religious professionals, military professionals, artists and performers, aristocrats, and merchants who lived by buying and selling goods produced by others.

The limited range of categories available in those societies was not the result of inadequate cleverness. If some Renaissance Italian despot or Tokugawa shogun had decided he needed a staff of human resource managers, corporate image consultants, strategic marketing specialists, and the rest of the occupational specialties of modern business life, say, he would have been out of luck. If he tried anyway, he would have been out of a job—the resources needed to train and employ some equivalent of modern office fauna would have had to be diverted from more immediate necessities such as training and employing a force of condottieri or samurai adequate to the military demands of the time. This is why Renaissance Italian despots and Tokugawa shoguns got by with relatively small staffs of clerks, scribes, feudal subordinates, and maybe an astrologer; that's what their economic systems could afford.

Equally, an aspiring craftsman or merchant in these societies faced real challenges in expanding his business beyond fairly sharp limits. In a few cases, a combination of luck, technical skill, and adequate transport allowed one region to take on a commanding role in some specific export market, profit considerably from that, and build up an impressive degree of infrastructure; the golden age of Greece was paid for by the profits from Greek wine and olive oil exports, for example, and the woolen trade brought similar benefits to late medieval Flanders. Far more often, though, local needs had to be supplied by local production, because the surplus energy that would have been needed to power long distance trade on a large scale simply didn't exist, or couldn't be spared from more pressing needs. Thus the institutional arrangements that governed economic life before the industrial age were as closely tailored to a world of relatively scarce energy, in which most people worked in the household or farming sectors of the economy, as today's institutional arrangements are tailored to a world awash in cheap abundant energy.

That last point defines the crisis of our times, however, because we no longer live in a world awash in cheap abundant energy. We've still got more energy than Renaissance Italy or Tokugawa Japan had, to be sure, but the per capita surplus is not what it once was, and a growing fraction of what we've got has had to be diverted to cover increases in direct and indirect energy costs of energy production. Meanwhile, the institutional arrangements are still firmly fixed in place, and they aren't optional; try starting a business without dealing with banks, real estate companies, licensing boards, tax authorities, et al., and you'll quickly discover how non-optional these arrangements are.

The mismatch between the economy we've got and the economy we can afford has many implications, but one of the largest is precisely that there are very few bankable projects to be found, even at a time when there are millions of people who need work, and who would happily buy products if they had the chance to earn the money to do so. Our economy is thus burdened with an unproductive superstructure it can no longer support. The globalization fad of the 1990s, which arbitraged the difference in wage costs between Third World sweatshops and industrial-world factories, was an attempt to evade the resulting difficulties by throwing the industrial nations' working classes under the bus, and it only worked for a decade or so; as so often happens in the declining years of a civilization, a short term fix was treated as a long term solution, and a brief remission of symptoms allowed the underlying crisis to worsen.

Over the long run, the mismatch is a problem that will solve itself. Once the unraveling of the industrial economy goes far enough, the superstructure will come apart, leaving a great many human resource managers, corporate image consultants, strategic marketing specialists, and the like with about as much chance of finding jobs in their fields as they would have had in 17th-century Osaka or 14th-century Milan. In the short and middle term, though, the mismatch will almost certainly continue to show itself in exactly the same way that it's been visible over the last few decades: more and more often, business ventures simply won't be able to make enough money to cover startup costs or to stay in business.

Of course there will be exceptions. Sweeping as it is, this change will appear, as it has appeared so far, as a shifting of statistical averages, and the background of ordinary economic fluctuations will make it difficult to tease out the signal from the noise. Even in hard times, some ventures make fortunes; what makes hard times differ from boom times is that the fortunes are fewer, and the odds of making one of them come more and more to resemble the odds of walking away from a Vegas casino with a six-figure jackpot.

While other economic arrangements are certainly imaginable, the one we have right now is strictly limited in what it can accomplish by what can make a profit. To repeat Daly's term, it has to be a bankable project, or it probably won't get done. This may just turn out to be a far more dangerous limitation than anybody has yet realized. There are, after all, any number of plans for grand projects in response to the end of the age of cheap abundant energy; each of them would require the investment of a great deal of capital, labor, raw materials, and other resources; and under present arrangements, none of them can go forward unless someone can count on making a profit from making them happen. Under present arrangements, in turn, it's likely that none of them will be profitable enough to get a construction loan or to cover their operating costs once they get built.

We've already seen a solid prefigure of this in the ethanol bubble of a few years ago, in which firms in corn states rushed to build ethanol plants. Even with government subsidies and a guaranteed market, a great many of those plants are now bankrupt and shuttered. It's an open secret that many recent solar and wind energy projects make money only because of government subsidies. Grandiose plans to turn large swathes of Nevada into algal biodiesel farms or vast solar arrays are even more likely to be subject to the same rule—and the subsidies in these latter cases would be ruinously expensive.

That arithmetic is currently playing out in a different way in Europe, sending out foreshocks of an economic earthquake that could level quite a bit of the industrial world's fiscal architecture. A diversity of forces have come together to turn Europe into the rolling economic debacle it is today, and not all of them are shared by industrial civilization as a whole. Still, a close look at the European crisis will make it possible to make sense of the broader predicament of the industrial world, on the one hand, and the way that predicament will likely play out in the collapse of what remains of the American economy on the other.

Let's begin with an overview. During the global real estate bubble of the last decade, European banks invested recklessly in a great many dubious projects, and were hit hard when the bubble burst and those projects moved abruptly toward their real value. Only one European nation, Iceland, did the intelligent thing: it allowed its insolvent banks to fail, paid off those depositors who were covered by deposit insurance, and drew a line under the problem. Everywhere else, governments caved in to pressure from the rentier class—the people whose income depends on investments rather than salaries, wages, or government handouts—and from foreign governments, and assumed responsibility for all the debts of their failed banks without exception.

Countries that did so, however, found that the interest rates they had to pay to borrow in credit markets quickly soared to ruinous levels, as investors sensibly backed away from countries that were too deeply in debt. Ireland and Greece fell into this trap, and turned to the IMF and the financial agencies of the European

Union for help, only to discover the hard way that the "help" consisted of loans at market rates—that is, adding more debt on top of an already crushing debt burden—with conditions attached. The conditions, to be precise, mirrored those that were inflicted on a series of Third World countries in the wake of the 1998 financial crash, with catastrophic results.

It used to be called the Washington Consensus, though nobody's using that term now for the austerity measures currently being imposed on most of Europe. Basically, it amounts to the theory that the best therapy for a nation over its head in debt consists of massive cuts to government spending and the privatization, at fire-sale prices, of government assets. In theory, debtor countries that embrace this set of prescriptions return promptly to prosperity. In practice—and it's been tried on well over two dozen countries over the last three decades or so, so there's an ample body of experience—debtor countries that embrace this set of prescriptions are stripped to the bare walls by their creditors and remain in an economic coma until populist politicians seize power, tell the IMF where it can put its economic ideology, and default on their unpayable debts. That's what Iceland did, as Russia, Argentina, and any number of other countries did before them, and it's the only way for a country drowning in debt to return to prosperity.

That reality, though, is not exactly welcome news to those nations profiting off the modern form of wealth pump, in which unpayable loans usually play a large role. Whenever you see the Washington Consensus being imposed on a country, look for the nations that are advocating it most loudly and it's a safe bet that they'll be the countries most actively engaged in stripping assets from the debtor nation; in today's Europe, that's usually Germany. It's one of the mordant ironies of contemporary history that Europe fought two of the world's most savage wars in the first half of the twentieth century to deny Germany a European empire, then spent the second half of the same century allowing Germany to attain, without a shot being fired, nearly every one of its war aims short of overseas colonies and a victory parade down the Champs Élysées.

Since the foundation of the Eurozone, in particular, European economic policy has worked out for German benefit even at the expense of other European nations. The single currency itself is an immense boon to the German economy, which spent decades struggling with exchange rates that made German exports more expensive, and foreign imports more affordable, to Germany's detriment. The peseta, the lira, the franc and other European currencies can no longer respond to trade imbalances by losing value relative to the deutschmark now that it's all one currency. The resulting system—combined with the free trade regulations demanded by economic orthodoxy and enforced by bureaucrats in Brussels—has functioned as a highly efficient wealth pump, and has allowed Germany and a few of its northern European neighbors to prosper while southern Europe stumbles deeper into economic collapse.

In one sense, then, it's no wonder that German government officials are insisting at the top of their lungs that other European countries have to bail out failing banks and then use tax revenues to pay off the resulting debt, even if that requires those countries to follow what amounts to a recipe for national economic suicide. The end of the wealth pump might not mean the endgame for Germany's current prosperity, but it would certainly make matters much more difficult for the German economy, and thus for the future prospects not only for the nation's chancellor, but of a great many other German politicians. Even the most blinkered of those ought to recognize that trying to squeeze the last drop of wealth out of southern Europe is simply going to speed up the arrival of the populist leaders mentioned a few paragraphs back, but I suppose it's possible that this generation of German politicians is too clueless or too harried to think of that.

Still, there may be more going on, because all these disputes are taking place in a wider context.

The speculative bubble that popped so dramatically in 2008 was by most measures the biggest in human history, considerably bigger than the one that blew the global economy to smithereens in 1929. Even so, the events of 1929 and the Great Depression that followed it remain the gold standard of economic crisis, and the managers of the world's major central banks in 2008 were not unaware of the factors that turned the 1929 crash into what remains, even by today's standards, the worst economic trauma of modern times. Most of those factors amount to catastrophic mistakes on the part of central bankers, so it's just as well that today's central bankers are paying attention.

The key to understanding the Great Depression lies in understanding what exactly it was that went haywire in 1929. In the United States, for example, all the factors that made for ample prosperity in the 1920s were still solidly in place in 1930. Nothing had gone wrong with the farms, factories, mines, and oil wells that undergirded the American economy, nor was there any shortage of laborers ready to work or consumers eager to consume. What happened was that the money economy—the system of abstract tokens that industrial societies use to allocate goods and services among people—had frozen up. Since most economic activity in an industrial society depends on the flow of money, and there are no systems in place to take over from the money economy if that grinds to a halt, a problem with the distribution and movement of money made it impossible for the real economy of goods and services to function.

That was what the world's central bankers were trying to prevent in 2008 and the years immediately afterward, and it's what they're still trying to prevent today. That's what the trillions of dollars that were loaned into existence by the Fed, the Bank of England, and other central banks, and used to prop up failing financial institutions, were meant to do, and it may well be part what's behind the frantic attempts already mentioned to stave off defaults and prevent banks from paying the normal price for the resoundingly stupid investments of the former boom—though of course the unwillingness of bankers to pay that price with their own careers, and the convenience of large banks as instruments of wealth pumping, also have large roles there.

In 1929 and 1930, panic selling in the US stock market erased millions of dollars in notional wealth—again, that was a lot of money then—and made raising capital next to impossible for businesses and individuals alike. In 1931, the crisis spread into the banking industry, kicking off a chain reaction of bank failures that pushed the global money system into cardiac arrest and forced most of the world's economies to their knees. The world's central banks set out to prevent a repeat of that experience. It's considered impolite in some circles to mention this, but by and large they succeeded; the global economy is still in a world of hurt, but the complete paralysis of the monetary system that made the Great Depression what it was has so far been avoided.

There's a downside to that, however, which is that keeping the monetary system from freezing up has done nothing to deal with the underlying problem driving the current crisis, the buildup of an immense dead weight of loans and other financial instruments that are supposed to be worth something, and aren't. Balance sheets throughout the global economy are still loaded to the bursting point with securitized loans that will never be repaid, asset-backed securities backed by worthless assets, derivatives wished into being by what amounts to make-believe, and equally dubious financial exotica acquired during the late bubble by people who were too giddy with paper profits to notice their actual value, which in most cases is essentially zero.

What makes this burden so lethal is that financial institutions of all kinds are allowed to treat this worthless paper as though it still has some approximation of its former theoretical value, even though everyone in the financial industry knows how much it's really worth. Forcing firms to value it at market rates would cause a catastrophic string of bankruptcies; even forcing firms to admit to how much of it they have, and of what kinds, could easily trigger bank runs and financial panic; while it remains hidden, though, nobody knows when enough of it will blow up and cause another financial firm to implode—and so the trust that's essential to the functioning of a money economy is trickling away. Nobody wants to lend money to a firm whose other assets might suddenly turn into twinkle dust; for that matter, nobody wants to let their own cash reserves decline, in case their other assets turn into the same illiquid substance; and so the flow of money through the economy slows, and fails to do the job it's supposed to do of facilitating the production and exchange of goods and services.

That's the risk you take when you try to stop a financial panic without tackling the underlying burden of worthless assets generated by the preceding bubble. Much more often than not, in the past, it's been a risk worth running; if you can only hold on until the impact of the panic fades, economic growth in some non-financial sector of the economy picks up, the financial industry can replace its bogus assets with something different and presumably better, and away you go. That's what happened in the wake of the tech-stock panic of 2000 and 2001: the Fed dropped interest rates, made plenty of money available to financial firms in trouble, and did everything else it could think of to postpone bankruptcies until the housing bubble started boosting the economy again. It doesn't always work—Japan has been stuck in permanent recession in the wake of its gargantuan 1990 stock market crash, precisely because the same program didn't work there—but in American economic history, at least, it's tended to work more often than not.

Still, there was a major warning sign in the wake of the tech-stock fiasco that should have been heeded, and was not: what boosted the economy anew wasn't an economic expansion in some non-financial sector, but a second and even larger speculative bubble in the financial sphere. The shortage of bankable projects already discussed is again at issue here. In an expanding economy, bankable projects are easy to find, since it's precisely the expansion of an expanding economy that makes a positive return on investment the normal way of things. If you flood your economy with cheap credit to counter the aftermath of a speculative bubble, and the only thing that comes out of it is an even bigger speculative bubble, something significant has happened to the mechanisms of economic growth.

More specifically, something other than a paralysis of the money system has happened to the mechanisms of economic growth. That's the unlearned lesson of the last decade. In the wake of the 2001 stock crash, and then again in the aftermath of 2008's even larger panic, the Fed flooded the US economy with quantities of cheap credit so immense that any viable project for producing goods and services ought to have been able to find ample capital to get off the ground. Instead of an entrepreneurial boom, though, both periods saw money pile up in the financial industry, because there was a spectacular shortage of viable projects outside it. Outside of manipulating money and gaming the system, there simply isn't much that makes a profit any more.

It's important to note what the twilight of investment means for the kick-the-can strategy that's guiding the Fed and other central banks in their efforts to fix the world economy. That strategy depends on the belief that sooner or later, even the most battered economy will finally begin to improve, and the upswing will make it possible to replace the temporary patches on the economy with something more solid. It's been a viable strategy fairly often in the past, but it worked poorly in 2001 and it doesn't appear to be working at all at this point. Thus it's probable that the Fed is treading water, waiting for a rescue that isn't on its way.

Since the crisis dawned in 2008, in the same way, EU policy has demanded that every other sector of the economy be thrown under the bus in order to prop up the tottering mass of unpayable debt that Europe's financial economy has become. As banks fail, governments have been strong-armed into guaranteeing the value of the banks' worthless financial paper; as governments fail in their turn, other governments that are still solvent are being pressured to fill the gap with bailouts that, again, amount to little more than a guarantee that even the most harebrained investment will not be allowed to lose money. The problem is that you can cash in the whole planet's gross domestic product—that was a little under $62 trillion in 2010—and not come anywhere close to the value of the mountain of increasingly fictive paper wealth that's been piled up by the financial industry in the last few decades. Thus the EU's strategy is guaranteed to fail, and the natural endpoint of that strategy is default.

There's been a lot of talk about default in the economic end of the blogosphere, and for good reason. No matter how you twist and turn the matter, Greece is never going to be able to pay its debts. Neither are Spain, Italy, or half a dozen other nations that ran up big debts when it was cheap and convenient to do so, and are now being strangled by a panicking bond market and a collapsing economy. Most of the countries on Earth have either defaulted outright on their debts or forced renegotiations on their creditors that left the latter with some equivalent of pennies on the dollar. The United States last did that in a big way in 1934, when the Roosevelt administration unilaterally changed the terms on billions of dollars in Liberty Bonds from "payable in gold" to "payable in devalued dollars," and proceeded to print the latter as needed. That or considerably worse will be happening in Europe in the near future, too.

A good deal of the discussion of these upcoming defaults, though, has insisted that these defaults will lead to a complete collapse of the world's financial economy, and from there to an equally complete collapse of the world's productive economy, leaving all seven billion of us to starve in the gutter.[12] It's an odd belief, since sovereign debt defaults have happened many times in the recent past, currency collapses are far from rare in economic history, and nation-states can do—and have done—plenty of drastic things to keep goods and services flowing in an economic emergency. Governments used to produce and circulate currency without benefit of banks until fairly recently, and banking services can be provided quickly and easily by a government that means business; in 1933 it took the US government just over a week, at a time when information technology was incomparably slower than it is today, to nationalize every bank in the country and open their doors under federal management. The other services the financial industry provides to the real economy can equally well be replaced by hastily jerry-rigged substitutes, or simply put on hold for the duration of the crisis.

So the downside of any financial crisis, no matter how alarming it appears, can be stopped promptly by proven methods. Then there's the upside, which is the ultimate secret of the financial crisis, the thing that nobody anywhere wants to talk about: if a country gets into a credit crisis, defaulting on its debts is the one option that leads to recovery.

That statement ought to be old hat by now. Russia defaulted on its debts in 1998, and that default marked the end of its post-Soviet economic crisis and the beginning of its current period of relative prosperity. Argentina defaulted on its debts in 2002, and the default put an end to its deep recession and set it on the road to recovery. Even more to the point, Iceland was the one European country that refused the EU demand that the debts of failed banks must be passed on to governments; instead, in 2008, the Icelandic government allowed the country's three biggest banks to fold, paid off Icelandic depositors by way of the existing deposit insurance scheme, and left foreign investors twisting in the wind. Since that time, Iceland has been the only European country to see a sustained recovery.

When Greece defaults on its debts, in turn, there will be a bit of scrambling, and then the Greek recovery will begin. That's the reason the EU has been trying so frantically to keep Greece from defaulting, no matter how many Euros have to be shoveled down how many ratholes to prevent it. Once the Greek default happens, and it will—the number of ratholes is multiplying faster than Euros can be shoveled into them—the other southern European nations that are crushed by excessive debt will line up to do the same. There will be a massive stock market crash, a great many banks will go broke, a lot of rich people and an even larger number of middle class people will lose a great deal of money, politicians will make an assortment of stern and defiant speeches, and then the great European financial crisis will be over and people can get on with their lives.

That's what will happen, too, at some point down the road, when the United States either defaults on its national debt or hyperinflates the debt out of existence. It's going to do one or the other, since its debts are already unpayable except by way of the printing press, and its gridlocked political system is unable either to rationalize its tax system or cut its expenditures. The question is simply what crisis will finally break the confidence of foreign investors in the dollar as a safe-haven currency, and start the panic selling of dollar-denominated assets that will tip the United States into its next really spectacular financial crisis. In the aftermath of that crisis, some form of economic recovery will be able to get under way, as the burden of unpayable debts will finally be lifted; the question that remains to be settled is how much of the United States as presently constituted will be around to witness that recovery.

THE SPECTER OF DEFEAT

A NY NUMBER OF EVENTS could bring about the crisis that, in the twilight years of most empires, pushes an already crumbling system into collapse. As already mentioned, though, I suspect the most likely trigger for an American imperial collapse will be military defeat. Given the gargantuan funding and global reach of today's US military machine, few suggestions fly more thoroughly in the face of the conventional wisdom. I'm not suggesting, though, that such a defeat will happen in spite of the immense power of the US military; Rather, if it occurs, it will almost certainly do so *because* of that vast preponderance of force.

The history of war is full of cases in which the stronger side—the side with the largest forces, the strongest alliances, the most advanced military technology—was crushed by a technically weaker rival. That unexpected outcome can take place in many different ways, but all of them are a function of one simple and rarely remembered fact: military power is never a single uncomplicated variable. In this light, I trust my readers will forgive a somewhat lengthy excursus into what, for most people these days, is an unfamiliar corner of the past. Those who know little and care less about the late Bronze Age Mediterranean should follow along anyway; once we get past the exotic details, the story may begin to seem oddly familiar.[1]

The eastern Mediterranean in the 13th century BCE was at or near the cutting edge of technological complexity at that time, and that inevitably expressed itself on the field of war. In previous centuries, battles were fought by lines of massed infantry using spears, but a new suite of technologies—the horse-drawn chariot and powerful composite bows—revolutionized warfare, allowing relatively small armies of highly mobile and mechanized troops to run rings around old-fashioned infantries and cut them down from a distance with lethal firepower. If you want to call the resulting mode of warfare "blitzkrieg," you won't be too far off.

Chariots, by the standards of the time, were a complex and expensive technology. They required highly trained personnel on the front lines, and large and expensive organizational systems behind the lines, as complex and expensive military technologies always do. The superpowers of the day, Egypt, Assyria, and the Hittite Empire, put quite a bit of their annual budgets into chariot procurement and related costs, fielding anything up to several thousand chariots for major battles; smaller nations, most of them client states of one of the big three, had their own more modest chariot armies. Since a relatively small chariot army could defeat a much bigger force of spearmen, most kingdoms didn't bother to have any more infantry than they needed to man the walls of fortresses and add a few extra pompous circumstances to the royal court.

It was a stable, rich, technologically advanced society—and then, over the course of a few decades to either side of 1200 BCE, it crashed into ruin. The Hittite capital was sacked, its empire collapsed, and the Hittites as an independent people vanished from history forever. City-states, from Mycenean Greece straight down the eastern Mediterranean littoral to the borders of Egypt, were sacked, burned, and abandoned. Surviving documents refer to unknown ships appearing suddenly off the coast, and record frantic pleas to allies for military aid. Finally, in 1179 BCE, the raiders come into the full light of history as the Sea Peoples—that's the name the Egyptians used for them—launched an all-out assault on Egypt itself.

What made the raiders all but unstoppable, as historian Robert Drews showed, was that they had come up with a suite of military technologies and tactics that efficiently crippled chariot armies. Their key weapon was the javelin. Chariot armies depended on mobility and the ability to maneuver in close formation; swarming attacks by light infantry, who could get in among the chariots and use javelins to injure, kill, and panic the chariot horses, shattered the maneuverability that made chariot armies otherwise invincible. Combine that with fast ships that allowed the raiders to come out of nowhere, annihilate armies sent to stop them, pillage and burn every town within reach, and vanish again, and you have the recipe for a shattering military revolution.

Egypt survived and triumphed, in a thoroughly Egyptian way. It was the oldest of the superpowers of its era, and the most conservative; it had a modern chariot army, but it also still had the knowledge base and infrastructure necessary to organize and use an old-fashioned army of massed infantry armed with spears and shields. That's what Ramses III and his generals did, scrapping their chariots and returning to an older and more resilient way of warfare, and so the Sea Peoples crashed headlong into an enemy that had none of the weaknesses on which their tactics depended. The resulting battles were the kind of straightforward slugging match where sheer numbers count most, and the numbers were on Egypt's side; the Sea Peoples got the stuffing pounded out of them, and scattered to the far corners of the Mediterranean world.

Egypt and the Hittite Empire were pretty much equal in military terms; the great battle between them at Kadesh in 1275 BCE ended in an Egyptian retreat, but the forces pitted against one another were of equivalent size and effectiveness. The loose co-alition of barbarian chiefdoms that the Egyptians called the Sea Peoples was immeasurably inferior to either one in conventional military terms—that is to say, they had no chariots, no chariot horses, no composite bows, and military budgets that were a tiny fraction of those of the superpowers of the day. Furthermore, the weapons systems used by the Sea Peoples were radically simpler than those of the superpowers, almost embarrassingly primitive compared to the complex technology of chariot warfare. That didn't keep them from bringing the Hittite Empire down in flames and posing a threat to Egypt that only a stroke of military genius nullified in time.

The central lesson to be learned from this bit of ancient history is that *military power is always contextual.* What counts as overwhelming power in one context can be lethal weakness in another, and the shift from one context to another can take place without warning. Thus it's never safe to say that because one nation has a bigger military budget, or more of whatever the currently fashionable military technology happens to be, than another, the first nation has more military power than the other. In fact, if the first nation has enough of an advantage, and the second nation has the brains the gods gave geese, the first nation is very possibly cruising for a bruising.

Let's look at another example, one cited here several times already: the British Empire on the eve of its dismemberment. In 1900, the official policy was that the British military was to be able to take on the next two largest powers in the world at any moment, and beat them both. That commitment drove a hugely expensive naval building program, backed by research and development so rapid that the world's most powerful battleship in 1906, the then-newly commissioned HMS Dreadnought, was hopelessly obsolete by the time war broke out in 1914.[2] That and millions of pounds spent elsewhere made Britain, by every conventional measure, the strongest military power in the world at that time.

The problem, as mentioned earlier, was that most of that gargantuan expenditure went into projects that proved to be useless when war finally came. Britain's vast naval fleet spent most of the war tied up to the quays, except for one inconclusive battle. If a fraction of the money wasted on battleships had been put into developing antisubmarine warfare, say, or jolting the British Army out of its nineteenth century notions of strategy and tactics, it might have had a significant impact on the war; battleships, however, were central to the British notion of how wars were fought, and so battleships were where the money went.

What's more, after the First World War ended and the Second loomed, the British military remained fixated on the same kind of thinking. While rising powers such as Japan and the United States flung their resources into aircraft carriers and laid the foundations for the future of naval warfare, Britain dabbled in naval aviation and entrusted its defense to battleships. Only a near-total failure of strategic imagination in the Kriegsmarine, Germany's naval arm, kept that from being fatal; if Nazi Germany had learned from its Japanese ally and built half a dozen aircraft carriers before the war instead of wasting its resources on battleships and cruisers, and had then used the carriers to launch a Pearl Harbor-style strike on the British Navy in the spring of 1940, Britain would have been left wide open to an invasion across the Channel once France fell.

Chariots and battleships are simply two examples of a common theme in military history: any military technology that becomes central to a nation's way of war attracts a constituency—a group that includes officers who have made their careers commanding that technology, commercial interests who have made their money building and servicing that technology, and anyone else who has an economic or personal stake in the technology—and that constituency will defend its preferred technology against competing projects until and unless repeated military defeat makes its abandonment inescapable. A common tactic such constituencies routinely use is to offer military scenarios that assume the enemy

must always make war in whatever way will bring out their preferred technology's strengths, and never exploit its weaknesses.

As far as I know, whatever literature ancient Egyptian chariot
officers, horse breeders, and bow manufacturers may have churned
out to glorify chariot warfare to the Egyptian reading public has
not survived, but there's an ample supply of books and articles
from British presses between 1875 or so and the Second World
War, praising the Royal Navy's invincible battleships as the inevitable linchpin of British victory. All this literature was produced
to bolster the case for building and maintaining plenty of battleships, which was to the great advantage of naval officers, marine
architects, and everyone else whose careers depended on plenty
of battleships. The fact that all this investment in battleships
was a waste of money that might actually have done some good
elsewhere did not register until it was too late to save the British
Empire.

If my readers have any doubt that the same sort of literature is
currently being marketed by the constituencies of today's popular
Pentagon weapons systems, I encourage them to check out Tom
Clancy's 1999 puff piece *Carrier: A Guided Tour of an Aircraft
Carrier*. It's a 348-page sales brochure for the most elaborate piece
of military technology ever built, a modern nuclear aircraft carrier, which currently fills the same role in the US military that the
battleship filled in that of imperial Britain. You needn't expect to
find substantive analysis of the strengths and weaknesses of this
hugely expensive technology, or of the global military strategy or
the suite of tactics that give it its context. This is a sales brochure,
and it's meant to sell carriers—or, rather, continued funding for
carriers—to that fraction of the American people that concerns
itself sufficiently with military affairs to write the occasional letter
to its congresscritters.

The inevitable military scenario comes in the last chapter,
where Clancy demonstrates conclusively that if a hopelessly outgunned and outclassed Third World nation were ever to launch

a conventional naval attack against a US carrier group, the carrier group will probably be able to figure out some way to win. It would be a masterpiece of unintended comedy, if it weren't for the looming shadow of all those other books before it, singing the praises of past military technologies whose many advantages didn't turn out to include any part in winning or even surviving the next war. Nor are carriers the only currently popular weapons system that benefits from this sort of uncritical praise; the US military is riddled with them, and thus with a series of potentially fatal vulnerabilities.

The best introduction to the crisis facing the American military, interestingly enough, is a piece of classic science fiction. Among science-fiction author Arthur C. Clarke's many gifts was a mordant sense of humor, and a prime example of that gift in action was his 1951 short story "Superiority."[3] It's the story of a space war narrated by the commanding general of the losing side, who is explaining to some interstellar equivalent of the Nuremberg war crimes tribunal how his forces were defeated. The question is of some interest, as the space fleets and resources of the losing side were far superior to those of the victors. So, however, was their technology. "However" is the operative word, for each brilliantly innovative wonder weapon fielded by their scientists turned out to have disastrous downsides when put into service, while the winning side simply kept on churning out unimaginative space battleships using old but proven technology. By the time the losing side realized that it should have done the same thing, it was so far behind that only a new round of wonder weapons seemed to offer any hope of victory—and a little more of that same logic finished them off.

It's been suggested by more than one wit that life imitates art far more often than art imitates life, and the United States military these days seems intent on becoming a poster child for that proposal. Industrial design classes at MIT used to hand out copies of "Superiority" as required reading; unfortunately that useful habit has not been copied by the Pentagon, and as a result, the US armed forces are bristling with brilliantly innovative wonder weapons that don't do what they're supposed to do.

The much-ballyhooed Predator drone is one good example among many. For those who don't follow military technology, it's a remote-controlled plane designed to fly at rooftop level, equipped with a TV camera and missiles. The operator, sitting in an air-conditioned office building in Nevada, can control it anywhere on Earth via satellite uplink, seek out suspected terrorists, and vaporize them. Does it work? Well, it's vaporized quite a few people; the Obama administration is even more drone-happy than its feckless predecessor, and has been sending swarms of drones around various corners of the Middle East to fire missiles at a great many suspected terrorists.

You'll notice that this has done little to stabilize US puppet governments in the Middle East these days, and did even less to decrease the rate at which American soldiers were getting shot and blown up in Afghanistan before the headlong US withdrawal from that unfortunate country. There's a reason for that. Targets for drone attacks have to be selected by ordinary intelligence methods, since terrorists don't go around with little homing beacons on them, and ordinary intelligence methods have a relatively low signal-to-noise ratio. As a result, a lot of wedding parties and ordinary households get vaporized on the suspicion that there might be a terrorist hiding in there somewhere. Since tribal custom in large parts of the Middle East makes blood vengeance on the murderers of one's family members an imperative duty—well, you can do the math for yourself.

Thus the Predator drone isn't a war-fighting technology, it's a war-losing technology, pursued with ever-increasing desperation by a military and political establishment that has no idea what to do but can't bear the thought of doing nothing. It appeals powerfully to the sort of squeaky-voiced machismo that played so large a role in the Bush administration's foreign policy and is shaping the Obama administration's actions just as extensively, but wars aren't won by imposing one's own delusions on a global battlefield; they're won by figuring out what's out there in the world, and responding to it.

Winning wars also requires remembering that what's out there in the world is responding to you. To grasp how this works, it's going to be necessary to borrow certain concepts from systems theory, and talk about the three ways a system can mess you over.

There may be official names for these somewhere in the neglected jungle of systems theory literature, but I've taken the liberty of borrowing a convenient set of terms from the Discordian religion, and calling them chaos, discord, and confusion.[4] For a handy example of chaos, the tropical storms that go surging through the world's warm oceans each year are hard to beat. As systems go, a tropical storm is a fairly simple one—basically, it's a heat engine in which all the moving parts are made of air and water, with a few feedback loops linking it to its environment. Those loops are what make it chaotic; a tropical storm's behavior is determined by its environment, but its environment is also constantly being reshaped by the tropical storm, so that perturbations too small to track or anticipate can spin out of control and drive major shifts in size, speed and direction.

Thus you can never know exactly where a tropical storm is going to go, or how hard it's going to hit. The most you can know is where, on average, storms like the one you're watching have tended to go, and what they've done when they got there. That's chaos: unpredictability because the other system's interactions with its environment are too complex to be accurately anticipated.

If we shift attention from tropical storms to the latest recall of bacteria-tainted produce, say, we move from chaos to discord. Individually, bacteria are nearly as dumb as storms, but a species of bacteria taken as a whole has a curious analogue to intelligence. All living systems are value-oriented—that is, they value some states (such as staying alive) more than other states (such as becoming dead) and take actions to bring about the states they value. That makes them considerably more challenging to deal with than storms, because they take active steps to counter any change that threatens their survival.

That's the factor that drives the evolution of antibiotic resistance in bacteria. Successful microbe species maintain a constant pressure on their ecological boundaries via genetic variation. The DNA dice are constantly rolling, and it doesn't matter if the odds against the combination of genes they need to survive in an antibiotic-rich environment are in the millions-to-one range; as long as they aren't driven to extinction, they'll roll boxcars sooner or later. That's discord: unpredictability because the other system is constantly modifying its own behavior to pursue values that conflict with yours.

Compare bacterial evolution to the behavior of a tropical storm and the difference between chaos and discord is easy to grasp. Tropical storms aren't value-oriented; they simply respond in complicated ways to subtle changes in environmental conditions they themselves play a part in causing. Imagine, though, a tropical storm that started seeking out patches of warm water and moving away from wind shear, so it could prolong its own existence and increase in strength. That's what all living things do. Tropical storms don't, which is a good thing, as there would be a lot more cataclysmic hurricanes if they did.

To go to the next level, let's imagine an ecosystem of living tropical storms: seeking out the warm water that feeds them, dodging the wind shear that can kill them, and competing against other storms. That's all in the realm of discord. Imagine, though, that a storm that achieves hurricane status becomes conscious and capable of abstract thought. It can think about the future and make plans. It becomes aware of other hurricanes, and realizes that those other hurricanes can frustrate its plans if they can figure out those plans in time to do something about them. The result is confusion: uncertainty because the other system is deliberately trying to fool you.

It's crucial to grasp that what I've called chaos, discord, and confusion are fundamentally different kinds of uncertainty, and the tricks that will help you deal with one will blow up in your face if you apply them to the others. Statistical analysis, for instance, can give you a handle on a chaotic system: meteorologists trying to predict the movements of a storm can study the trajectories of past storms and get a good idea of where the storm is most likely to go. Apply that to bacteria, and you'll be blindsided sooner or later, because the bacteria are constantly generating genetic novelty and thus shifting the baseline on which the statistics rely. Apply it to an enemy in war, and you've just made a lethal mistake; once your enemy figures out what you're expecting, they'll play along to lull you into a sense of false security, and then come out of the blue and stomp you.

This bit of systems theory is relevant here because American culture has a very hard time dealing with any kind of uncertainty at all. That's partly the legacy of Newtonian science, which saw itself—or at least liked to portray itself in public—as the quest for absolutely invariant laws of nature. If X occurs, then Y must occur: that sort of statement is the paradigmatic form of knowledge in industrial societies. One of the great scientific achievements of the 20th century was the expansion of science into fields that can only be known statistically—quantum mechanics, meteorology, ecology, and more. Even there, though, the lure of the supposedly invariant has been a constant source of trouble, while those fields that routinely throw discord and confusion at the researcher are by and large the fields that have remained stubbornly resistant to scientific inquiry and technological control.

It also explains a good bit of why the United States has stumbled from one failed counterinsurgency after another since the Second World War. There's more to it than that—I'll explain later why the American way of war guarantees that any country invaded and occupied by the United States is sure to pup an insurgency in short order—but the American military fixation on certainty and control, part and parcel of the broader American obsession with these notions, has gone a long way to guarantee the litany of failures. You can't treat a hostile country like a passive object that will respond predictably to your actions. You can't even treat it as a chaotic system that can more or less be known statistically. At the very least, you have to recognize that it will behave as a discordant system, and react to your actions in ways that support its values, not yours: for example, by shooting or blowing up randomly chosen American soldiers to avenge family members killed by a Predator drone.

Still, it's crucial to be aware of the possibility of the third level of uncertainty, the one that I've called confusion. Any hypothesis you come up with, if it becomes known or even suspected by the enemy, becomes a tool he can use to clobber you. The highly political and thus embarrassingly public nature of American military doctrine and strategy pretty much guarantees that this will happen—does anyone really believe, for example, that the Taliban weren't reading online news stories about the much-ballyhooed American "surge" for months before it happened, and combining that with information from a global network of intelligence sources to get a very clear picture of what was coming and how to deal with it?

So far, the consequences of confusion have been limited, because the United States has been careful to pick on nations that couldn't fight back. We could pound the rubble in Vietnam and Iraq, invade Panama and Grenada, and stage revolutions in Libya and a bunch of post-Communist nations, because we knew perfectly well that the worst they could do in response was kill a bunch of American soldiers. Several trends, though, suggest that this period of relative safety may be coming to an end.

The spread of digital technology is part of it—the ease with which Iraqi insurgents figured out how to use cell phones to trigger roadside bombs is only the first foreshock of a likely tectonic shift in warfare, as DIY electronics meets DIY weapons engineering to produce cheap, homemade equivalents of smart bombs and Predator drones. The United States' increasing dependence on the rest of the world is another part—the number of soft targets that, if destroyed, would deal a punishing blow to America's economy has soared in recent years, and a great many of those targets are scattered around the world, readily accessible to those with a grudge and a van full of fertilizer. Still, there's a third factor, and it's a function of the increasingly integrated and highly technological American military machine.

As the most gizmocentric culture in recorded history, America was probably destined from the start to end up with a military system in which most uniformed personnel operate machinery, and every detail of making war involves a galaxy of high-tech devices. The machines and devices have been so completely integrated into military operations that they are necessities, not conveniences; I've been quietly informed by several people in the militaries of the United States and its allies that a failure of the GPS satellite system, for example, would cripple the ability of a US military force to do much of anything. It's far from the only such vulnerability. Today's US military is tightly integrated with a global technological infrastructure of fantastic complexity. That structure is immensely powerful and efficient, but the power and efficiency were bought at the cost of resilience.

That's why I discussed the abrupt termination of Bronze Age chariot warfare by javelin-throwing raiders. If you have to fight an enemy armed with an extremely efficient military technology, one of the most likely ways to win is to find and target some previously unexploited weakness in the technology itself. Complex as they were by the standards of the time, chariots had a very modest number of vulnerabilities, one of which the Sea Peoples attacked and exploited. By contrast, the hypercomplex American military machine is riddled with potential vulnerabilities—weak points that a hostile force might be able to monkeywrench in some unexpected way.

It's only fair to note that the Pentagon is thinking about this as well. The famous military penchant for endlessly refighting the last really successful war, however, and the tendency for weapons systems to develop political constituencies that keep them in service long after they're obsolete militate against a meaningful response. US military planners in recent decades have followed the lead of the sciences to embrace the form of uncertainty I've called chaos, and so you get plenty of scenarios of future war that extrapolate current trends out fifteen or fifty years, with a few new bits of gosh-wow technology and a large role reserved for those weapons systems, such as carriers, with constituencies that have enough clout.[5] The thought that hostile forces may be evolving resistance to our military equivalent of antibiotics rarely gets a look in, and the thought that at least some of those hostile forces may be reading those same scenarios and brainstorming ways to toss a monkey wrench into the machinery—well, let's just say that making such suggestions will be about as helpful for the career of a military officer today as the same habit was for Col. Billy Mitchell back in his day.

This is one reason why I have come to believe that of the shocks that could cause the US empire to collapse, one of the most likely is a disastrous and unexpected military defeat. At this point, very nearly the only thing that maintains US power, and the disproportionate share of the world's wealth that is the payoff of that power, is our readiness to pound the bejesus out of Third World nations at the drop of a hat. If we lose that capacity, we could end up neck deep in serious trouble very quickly indeed. Yet the military downsides of America's obsession with high-tech gizmos, in a world where complexity just gives the other guy more opportunities to mess with you, are taking shape in a wider context that has its own bad news to deliver to fans of US global dominance.

To make sense of that context, though, it's going to be necessary to talk about the pervasive misunderstanding of evolution you'll find straight across the cultural landscape of today's America. Since

Darwin first proposed his eminently simple theory more than a century and a half ago—"How stupid not to have thought of it before," Thomas Henry Huxley is reported to have said—the great majority of Americans, believers and critics alike, have insisted on redefining evolution as progress: what is "more evolved" is better, more advanced, more progressive than the competition.

Not so. Evolution is adaptation to changing circumstances, and that's all it is. In some cases, evolution moves organisms in the direction of greater complexity, but in plenty of other cases it's gone the other direction. Over the two billion years or so since the first self-replicating organisms first appeared on this planet, the no-holds-barred wrestling match between genetic variation and a frighteningly unstable environment has turned out some remarkably weird adaptations—pterodactyls, uintatheria, Khloe Kardashian—but they aren't the organisms that endure over the long term. The dragonflies who visit my backyard regularly haven't changed much since the Devonian period, the box turtle we see at intervals out front had relatives munching slugs in the Cretaceous, while the adolescent bats who stray into our basement every so often would not have been out of place in the forests of the Eocene. They and organisms like them are survivors because they found a good stable adaptation and stuck with it; while other organisms adapted in ways that turned out to be dead ends.

It's precisely because evolution is adaptation to circumstances, no more and no less, that it's possible—and indeed easy—to find precise analogues to Darwinian evolution in fields far removed from biology. War is one of these. Nations competing for survival, prosperity, and power show plenty of equivalencies to species doing the same thing for the same reasons, and war—now as always, the final arbiter of national survival—follows patterns of adaptation that a Darwinian analysis explains well.

The collapse of Bronze Age chariot warfare discussed earlier offers a useful example. The chariot armies of the late Bronze Age were superbly adapted for their military environment, but like so many highly specialized life forms in evolutionary history, their adaptations limited their ability to further adapt to rapidly changing circumstances. That limit proved to be fatal to many societies along the eastern Mediterranean littoral, and might well have done so even for Egypt if that ancient society had not been willing and able to return to an older and more resilient set of military adaptations.

Our chances are fairly high of witnessing an even more striking example of the same process in the not too distant future. The current American way of war was originally pioneered by the German and Japanese militaries in the years before the Second World War, as both nations explored the extraordinary new possibilities that petroleum had opened up in war. The destruction of the French army in the spring of 1940 by a German invasion force that had fewer men, cannons, and tanks than its Allied opponents put the world on notice that the old ways of war no longer mattered; the Japanese conquest of the entire western Pacific in a few weeks at the end of 1941 made that memo impossible to ignore, and the United States—to the lasting regret of Germany and Japan—proved to be a quick learner.

The new warfare depended on the mobility that planes, tanks, and trucks made possible, but it had another dimension that is not always recognized. The German conquest of France in 1940, for example, did not succeed because the Germans met and crushed the Allied armies in a head-on battle. Rather, the Panzer divisions of the Wehrmacht dodged the big battle the Allies wanted to fight on the plains of Belgium, and cut across France south of the Allied forces, breaking their communication and supply lines, while the Luftwaffe carried out air strikes to disorganize Allied units and cripple their ability to respond to a rapidly changing situation. Compare it to the US invasions of Iraq in 1990 and 2003 and it's hard to miss the precise parallels; in both these cases, as in 1940 France, what handed a quick victory to the invaders was a strategy that focused on shredding the ability of the enemy government and military commanders to respond to invasion.

The aftermath, though, is telling. In 1940 as in 2003, the invader's victory was followed promptly by a sustained insurgency against the occupying forces. (The only reason that didn't happen in 1990 was that the elder Bush and his generals had the great common sense to declare victory and get out.) The same thing has happened far more often than not whenever gasoline warfare on the blitzkrieg model has taken place in the real world.

There are good reasons for that. Military theorists have postulated any number of conditions that define victory in war, but in practice these all come down to one requirement, which is that the losing side has to be convinced that giving up the fight is the best option it has left. That was the point of the old-fashioned pitched battle, in which one army offered to fight at a chosen location, the other army accepted the invitation, both sides got into position, and then they hammered away at each other for a day or two until one side or the other had the stuffing pounded out of it. After a few battles of that kind, everyone from the king to the lowliest foot soldier knew exactly which side was going to keep on beating the other if the war went on, and so a peace treaty was normally negotiated in short order.

Gasoline warfare rarely has the same result. For those on the losing side—I'm relying here on accounts by French and British officers who were in the Battle of France in 1940[6]—the war is a roller-coaster ride through chaos. Many, sometimes most, units never have the chance to measure their strength against the enemy in combat, because the other side has gone past them and is deep behind their lines; orders from their own commanders are confused, contradictory, or never arrive at all; and then suddenly the war is over, the government has surrendered, and the other side is parading through Paris or Baghdad. So there you are; your government's will to resist may be broken, but yours isn't, and pretty soon you're looking for ways to carry on the fight. That way lies the French Resistance—or, for that matter, the Iraqi one.

This is why resistance movements sprang up so promptly in every nation conquered by Nazi Germany, and why insurgencies have done the same so often in nations conquered by the United States. It's the natural result of a way of war that's very good at bullying governments into fast collapse but very poor at convincing the ordinary grunt in uniform, or for that matter the ordinary person on the street, that the other side's triumph ought to be accepted without further fuss.

It's here that the Darwinian analysis of war mentioned earlier is most relevant, because insurgency is not a fixed thing. It evolves over time, as different insurgent groups try new tactics, strategies and weapons, and draw on the experience of past insurgencies. The evolution of insurgency, as it happens, dates from before the birth of gasoline warfare; it emerged as opponents of European colonial regimes in the Third World began to adapt the methods of European revolutionary warfare to the distinctive conditions of their time. The new model of insurgency saw its first trial runs in South Africa and the Philippines right around 1900; both insurgencies were eventually defeated, but not without serious cost to the two imperial powers in question, and the lessons learned in those wars spread widely—it's not accidental, for example, that the word "commando" entered military parlance in the very early 20th century from Afrikaans, where it was used for Boer insurgent groups fighting the British.

The evolutionary struggle between gasoline warfare and insurgency has been much discussed in recent years in military journals.[7] These discussions have brought up a crucial issue, which is that insurgent groups have been at least as quick to innovate and to adopt the latest technology as their well-funded opponents in the Pentagon and its equivalents elsewhere. Darwinian selection works just as effectively on insurgencies as on species, and the mechanism is much the same—a constant pressure on ecological boundaries, which sooner or later stumbles across every available option for greater success. So far, the military bureaucracies in the world's great powers have been able to stay more or less abreast of the resulting transformations, but their situation has a lot in common with that of physicians today faced with antibiotic-resistant bacteria: you can keep on inventing new antibiotics for a while, but the law of diminishing returns is always working against you, the germs are gaining ground, and you know that sooner or later something lethal, communicable, and resistant to all known antibiotics is pretty much certain to make an appearance.

Exactly what form the next military revolution will take is an interesting question. Some days I suspect that a first draft of it was field-tested by the Hezbollah militia in southern Lebanon in 2006. To deal with an invasion by an Israeli Army as thoroughly committed to gasoline warfare as any army on earth, Hezbollah adopted a strategy that might be called preventive insurgency. Soldiers, weapons, ammunition and supplies were carefully stashed in underground hideouts all over southern Lebanon in advance of the Israeli invasion, where they could wait out the aerial bombardment and the initial assault, and then popped up unexpectedly behind Israeli lines with guns and antitank rocket launchers blazing. While both sides claimed victory in the resulting struggle, the fight was nothing like as one-sided as Israel's two earlier invasions of Lebanon had been. Could the same strategy be taken further, and turned into a wickedly effective defense in depth against a conventional invasion? I suspect so.

On other days, I remember the war between Libya and Chad in 1987, when Libya was a client state of the Soviet Union and had an extensive army and air force equipped with second-hand Russian tanks and planes, and Chad had an army equipped mostly with Toyota pickups packing 50-caliber machine guns, rocket launchers, and half a dozen infantrymen in back. The Chadian forces won an overwhelming victory, whipping around the Libyan forces via goat trails in the mountains and leaving the plains of northern Chad littered with burning Libyan tanks. Those armed pickups are called "technicals" in African jargon; for decades now, they've been standard military vehicles all over the continent, and my guess is that it's only a matter of time before they are used elsewhere in the world. Could an army equipped with technicals, and with anti-aircraft and antitank rocket launchers a little more sophisticated than the ones in common use just now, copy the Chadian victory against a major power? Again, I suspect so.

Whether or not these speculations have any bearing on the way things work out, though, the age of gasoline warfare that began with Stukas screaming out of the sky in the spring of 1940 is guaranteed to come to an end sooner or later. There are two reasons that can be said with a fair degree of assurance. First, of course, is the simple fact that every way of making war eventually runs into something it can't handle. If military history shows anything, it's that the invincible army of one era is the crow food of the next, and far more likely than not the switchover has nothing to do with technological progress; it simply takes a certain amount of time for potential enemies to stumble on whatever trick or tactic will do the job.

Still, even this factor is less certain than the other, which is that gasoline warfare is only possible in the presence of ample supplies of gasoline. More generally, the contemporary American way of war can only be carried out if huge amounts of cheap energy can be provided, not only to fuel planes and tanks and ships, but to support the immense infrastructure that makes modern war possible. As that surplus of energy wanes, so will gasoline warfare, and the successful military powers of the future will be those that can figure out ways to project power and win battles with less of an outlay of energy and raw materials than their rivals.

To be sure, some amount of gasoline or the equivalent will be going into war for a very long time to come—the advantages provided by the internal combustion engine are real enough that gasoline will probably still be used for military purposes long after the private automobile has retreated into legend. My guess, though, is that the last gallons of gasoline used in warfare will be fueling technicals, not tanks. Long before that happens, a way of war dependent on the extravagant consumption of energy and raw materials will have gone whistling down the wind alongside a civilization that tried to support itself on the same unsustainable basis. Since America's current empire survives only because of its ability to threaten potential rivals and insurgents with that kind of war, the implications of this shift pose perhaps the largest single threat to the survival of that empire, and thus to the world order built around it.

THE CONSEQUENCES OF COLLAPSE

WHETHER OR NOT it ends in a military debacle, the decline
and fall of America's empire will have an immense impact
on nearly every aspect of life across much of the globe, just as the
parallel implosion of the British Empire had in its day. A book
much bigger than this one could be filled with speculations and
educated guesses about how that impact will play out. For our purposes, though, it's enough to focus on the way the end of American
empire will affect three parts of the contemporary world order:
the calculus of nuclear deterrence, the survival of American client states such as Israel, and the troubled southern border of the
United States.

All three of these have gathered a bumper crop of misunderstanding and mythology in recent years. It's remarkable, for example, how many people seem to forget that a nuclear weapon
is simply an explosive. It's a very powerful explosive, and one
that produces some dangerous residues when it blows up, but it's
still just an explosive. All it can do is blow things to smithereens,
and unless your problem can be solved by blowing something to

smithereens—or threatening to do so—a nuclear weapon will do you no good at all. You'd have a hard time figuring that out from the way nuclear weapons get discussed in this country, though. Once the prospect of using a nuclear weapon enters the discussion, even the most basic sort of rational thought waves goodbye and sends back a forwarding address from another state.

Follow military debates on the blogosphere and you can find plenty of examples of nuclear irrationality. Every time the United States and China end up at loggerheads, for example, it's a safe bet that online forums will be swamped with claims that the United States ought to carry out a nuclear first strike on the Chinese. It's hard to think of a better example that people simply aren't thinking things through.

Let's suppose that a US president, faced with a crisis, does in fact order a nuclear first strike on China's strategic nuclear arsenal. Let's also suppose that, ignoring all the rules of strategy from Sun Tsu on down, the Chinese haven't anticipated the possibility, don't have their arsenal ready to launch, and haven't informed the American government that the bombs will go up and the boom will come down the moment an American missile crosses into Chinese airspace. We'll say that the US strike is enormously, un-realistically effective; of the 175 or so Chinese nuclear weapons, 174 of them are vaporized on the ground along with their launch systems, and only one missile, with a single 100-kiloton warhead on the business end, arcs through the ionosphere and explodes in a low air burst over San Francisco.

The result? The United States has just suffered the greatest di-saster in its history.[1] The total death toll from that one warhead would likely exceed the 600,000 military deaths in the Civil War, our nation's bloodiest conflict to date. Hundreds of billions of dol-lars of immediate damage would deliver a body blow to the nation's economy, and a galaxy of long-term costs could well raise the final cost by an order of magnitude or more. The impact of Hurricane

Sandy on the East Coast and Katrina on New Orleans combined would be a puny fraction of what we're discussing here.

Now ask yourself this: What has the United States gained in exchange for those huge losses? In terms of actual strategy, it gets a slightly better military position vis-a-vis the Chinese. That is to say, not much compared to the cost.

That's the rarely discussed logic behind nuclear deterrence. None of the concrete gains a nation can achieve by launching a nuclear strike on another nation comes anywhere near the scale of the costs that would be inflicted by even the feeblest nuclear response. If the US first strike just described does not quite turn out to be quite so improbably flawless, in turn, the costs go up accordingly. Ten mushroom clouds over large American cities would leave the US economy as crippled as the economies of Europe were after the Second World War, with no Marshall Plan in sight; the impact of the full Chinese arsenal, small as it is by American or Russian standards, would likely mean the end of the United States as a functioning First World nation. Sure, much of China would be pounded into radioactive rubble; what imaginable advantage would this give to whatever was left of the United States?

This is why, in turn, the Peoples Republic of China contents itself with so small a nuclear arsenal. It doesn't need anything bigger; all that's necessary is that any other nuclear power that might think of launching a strike on China be faced with utterly unacceptable losses. It's why Israel clings so tightly to its nuclear weapons, why India and Pakistan have been so much more polite to each other since both became nuclear powers, and why Iran will inevitably join the nuclear club in the next few years—and the harder the United States backs Iran into a corner, by the way, the more overwhelming will be the pressure on Iran's leadership to assemble and test a warhead, and so provide itself with the one truly effective way of telling hostile countries to back off.

The mistake made by most people who try to reason about nuclear weapons can be summed up very simply: They think that nuclear weapons exist to fight nuclear wars. That was true of the first two fission bombs ever made, Little Boy and Fat Man, but it hasn't been true of any nuclear weapon since that time. They exist not to fight but to threaten. Those people who speculate about when and if nuclear weapons will be used are missing the point; they're used all the time, with great effectiveness, by everyone who has them, to guarantee national survival and draw hard lines that other nations will not cross.

A common objection probably needs to be dealt with at this point. This is the insistence that such logic may be all very well for ordinary leaders and ordinary countries, but what if nuclear weapons get into the hands of a mad dictator? It's a common argument, but the simple fact is that nuclear weapons have already fallen into the hands of mad dictators. Josef Stalin and Mao Zedong can hardly be described in any other terms; both were homicidal megalomaniacs who were directly responsible for annihilating tens of millions of the people they ruled, both of them had nuclear weapons, and we're still here.

For that matter, let's look at the mad dictator who comes first in almost everyone's list, Adolf Hitler. Hitler didn't have nuclear weapons, but he did have the next best thing, massive stockpiles of three highly lethal nerve gases, and delivery systems that could readily have landed decent quantities of them on London and a variety of other military and civilian targets.[2] He never used them, even when the Wehrmacht's last battalions were fighting Russian troops in the suburbs of Berlin and his own death was staring him in the face. Why? Because he believed that the Allies also had them, and could be counted on to retaliate in kind; the military benefits of gassing London, or even the D-Day beaches, paled in contrast to the military impact of Allied nerve gas attacks, say, against German armies on the Eastern Front. That is to say, like most mad dictators, Hitler may have been crazy but he wasn't stupid.

The same logic applies to all weapons of mass destruction. Unless you're the only nation in a given conflict that has the power to annihilate huge numbers of people with a single weapon, it's never worth your while to use your weapons of mass destruction, because the retaliation will cost you at least as much as, and usually more than, the use of the weapon will gain you. That's why the plans to equip infantry divisions with truck-launched nuke-tipped rockets that filled the dreams of US military planners in the 1950s went the way of the Ford Nucleon, a 1957 concept car that was expected to be powered by a pint-sized nuclear reactor, and why the huge multimegaton bombs of the same era were quietly disassembled and replaced by much smaller warheads in the following decades.

It's very likely, in fact, that in the decade or two that lies ahead, an American president will earn a Nobel peace prize—as opposed to being handed one more or less at random, as Barack Obama was in 2009—by completing the process, and signing a treaty with Russia scrapping most of both sides' arsenals. Two hundred fifty warheads each, say, would be more than enough to deter all comers, and the savings in money and resources would be considerable. That latter may turn into a major issue in the decades to come, as the age of cheap abundant energy comes to an end.

One thing about nuclear weapons that's too rarely remembered is that they are surprisingly delicate devices, and don't store well.[3] Certain components of hydrogen warheads, for example, have to be replaced every six months or so because the radioactive material in them undergoes normal decay, and enough of it changes into another element that it stops working. Other components have to be remachined at regular intervals, because plutonium is a relatively soft metal and won't stay within the necessary ultrafine tolerances indefinitely. The missiles and other delivery systems have maintenance issues of their own. The science fiction cliché of abandoned nuclear missiles in forgotten silos, ready to spread devastation far into the future, thus deserves decent burial.

As the world's remaining supplies of cheap energy deplete, in turn, the costs in energy, raw materials, and labor needed to keep existing nuclear arsenals functioning will be an increasingly large burden. As resource depletion proceeds, systems dependent on scarce supplies will be forced to compete with one another for what's left, some will inevitably lose, and each loss will mark the disintegration of some part of business as usual in the industrial world. The elaborate arrangement that keeps nuclear weapons and their delivery systems ready for use at any moment is simply one energy- and resource-dependent system among many.

That's one of the reasons why I expect the treaty mentioned above to be signed at some point in the next couple of decades. Applied more generally, though, the same logic makes nuclear war an unlikely event. As costs mount and industrial infrastructure comes apart, the challenge of maintaining a nuclear arsenal in usable condition will be balanced by the need to maintain the appearance of a credible nuclear threat. The most likely outcome would be a strengthening of the logic of deterrence.

It's a safe bet that as technological capabilities and access to resources decline, nations that have nuclear weapons will continue to claim that they are ready, willing, and able to blow their adversaries to kingdom come. It's an equally safe bet in an age of continuing decline that, given the increasingly harsh limits on resources and technology, the ability of any given nation to make good on those threats will fail to keep up with the appearances it projects to the rest of the world. The problem is that, barring a really spectacular intelligence failure, nobody will know just how wide the gap has become in any given case.

Sixty years from now, as a result, the United States, or whatever successor nations inherit a share of its nuclear weapons, will doubtless still appear to have a substantial nuclear arsenal. Just how many of its missiles and bombs can still be counted on to follow gravity's rainbow and ignite a second sun over an overseas target, though, will be one of the most closely guarded of the nation's secrets. The same will be true of every other nuclear power. As the effects of the peak and decline of oil production continue to manifest, it's very likely that we will reach a point when no nation on Earth still has the effective means to wage nuclear war, but every significant power still claims that capacity, and nobody can be quite sure that everyone else is bluffing—after all, what if the other side has managed to maintain a small arsenal in working order?

Now of course it's entirely possible that a few nuclear weapons will end up being used over the decades ahead. There's always the risk that terrorists will seize or manufacture one and blow it up somewhere—though it's only fair to note that most terrorist organizations depend on covert support from nation-states, who are generally not interested in supporting any operation for which the blowback arrives on the business end of an ICBM. (If the people responsible for the September 11, 2001, attacks in the United States had used a stolen nuclear weapon rather than hijacked aircraft, for example, there's a significant chance that the response might have included the thermonuclear annihilation of the city of Kabul; this was presumably not a risk the Taliban would have wanted to run.)

It's also possible that some conventional war or political crisis might trigger a series of miscalculations that could go nuclear. Accidents happen and mistakes are made. Still, that doesn't justify the repeated insistence in various corners of the internet that a nuclear war has to happen sometime soon—an insistence driven by the same habit of collective fantasy that makes apocalyptic imaginings of all kinds so common these days.

While the logic of deterrence will almost certainly be strengthened by the twilight of American empire, not to mention the parallel decline of the "empire of time" that allows industrial societies around the world to maintain nuclear deterrents and other costly toys, the position of many of America's client states will be considerably weakened. The most vulnerable of those client states, in many ways, is the nation of Israel, and its future and fate is thus worth discussing here.

By this I don't mean that we need to go through yet another round of who-did-what-to-whom rhetoric in the tones of moral absolutism that pervade the subject these days. There's a point to discussing ethical issues surrounding the origins, conduct, and future of the nation-state of Israel, to be sure, but that discussion is already happening elsewhere, or more precisely would be happening if most of the potential participants weren't too busy shouting past each other. What gets misplaced in all the noise, though, is that this is not the only discussion worth having.

In particular, the decline and fall of America's global empire has aspects that are easiest to see from the perspective of one of America's most vulnerable client states. Those aspects are not particularly moral in nature, and the self-righteous arguments that fill most current discussions of Israel's fate have nothing to contribute here. For the moment, then, I'd like to set aside squabbles about whether the nation-state of Israel as currently constituted *should* survive, and ask instead whether, in the post-American world of the not too distant future, it *can* survive. That's a much simpler question, and the answer is equally simple: no.

To explain that answer, I'd like to tell a story. Once upon a time—isn't that how stories are supposed to begin?—there was a group of people who believed that their god had promised them a particular corner of the Middle East, and decided to take him up on the offer. It so happened that conditions just then were propitious for their project. The cultural politics of the major Western powers of the time favored it, and not merely in an abstract sense: money and weapons could be had for the attempt, and a great deal more could be made available if the project succeeded in establishing a foothold.

Even more crucial was the state of the Middle East at that time. The history of that region has a regular rhythm of systole and diastole that can be traced back very nearly to the earliest clay-tablet records: periods of centralization, in which a single major Middle Eastern power dominates as large a fraction of the world as the current transport technology will allow, alternate with periods of disintegration, in which the region fragments and turns into a chessboard on which powers from outside the region play their own power games. At the time we're discussing, the Middle East was in one of its diastole phases, fractured into small quarrelling states, and the sudden seizure of a strategically important part of the region drew only a local and ineffective response.

So a new state came into being, surrounded by hostile neighbors, and a great deal of the shrill self-justifying rhetoric already described came from both sides of the new frontier. Several of the major Western powers supported the new state with significant financial and military aid; of at least equal importance, members of the religious community responsible for creating the new state, who remained back in those same Western nations, engaged in vigorous fundraising efforts to support the new state, and equally vigorous political efforts to get the existing governmental support maintained or increased. The resources thus made available to the new state gave it a substantial military edge against its hostile neighbors, and its existence became enough of a *fait accompli* that some of its neighbors backed away from a wholly confrontational stance.

Still, the state's survival depended on three things. The first, and by far the most crucial, was the ongoing flow of support from the Western powers to pay for a military establishment far larger than the economic and natural resources of the territory in question would permit. The second was the continued fragmentation and relative weakness of the surrounding states. The third was the maintenance of internal peace and of collective assent to a clear sense of priorities, so that it could respond with its full force to threats from outside instead of squandering its resources on civil strife or popular projects that contributed nothing to its survival.

In the long run, none of these three conditions could be met indefinitely. Shifts in cultural politics and in the economic stability of the Western powers of the time turned the large subsidies supporting the state into a political liability that eventually lost out in the struggle for available funds. Meanwhile, in the Middle East, the power struggles between competing statelets began to give way to a new era of centralization. Finally, the internal cohesion of the state broke down in power struggles between different factions, and too many resources had been committed to politically necessary but practically useless projects such as the support of large religious communities that did nothing but pray and study the scriptures. The arrogant certainty that the state could always overcome its enemies, and that the Western powers owed it the subsidies that paid for its survival, put bitter icing on an already overbaked cake, and all but guaranteed the final disaster.

And that, dear reader, was why the Crusader kingdom of Jerusalem fell to the armies of Saladin in 1187, and why the last scraps of the kingdoms of Outremer, as the Crusaders called the land now known as Israel, were mopped up by Muslim armies over the century that followed.[4]

Now I'm quite aware that comparing the current state of Israel to the Crusader states of Outremer is waving a red flag at some already overexcited bulls. Any of my readers who are ready to leap up and insist that Israel either can or can't be compared to the Crusaders on moral grounds are encouraged to stop, and remember that that's not what we're talking about. The relative moral standing of Crusaders and Israelis is irrelevant to the issues we're discussing here; what's relevant is that, in the purely pragmatic realms of politics and war, there are a great many parallels between the two examples.

To begin with, Israel, as Outremer did in its time, depends for its survival on very large subsidies from the major Western powers. In the case of Israel, those mostly come from the United States. The US government spends a little over $3 billion a year on direct aid to Israel,[5] while America's large and relatively wealthy Jewish community sends something in excess of $1 billion a year to Israel on its own account. Many synagogues and other Jewish community institutions in America thus serve just as effectively to channel resources to Israel as, say, the European properties and chapter houses of the Knights Templar and Knights Hospitaller did to keep wealth and weapons flowing to the kingdoms of Outremer. Without that aid, governmental and private, the large and well-equipped Israeli military would be far too great a burden on the economy of what is, after all, a very small and resource-poor country, and the balance of power in the region would shift dramatically to Israel's disadvantage.

Equally, the continued fragmentation of the Middle East is a crucial factor in Israel's survival. The last two centuries or so have seen the long rhythm of Middle Eastern history enter a diastole period, splintering the once-powerful Ottoman Empire into more than two dozen small, quarrelsome, and vulnerable nations that have generally been unable to counter incursions from Europe and America. To a real extent, the current condition of the Middle East is one of waiting for the next Saladin, with Iran, Turkey, or a future Islamic Republic of Arabia likely contenders for the center around which the next Middle Eastern superstate will coalesce. Of course it's a core principle of Israeli diplomacy and military strategy to prevent the emergence of a single center of power capable of mobilizing any large fraction of the resources of the Arab world. It bears remembering that this was an equally central principle of the strategy of Outremer, and the Crusaders' efforts in this direction eventually failed.

I don't propose to pass judgment on the current state of Israeli politics and culture, even to the extent of deciding whether current trends toward political factionalism and the support of Orthodox communities at state expense do or don't mirror the vicious political infighting of the Kingdom of Jerusalem's final decades and the economic burden of Christian monasteries and nunneries that played so large a role in weakening Outremer.

The crucial point just now, it seems to me, is Israel's dependence on a constant inflow of funds from the United States. If that goes away, the military balance of power shifts irrevocably, and so does the Israeli government's capacity to afford the unproductive but politically necessary payoffs that maintain such social cohesion as there is; these shifts, in turn, promise an outcome as unwelcome to Israel, at least as currently constituted, as the equivalent was to Outremer.

One of the central consequences of the trajectory of imperial decline discussed in this book, in turn, is that the capacity of the United States government to afford lavish subsidies to client states overseas, as well as the capacity of any significant group of American citizens to carry out large-scale fundraising projects on their own, will not last indefinitely. The United States has the ample wealth that allows it to support Israel because of the imperial wealth pump, that is to say, the systematic patterns of unbalanced exchange that funnel an oversized share of the world's wealth into American hands. As those patterns break down—and they are breaking down already—the subsidies that keep the Israeli economy afloat and make its current rate of military expenditure possible will inevitably slow to a trickle and then stop.

When that happens, Israel will find itself backed into a corner with no readily available means of escape. Finding another nation willing to take over the American role as sugar daddy is easier said than done; much of the support Israel gets from the United States comes out of the fact that the American Jewish community is one of the better organized veto groups in American politics just now, with the votes and funding to swing a close election, while none of the rising powers likely to take over America's role in the world has either a large enough Jewish minority or a political system sufficiently gridlocked to allow the same sort of pressure to be applied. Given a choice between funding Israel and placating the petroleum-rich nations and ample export markets of the Arab world, it's not hard to see where, for example, China's interest lies.

Lacking outside support, in turn, Israel faces a future in which it can no longer dominate its region and may not be able to ward off military threats. Its military depends, like most modern militaries, on large and reliable inputs of petroleum products, and petroleum is one of the many resources that Israel lacks. Its ability to import as much gasoline, diesel fuel, jet fuel, and so on as it needs depends, like so much else, on the subsidies it gets from the United States. The ability to field a large and technically advanced military machine also depends on those direct and indirect subsidies. Lacking them, Israel's military potential is not much greater than, say, Lebanon's or Jordan's—not enough, in other words, to sustain anything like its current dominance. Its nuclear arsenal gives it a temporary edge, but one that will last only until a rival power in the region equips itself with its own stockpile of warheads and delivery systems.

It's probably necessary at this point to put paid to one of the widely repeated fantasies of our time: the notion that Israel might set out to guarantee its survival by threatening the rest of the world with nuclear war, or might simply start flinging warheads around in the event of its imminent demise. That's one of those theories that seems to make sense as long as no one asks what happens next. The downside to any such action on Israel's part, of course, is that the nations threatened or attacked would be able to respond with far more compelling threats and far more devastating reprisals.

To begin with, Israel is a very small country. Any nation with a significant nuclear arsenal could turn the whole of it into incandescent ash, along with its entire population, and still have bombs left over. The threat to wreck a city or two has very little clout when the cost of following through on that threat could quite easily amount to immediate national annihilation.

Furthermore, many of the nations that might plausibly be threatened with a bomb or two can respond at least as effectively by means of conventional warfare. Let's imagine, for example, that Israel were to threaten Russia with nuclear bombs unless something is done to stop an otherwise unstoppable Arab advance. We'll assume, borrowing one of the common tropes, that the bombs in question have been smuggled into Saint Petersburg and Moscow. Anyone who thinks that Russia would respond in a manner favorable to Israel knows nothing of Russian culture or history, but then that's a common mistake on this side of the Atlantic.

We'll assume, for the moment, that for some reason the Russian government decides not to inform the Israelis calmly that thirty minutes after either bomb goes off, a MIRV-tipped missile or two will return the favor to Tel Aviv with several hundred kilotons of interest. The obvious alternative is to inform the Israelis with equal sang-froid that if either bomb goes off, Russia will declare war on Israel, and twenty or thirty Russian divisions with air support and all the other desiderata of modern warfare will join the Arab forces assaulting Israel. We don't even need to talk about what additional threats the Russian government might quietly make concerning, for example, Russia's remaining Jewish population.

Israel could make a similar blustering threat toward another country, of course, but the same logic applies. The only nation that would face assured destruction in any nuclear exchange with Israel is Israel.

The existence of Israel's nuclear arsenal, mind you, makes it unlikely that the sort of final Arab assault beloved of American fundamentalist apocalypse-mongers will happen at any point in the near or middle future. A far more likely scenario, as America's empire enters its twilight, would see economic and political crisis in Israel spiraling out of control as moderate and extremist factions scramble for control of a dwindling stock of wealth and resources, and everyone who has the resources and common sense to flee the country gets out. How the endgame would play out is anyone's guess at this point, and it's not impossible that a few mushroom clouds might have a part in it one way or another.

The western shores of the Pacific Ocean include a similar flashpoint. Taiwan is another American client state that has everything to lose as America's global empire goes down, and it's also a likely focus of the old and bitter rivalry between China and Japan. It's a core requirement of Chinese policy to regain control of Taiwan in order to secure the Chinese coast against any hostile power; it's an equally core requirement of Japanese policy to keep China from regaining control of Taiwan, in order to secure the sea lanes that carry Japan's fuel and food supplies against Chinese interdiction. It's hard to think of a more perfect zero-sum game in the post-American world. Japan's position is by far the weaker, and it will face the difficult choice of either submitting to Chinese suzerainty, or going to war, as it did in 1941, against a rising superpower with vastly greater resources. Either way, it's not going to be pretty.

That's the sort of thing that happens routinely in the twilight of empires, when client states that have staked everything on support from an imperial patron find themselves twisting in the wind. In empires that expand by annexing territory, it's the frontier provinces that get clobbered first and hardest when decline sets in. In empires that expand by building a network of client states, it's the client states closest to major hostile powers that generally pay the heaviest price when the empire falters. Israel and Taiwan are wedged tightly into such positions, and their fate will be the result of the hard realities of history, not of any set of ethical consider-ations—nor, it probably has to be said, of which side in the current debates claims the moral high ground most loudly.

Israel's future also highlights a major source of international tension that bids fair to bring in a bumper crop of conflict in the decades before us. The word "irredentism" doesn't get a lot of play in the media just now, but my readers may wish to keep it in mind; there's every reason to think they will hear it fairly often in the future. It's the conviction, on the part of a group of people, that they ought to regain possession of some piece of real estate that their ancestors owned at some point in the past.

It's an understandably popular notion, and its only drawback is the awkward detail that every corner of the planet, with the excep-tion of Antarctica and a few barren island chains here and there, is subject to more than one such claim. The corner of the Middle East currently occupied by the state of Israel has a remarkable number of irredentist claims on it, but there are parts of Europe and Asia that could match it readily—and of course it only takes one such claim on someone else's territory to set serious trouble in motion.

It's common enough for Americans, if they think of irredentism at all, to think of it as somebody else's problem. Airily superior articles in the New York Times and the like talk about Argentina's claim to the Falklands or Bolivia's demand for its long-lost corridor to the sea, for example, as though nothing of the sort could possibly spill out of other countries to touch the lives of Americans. I can't think of a better example of this country's selective blindness to its own history, because the great-grandmother of irredentist crises is taking shape right here in North America, and there's every reason to think it will blow sky-high in the not too distant future.

Many Americans barely remember that the southwestern quarter of the United States used to be the northern half of Mexico. Most of them never learned that the Mexican War, the conflict that made that happen, was a straightforward act of piracy.[6] (As far as I know, nobody pretended otherwise at the time—the United States in those days had not yet fallen into the habit of dressing up its acts of realpolitik in moralizing cant.) North of the Rio Grande, if the Mexican War comes to mind at all, it's usually brushed aside with bland insouciance: we won, you lost, get over it. South of the Rio Grande? Every man, woman and child knows all the details of that war, and they have not gotten over it.

That might not matter much on this side of the border, except for two things. The first is the dominant fact of 21st century North American geopolitics, the failure of US settlement in the dryland West. In the heyday of American expansion, flush with ample wealth from undepleted resources and unexhausted topsoil, the United States flung a pattern of human ecology nurtured on the well-watered soils of the Ohio and upper Mississippi valleys straight across the continent, dotting the Great Plains and the dry lands between the mountains with farms and farm towns. The dream was that these would follow the same trajectory as their predecessors further east, and turn into a permanently settled agricultural hinterland feeding wealth into newborn cities.

The Dust Bowl of the 1930s was the first sign that this grand fantasy was not going to be fulfilled. The details of the resulting decline have varied from region to region, but the effect is the same. Across the dryland West, from the Great Plains to the Cascade and Sierra Nevada ranges, a new kind of ghost town is emerging alongside the old breed from the days of the gold and silver rushes. Homes, churches, schools, city halls sit empty as tumbleweeds roll down the streets; with the decline of the old agricultural economy, all the townsfolk, or all but a few stubborn retirees, have gone elsewhere. There are county-sized areas in several of the Plains states these days that once again fit the old definition of frontier: fewer than two non-Native American people per square mile. In response, the vacuum is being filled by the nearest nation that has enough spare people and cultural vitality for the job.

I encourage those of my readers who doubt this claim to book a long bus trip through any of the major agricultural regions of the United States from the Mississippi valley all the way to the Pacific Ocean. You'll want the run that stops at every farm town along the way, because that's where you're going to see a significant part of America's future: the towns that are Mexican by every standard except for a few lines on a map. It's not just that the signs are all in Spanish; the movie posters in the video shop windows are for Mexican movies, the snacks in the gas stations are Mexican brands, the radio announcers are talking excitedly about Mexican sports teams and the people on the street are wearing Mexican fashions. Such towns aren't limited these days to the quarter of the United States that used to be half of Mexico; they can be found in most of the country's agricultural regions, and increasingly beyond them as well.

In the United States, this isn't something you talk about. There's plenty of rhetoric about immigration from Mexico, to be sure, but nearly all of it focuses on the modest fraction of those immigrants who cross into the United States illegally. Behind that focus is another thing people in the United States don't talk about, which is the bitter class warfare between America's middle class and its working class. Illegal immigration is good for the middle class, because illegal immigrants—who have effectively no rights and thus can be paid starvation wages for unskilled and semiskilled labor—drive down the cost of labor, and thus decrease the prices of goods and services that middle class people want. By the same token, illegal immigration is bad for the working class, because the same process leaves working class Americans with shrinking paychecks and fewer job opportunities.

Nobody in the middle class wants to admit that it's in their economic interest to consign the working class to misery and impoverishment; nobody in the working class wants to use the language of class warfare, for fear of handing rhetorical weapons to the next class down; so both sides bicker about a convenient side issue, which in this case happens to be illegal immigration, and they bicker about it in the shrill moral language that afflicts discussions of most issues in today's America, so that the straight-forward political and economic issues don't come up. Meanwhile, the demographic shift continues, redefining the future history and cultural landscape of the North American continent.

Students of history will recognize in the failure of US settlement in the dryland West a familiar pattern, one that is also under way on the other side of the Pacific—the Russian settlement of Siberia is turning into a dead end of the same kind, and immigrants from China and other Asian countries are flooding northwards there, quite probably laying the foundations for a Greater China that may someday extend west to the Urals and north to the Arctic Ocean.[7] Still, there's another pattern at work in North America.

To make sense of it, a glance at the writings of Arnold Toynbee will be helpful.[8]

Central to Toynbee's project was the idea of putting corresponding stages in the rise and fall of civilizations side by side, and seeing what common factors could be drawn from the comparison. Simple in theory, that proved to be a gargantuan undertaking in practice, which is why nearly all of Toynbee's career as a writer of history was devoted to that one project. One pattern he found consistently repeated is the evolution of borderland regions caught between an imperial power and a much poorer and less technologically complex society.[9] Imperial China and central Asia, the Roman world and the Germanic barbarians, the Toltecs of ancient Mexico and their Chichimec neighbors to the north—well, the list goes on. It's a very common feature of history, and it unfolds in a remarkably precise and predictable way.

The first phase of that process begins with the rise and successful expansion of the imperial power. That expansion quite often involves the conquest of lands previously owned by less wealthy and powerful nations next door. For some time thereafter, neighboring societies that are not absorbed in this way are drawn into the imperial power's orbit and copy its political and cultural habits—German tribal chieftains mint their own pseudo-Roman coins and drape themselves in togas, people very far from America copy the institutions of representative democracy and don blue jeans, and so on. A successful empire has a charisma that inspires imitation, and while it retains its ascendancy, that charisma makes the continued domination of its borderlands easy to maintain.

It's when the ascendancy fails and the charisma crumbles that things get difficult. Toynbee uses a neat, if untranslatable, Latin pun to denote the difference: the charisma of a successful imperial power makes its borderlands a *limen* or doorway, while the weakening of its power and the collapse of its charisma compels it to replace the *limen* with a *limes*, a defensive wall. Very often, in fact, it's when a physical wall goes up along the border that the imperial power, in effect, serves notice to its historians that its days are numbered.

Once the wall goes up, literally or figuratively, the focus shifts to the lands immediately outside it, and those lands go through a series of predictable stages. As economic and political stresses mount along the boundary, social order collapses and institutions disintegrate, leaving power in the hands of a distinctive social form, the warband—a body of mostly young men whose sole trade is violence, and who are bound by personal loyalties to a charismatic warlord. At first, nascent warbands strive mostly with one another and with the crumbling institutions of their own countries, but before long their attention turns to the much richer pickings to be found on the other side of the wall. Raids and counter-raids plunge the region into a rising spiral of violence that the warbands can afford much more easily than the imperial government.

The final stages of the process depend on the broader pattern of decline. In Toynbee's analysis, a civilization in decline divides into a dominant minority, which maintains its power by coercive means, and an internal proletariat—that is, the bulk of the population, who are formally part of the civilization but receive an ever smaller share of its benefits and become ever more alienated from its values and institutions. This condition applies to the imperial state and its inner circle of allies; outside that core lies the world of the external proletariat—in the terms used earlier, these are the peoples subjected to the business end of the imperial wealth pump, whose wealth flows inward to support the imperial core but who receive few benefits in exchange.

The rise of warband culture drives the collapse of that arrangement. As warbands rise, coalesce, and begin probing across the border, the machinery that concentrates wealth in the hands of the dominant minority begins to break apart; tax revenues plunge as wealth turns into warband plunder, and the imperial state's capacity to enforce its will dwindles. The end comes when the internal proletariat, pushed to the breaking point by increasingly frantic demands from the dominant minority, throws its support to the external proletariat—or, more to the point, to the successful leadership of one or more of the external proletariat's biggest warbands—and the empire begins its final collapse into a congeries of protofeudal statelets. Much more often than not, that's how the final crisis of a civilization unfolds; it's also one standard way that garden-variety empires fall, even when they don't take a civilization down with them.

As the United States faces the end of its overseas empire and the drastic contraction of an economy long inflated by imperial tribute, in other words, it faces a massive difficulty much closer to home: a proud and populous nation on its southern border, with a vibrant culture but disintegrating political institutions, emergent warbands of the classic type, a large demographic presence inside US borders, and a burning sense of resentment directed squarely at the United States. This is not a recipe for a peaceful imperial decline.

Nor is there much hope that the classic pattern can be evaded: the wall has already gone up, in the most literal sense, and the usual consequences are following. The warbands are here too. The US media calls them "drug gangs," since their involvement in drug smuggling across the border makes good copy. They haven't yet completed the trajectory that will make them the heirs of the Huns and Visigoths. The rock-star charisma that surrounds great warlords in an age of imperial collapse has only just begun to flicker around the most successful leaders of the nascent Mexican warbands. Give it time; the glorification of the gangster life that pervades popular culture toward the bottom of the socioeconomic pyramid these days shows that the seeds of that change have long since been planted.

Can anything be done to prevent this from proceeding all the way to its normal completion? At this stage in the game, probably not. An empire in the days of its power can sometimes stop the spiral by conquering the entire region—not merely the border area, but all the way out to the nearest major geographical barrier—and absorbing it fully into the imperial system. That's why Gaul, which had been a source of constant raids against Roman interests early on, didn't produce warbands of its own in the years of decline until it was conquered and settled by tribes from points further east. Had the United States conquered all of Mexico in the 1870s, admitted its states into the Union, and integrated Mexican society fully into the American project, that might have worked, but it's far too late for that; the polarization of the borderlands is already a fact, so is the bitterness of a dispossessed people, and so is the ongoing unraveling of American power.

The other endpoint of the process—the *only* other endpoint of the process that can be found anywhere in recorded history—is the collapse of the imperial power. The United States has prepared plenty of other disasters for itself, by way of clueless choices in recent decades, and some of them are likely to hit well before the defense of the southern border becomes its most pressing and insoluble security problem. Still, I would encourage those readers who live in the dryland West, especially those within a state or so of the southern border, to keep an eye open for the first tentative raids, and perhaps to read up on what happened to those parts of the Roman Empire most directly exposed to warband incursions in the twilight years of Roman rule.

I would also like to ask any of my readers who are incensed by the above to stop, take a deep breath, and pay attention to what is and is not being said here. Again, the shrill rhetoric of moral judgment that treats every political question as an opportunity for self-righteous indignation, popular as it is, has no particular value in this context. More than a century and a half ago, American politicians decided to go to war with Mexico; over the next century or so, as a result of that decision and its cascading consequences, the social order basic to any viable society will most likely be shredded over a sizable part of what is now the United States, and stay that way for a good long time. That's simply one of the things that can happen when an empire falls, and it's something many of us can expect to see here in America in the years ahead.

part THREE

A REPUBLIC,
IF YOU CAN KEEP IT

THE FUTURE OF DEMOCRACY

THE PROSPECTS FOR America's future described in previous chapters may seem to foreclose any hope of positive change. A failing imperial power hindered by a political system in an advanced state of rigor mortis, a corrupt and dysfunctional economy dependent on foreign tribute it can't expect to receive indefinitely, and a hugely expensive military machine increasingly vulnerable to asymmetric attack, is facing a very hard time in the very near future. Nonetheless, I propose to outline a number of ways in which the end of America's empire might, given a great deal of hard work and forbearance, mark the beginning of a movement back toward the democratic ideals to which so much lip service is paid these days.

My suggestions for dealing with this will not involve some grandiose scheme for salvaging, replacing, transforming, or dismantling America's empire, of the sort popular these days with activists on both sides of an increasingly irrelevant political spectrum—the sort of project that merely requires all those who hold political and economic power to hand it over meekly to some cabal of unelected ideologues, so that the latter can once again learn the hard way that people won't behave like angels no matter what set of abstract theories is applied to them. At the same time, there are choices still open to Americans and others in an era of imperial decline; we're not limited to huddling in our basements until the rubble stops bouncing, unless we choose to be.

One of the lessons of history is that peoples with nearly identical economic arrangements can have radically different political institutions, affording them equally varied access to civil liberties and influence on the decisions that shape their lives. Thus it's reasonable and, I think, necessary to talk about the factors that will help define the political dimension of America's post-imperial future—and in particular, the prospects for democracy in the wake of imperial collapse. Those prospects may be brighter than many people currently suppose; it will take a great deal of work, and the abandonment of some popular but hopelessly misguided attitudes, to bring about a rebirth of democracy in post-imperial America, but I would argue that the effort involved in worth making.

To get to work on that task, though, it's going to be necessary to confront the weird but widespread notion that the word "democracy"—or, if you will, "real democracy"—stands for a political system in which people somehow don't do the things they do in every other political system, such as using unfair advantages of various kinds to influence the political process. Let's start with the obvious example: How often, dear reader, have you heard a pundit or protester contrasting vote fraud, say, or bribery of public officials with "real democracy"?

Across the spectrum of American politics, democracy is for all practical purposes defined as a political system in which a majority of voters will support whatever group happens to be using the word at that moment. That definition can be seen at work most clearly in the common insistence that the United States isn't a democracy; after all, the argument runs, if the United States was a democracy, the people would vote in favor of their own best interests, which of course just happen to be identical with the platform of whoever's talking. The fact that this claim can be heard from groups whose ideas of the people's best interests differ in every conceivable way—for example, the Tea Party and Occupy Wall Street—simply adds to the irony.

Behind the rhetoric is a conception of democracy that has nothing in common with the real world, and everything in common with the Utopian fantasies that have come to infest today's political discourse. When Americans talk about democracy or, with even richer irony, "real democracy," they usually mean a system that does not exist, has never existed, and can never exist—a system in which the free choices of millions of individual voters somehow always add up to an optimal response to the challenges of a complex age, without ever running afoul of the troubles that inevitably beset democratic systems in the real world.

Here's an example. Nearly all those who insist that the United States is not a democracy cite, as evidence for that claim, the fact that our elections are usually corrupt and sometimes fraudulent. Now of course this is quite true; the winner in an American election is generally, though not always, the candidate that has the most money to spend. The broader influence of wealth over America's media and political parties is pervasive; and a strong case could be made that election fraud is as much a part of American culture as baseball and apple pie.

Does this prove that the United States isn't a "real democracy"? Not at all. This is how democracies actually function in the real world. Under a system of representative democracy, the people who have wealth and the people who have power are by no means always the same. Some of those who have wealth want power, some of those who have power want wealth, and the law of supply and demand takes it from there. That extends all the way down to the individual voter: give citizens the right to dispose of their votes freely, and a significant number of them will use that freedom to put their votes up for sale—directly, as in old-fashioned machine politics, or indirectly, by voting for candidates who promise to provide them with largesse at the public expense. There's no way to prevent that without depriving citizens of the right to vote as they choose, and you can't eliminate that and still have a democracy.

By this point I suspect some of my readers may think I'm opposed to democracy. Quite the contrary, I'm very much in favor of it. Despite its usual problems, it's preferable to any other form of government. It has three benefits in particular that other systems very rarely provide.

First, democracies tolerate much broader freedom of speech and conscience than countries ruled by other systems. I can critique the personalities, policies, and fundamental concepts of American government without having to worry that this will bring jackbooted thugs crashing through my door at three in the morning; in nondemocratic countries, critics of the government in power rarely have that security. Equally, I can practice the religion I choose, read the books I prefer, carry on conversations with people in other democratic countries around the world, and exercise a great many other freedoms that people in nondemocratic countries simply don't have. These things matter; people have fought and died for them, and a system that makes room for them is far and away preferable to one that doesn't.

Second, democracies don't kill anything like as many of their own citizens as most other forms of government do. The history of the twentieth century, if nothing else, should have been enough of a reminder that authoritarian governments come with a very high domestic body count. All governments everywhere kill plenty of people whenever they go to war, and all governments everywhere go to war when they think they can get away with it; imperial democracies also tend to build up very large prison populations—the United States just now has more people in prison than any other nation on Earth,[1] just as Britain in its age of empire shipped so many convicts to Australia that they played a sizable role in the settling of that continent. Still, all other things being equal, it's better to live in a nation where the government doesn't dump large numbers of its own citizens into mass graves, and democracies do that far less often, and to far fewer people, than nondemocratic governments generally do.

Finally, democracies undergo systemic change with less disruption and violence than nondemocratic countries do. Whether we're talking about removing a failed head of state, coping with an economic depression, surviving military defeat, or winning or losing an empire, democracies routinely manage to surf the wave of change without the sort of collapse such changes very often bring to nondemocratic countries. The rotation of leadership hardwired into the constitutions of most successful democracies builds a certain amount of change into the system, if only because different politicians have different pet agendas, and pressure from outside the political class—if it's strong, sustained, and intelligently directed—very often has an impact. It does not come quickly, easily, or without a great deal of bellowing and handwaving, but the thing does happen eventually.

All three of these benefits, and a number of others of the same kind, can be summed up in a single sentence: democracy is resilient. Authoritarian societies, by contrast, are brittle; that's why they can't tolerate freedom of speech and conscience, why they so often murder their citizens in large numbers, and why they tend to shatter when they are driven to change by the pressure of events. Democratic societies can also be brittle, especially if they're newly established, or if too many of their citizens reject the values of democracy, but in general, democratic societies weather systemic change with less trauma than authoritarian ones.

One measure of this greater resilience, ironically enough, may be seen in the lack of success radical groups generally have when they try to delegitimize and overturn an established democratic society. Rhetoric that would bring a brutal response from authoritarian governments gets little more than a yawn from democratic ones. A few years back, the phrase "repressive tolerance" was the term for this on the American far left. I doubt those who did the denouncing would have preferred to be dragged from their beds in the middle of the night, shot through the head, and tumbled into an unmarked grave; the rest of us have good reason to be thankful that that's not the way America generally deals with its dissidents.

Just now, furthermore, democracy has another significant advantage: it doesn't require the complicated infrastructure of industrial society. The current United States constitution was adopted at a time when the most technologically sophisticated factories in the country were powered by wooden water wheels, and presidents used to be inaugurated on March 4th to give them enough time to get to Washington on horseback over muddy winter roads. (The date wasn't moved to January 20 until 1933.) America was still anything but industrialized in the 1820s, the decade that kickstarted the boisterous transformations that sent an aristocratic republic where only the rich could vote careering toward ever more inclusive visions of citizenship. In the deindustrial future, when the prevailing economic forms and standards of living might resemble those of the 1790s or 1820s much more closely than they do those of today, that same constitution will be right at home, and will arguably work better than it has since the imperial tribute economy began flooding the country with unearned wealth.

The problem with this otherwise appealing prospect, as discussed in an earlier chapter, is that American democracy is very nearly on its last legs. A great many people are aware of this fact, but most of them blame it on the machinations of some evil elite or other. Popular though this notion is, I'd like to suggest that it's mistaken. Of course there are plenty of greedy and power-hungry people in positions of wealth and influence, and there always are. By and large, people don't get wealth and influence unless they have a desire for wealth and influence, and "having a desire for wealth and influence" is simply a more polite way of saying "greedy and power-hungry." Every political and economic system attracts people who are greedy and power-hungry. Political systems that work, by definition, are able to cope with the perennial habit that human beings have of trying to get wealth and power they haven't earned. The question that needs to be asked is why ours is failing to cope with that habit today.

The answer is going to require us to duck around some of the most deeply ingrained habits of popular thought, so we'll take it a step at a time.

We can define democracy, for the sake of the current discussion, as a form of government in which ordinary citizens have significant influence over the people and policies that affect their lives. That influence—the ability of citizens to make their voices heard in the corridors of power—is a fluid and complex thing. In most contemporary democracies, it's exercised primarily through elections in which officials can be thrown out of office and replaced by somebody else. When a democracy's more or less healthy, that's an effective check; there are always other people angling for any office, whether it's president or town dogcatcher, and an official who wants to hold onto her office needs to glance back constantly over her shoulder to make sure that her constituents aren't irritated enough at her to throw their support to one of her rivals.

The entire strategy of political protest depends on the threat of the next election. Why would it matter to anybody anywhere if a bunch of activists grab signs and go marching down Main Street, or for that matter down the Mall in Washington, DC? Waving signs and chanting slogans may be good aerobic exercise, but that's all it is; it has no effect on the political process unless it delivers a meaningful message to the politicians or the people. When protest matters, the message to the politicians is blunt: "This matters enough to us that we're willing to show up and march down the street, and it should matter to you, too, if you want our votes next November." The message to the people is less direct but equally forceful: "All these people are concerned about this issue; if you're already concerned about it, you're not alone; if you aren't, you should learn more about it"—and the result, again, is meant to show up in the polls at the next election.

You'll notice that the strategy of protest thus means anything only if the protesters have the means, the motive, and the opportunity to follow through on these two messages. The politicians need to be given good reason to think that ignoring the protesters might indeed get them thrown out of office; the people need to be given good reason to think that the protesters speak for a significant fraction of the citizenry, and that their concerns are worth hearing. If these are lacking, again, it's just aerobic exercise.

That, in turn, is why protest in America has become as toothless as it is today. Perhaps, dear reader, you went to Washington, DC, sometime in the last decade to join a protest march to try to pressure the US government into doing something about global warming. If the president just then was a Democrat, he didn't have to pay the least attention to the march, no matter how big and loud it was; he knew perfectly well that he could ignore all the issues that matter to you, break his campaign promises right and left, and plagiarize all the most hated policies of the previous occupant of the White House, without the least political risk to himself. All he had to do come election time is wave the scary Republicans at you, and you'd vote for him anyway. If he was a Republican, in turn, he knew with perfect certainty that you weren't going to vote for him no matter what he did, and so he could ignore you with equal impunity.

No matter what party he belonged to, furthermore, the president also had a very good idea how many of your fellow protesters were going to climb into their otherwise unoccupied SUVs for the drive back home to their carbon-hungry lifestyles; he knew that if he actually wanted to make them change those lifestyles—say, by letting the price of gasoline rise to European levels—most of them would chuck their ideals in an eyeblink and turn on him with screams of indignation; and a phone call to the Secretary of Energy would remind him that any meaningful response to climate change would require such steps as letting the price of gas rise to European levels. He knew perfectly well, in other words, that most of the protesters didn't actually want him to do what they claimed they wanted him to do. They wanted to feel good about doing something to save the Earth, but didn't want to put up with any of the inconveniences that would be involved in any real movement in that direction, and so attending a protest march offered them an easy way to have their planet and eat it too.

It's only fair to say that the same logic applies with precisely equal force on the other side of the line. If, dear reader, the protest march you attended was in support of some right-wing cause, the man in the White House had no more reason to worry about your opinions than he had to fret about the liberal protest the week before. If he was a Republican, he knew that he could ignore your concerns and his own campaign promises, and you'd vote for him anyway once he waved the scary Democrats at you. If he was a Democrat, he knew that you'd vote against him no matter what. Either way, he also had a very good idea how many of the people out there who were denouncing drug abuse and waving pro-life and family-values placards fell all over themselves to find excuses for Rush Limbaugh's drug bust, and paid for abortions when they knocked up the teenage girlfriends their wives don't know about.

Does this mean that protest marches are a waste of time? Not at all. Nor does it mean that any of the other venerable means of exerting pressure on politicians are useless. The problem is not in these measures themselves; it's the absence of something else that makes them toothless.

That something else was discussed back in Chapter Four: grassroots political organization. That's where political power comes from in a democratic society, and without it, all the marches and petitions and passionate rhetoric in the world are so much empty noise. Through most of American history, the standard way to put this fact to work was to get involved in an existing political party at the caucus level and start leaning on the levers that, given time and hard work, shift the country's politics out of one trajectory and into another. These days, both parties have been so thoroughly corrupted into instruments of top-down manipulation on the part of major power centers and veto groups that trying to return them to useful condition is almost certainly a waste of time. At the same time, the fact that US politics is not currently dominated by Federalists and Whigs shows that even a resolutely two-party political culture is now and then subject to the replacement of one party by another, if the new party on the block takes the time to learn what works, and then does it.

The point I'm trying to explore here can be made in an even more forceful way. Protest marches, like letter-writing campaigns and other means of putting pressure on politicians, have no power in and of themselves; their effect depends on the implied promise that the politicians will be held accountable to their choices come election time, and that promise depends, in turn, on the existence of grassroots political organization strong enough to make a difference in the voting booth. It's the grassroots organization, we might as well say, that produces democracy; marches and other methods of pressuring politicians are simply means of consuming democracy—and when everyone wants to consume a product but nobody takes the time and trouble to produce it, sooner or later you get a shortage.

Thus we have a severe and growing democracy shortage here in America. Most currently popular ways of trying to put pressure on the American political system, in effect, presuppose that the politicians will pay attention if the people, or the activists who claim to speak in their name, simply make enough noise. The difficulty is that the activists, or for that matter the people, aren't giving the politicians any reason to pay attention; they're simply making noise, and the politicians have long since realized that the noise can be ignored with impunity.

That's what's implied by saying that protest marches, petitions, letter-writing campaigns, and the like consume democracy. These standard modes of activism only work if the officials who make decisions have some reason to think that the activists can follow through with some more effective action, such as a serious challenge in the next election, if they're ignored. It's those other actions that produce democracy or, in less metaphoric terms, convince elected officials that ignoring the activists could put their careers at risk.

What sets democracy apart from most other systems of government is that it gives citizens a peaceful way to make good on such threats. This is a huge advantage, for the most pragmatic of reasons. In autocratic societies, where the populace has no way to get rid of inept officials short of revolution, a vast amount of administrative idiocy and incompetence goes unpunished. The notion that autocracies are by definition more competent than democracies is quite simply untrue; the annals of autocratic states such as *ancien régime* France and Communist Russia are packed with examples of the most egregious incompetence—and no, despite the slogans, Mussolini didn't make the trains run on time, either. It's simply easier to cover up governmental stupidity in an autocracy, since there aren't media independent of government control to spread the word and embarrass the powers that be.

Yet that advantage, again, depends on the ability of citizens to vote the rascals out when they deserve it. In today's America, that ability is little more than theoretical these days. What was once one of the world's liveliest and most robust democratic systems has lapsed into a sham democracy uncomfortably reminiscent of the old Eastern Bloc states, where everyone had the right to vote for a preselected list of candidates who all support the same things. The reasons for that decay are complex, and I've talked about them in detail already. What I want to address here is what might be done about it—and that requires a second look at the countervailing forces that were once hardwired into the grassroots level of the American system.

A thought experiment might help clarify the issues here. Imagine, dear reader, that a couple of years from now you hear that a couple of legislators and popular media figures are talking about forming a new political party that will offer a meaningful alternative to the stalemate in Washington, DC. The two major parties ignore them, but by early 2018 the new party is more or less in existence, and candidates under its banner are running for Congress and a range of state offices. The morning after the 2018 election, Republicans and Democrats across the nation wake up to discover that they are going to have to deal with a significant third-party presence in Congress and a handful of state governments controlled lock, stock and barrel by the new party.

The two years leading up to the 2020 election pass by in a flurry of political activity as the old parties struggle to regain their joint monopoly over the political process and the new party scrambles to build a national presence. In 2020, the new party nominates its first presidential candidate, a longtime activist and public figure. The campaign faces an uphill fight, and loses heavily; some of the new party's people in Congress and state governments are ousted as well. Pundits insist that the new party's earlier success was a flash in the pan, but they're discomfited in the midterm elections in 2022 when the new party scores a major upset, winning a majority in the House of Representatives and nearly doubling its Senate presence.

That achievement strains the existing structure of American partisan politics to the breaking point. As the 2024 election nears, the Democratic Party, outflanked and marginalized by the rising new party, disintegrates in internecine feuding and fails to field a presidential candidate at all. The Republican Party breaks in two, with Tea Party and country-club Republicans holding competing conventions and nominating separate presidential tickets. Yet another new party springs up, composed mostly of old guard politicians from what used to be the middle of the road, and nominates its own candidate. Under US law, whatever party gets the most votes in any state wins that state's votes in the electoral college— and so the new party, by winning a plurality of the popular vote in just enough states to matter, sees its candidate raising his hand on January 20, 2025 to take the oath of office as the nation's next president.

Suggest a scenario of that kind to most Americans today and they'll dismiss it as impossible. That's all the more curious, in that every detail of the thought experiment I've just sketched out is drawn from an earlier period in American history. The years in question ran from 1854 to 1860, and the new party was the Republican Party; the Whigs were the party that imploded, the Democrats the party that split in two, the short-lived fourth party was the Constitutional Union Party and, of course, the tall figure taking the oath of office in 1861 was Abraham Lincoln.

It's true that an upset of the same kind would be much more difficult to pull off today. Several different factors combine to make that the case, but to my mind, the most important of them is the simple and awkward fact that the skills that would be needed to make it happen are no longer to be found among activists or, for that matter, American citizens in general. Organizing a new political party, building up a constituency on a national level, and making the machinery of democracy turn over in response, requires the pragmatic application of certain skill sets that most people in America today do not know and are, by and large, uninterested in learning. There are, broadly speaking, three such skill sets, and we'll take them one at a time.

The best way to start talking about the first is to pay attention to the way that words in modern American public life have been stripped of any content but raw emotion. The word "democracy," as suggested earlier, has suffered substantially from this treatment. In the mouths of most of the people who use it, that word has lost any connection it once had to elections, checks and balances, limitation of powers, theories of the nature of law, or any of the other things it means when it's treated as a descriptive label for a certain class of systems of government. Instead, it's a verbal noise linked to warm and fuzzy feelings. The word "empire," as mentioned at the beginning of this book, has come in for similar treatment in the opposite direction; to many people nowadays, it's merely a verbal noise linked to cold and prickly feelings.

The word "America" can have either set of feelings associated with it, depending on the political loyalties of the speaker or listener. Thus you can count on angry emotional outbursts from one set of Americans if you say "America is a democracy," because the verbal noise "America" is linked in their minds to cold prickly feelings while "democracy" links to warm fuzzy feelings, and these two are incompatible. You can get exactly the same reaction from another set of Americans by saying "America has an empire," and the possibility that both these utterances might be saying something specific rarely enters the discussion. It's a fine example of the lumpen-Aristotelianism against which Alfred Korzybski contended in vain:[2] A is A and therefore A cannot be not-A, even if A is a poorly chosen hypergeneralization that relates primarily to an emotional state and embraces an assortment of vaguely defined abstractions with no connection between them other than a nearly arbitrary assignment to the same verbal noise.

That is to say, the great majority of Americans have never learned how to think. I stress the word "learned" here; thinking is a learned skill, not an innate ability. The sort of mental activity that's natural to human beings is exactly the sort of linkage of verbal noises to emotional states and vague abstractions that I've outlined above. To get beyond that—to figure out whether the verbal noises mean anything, to recognize that an emotional state is not an objective description of the thing that triggers it, and to replace vague abstractions with clearly defined concepts that illuminate more than they obscure—takes education.

Now of course we have an educational system in the United States. More precisely, we have two of them: a public school system that reliably provides some of the worst education in the industrial world, and a higher education industry that provides little more than job training—and these days it's usually training for jobs that don't exist. You can easily pass through both systems with good grades, and never learn how to work through an argument to see if it makes sense or check the credentials of a purported fact. That's a problem for a galaxy of reasons, but one of them bears directly on the future of democracy in America, for it's a matter of historical record that democratic politics work only when the people who have the right to vote—however large or small that class happens to be—get an education in the basic skills of thinking.

That's why the first-draft versions of Western democracy emerged in the ancient Mediterranean world, especially but not only in the city-states of Greece, at a time when the replacement of hieroglyphs with alphabets had made literacy a common skill among urban citizens and one of history's great intellectual revolutions was inventing logic and formal mathematics. It's why democratic ideas began to spread explosively through western Europe once education stopped being a monopoly of religious institutions and refocused on the same logical and mathematical teachings, courtesy of the Renaissance and its aftermath. It's why the extension of democracy to previously excluded groups in the United States followed, after varying lag times, the extension of public education to these same groups—and it's also why the collapse of American education in recent decades has been promptly followed by the collapse of American democracy.

It's common enough to hear claims that American voters of previous generations must have been as poorly equipped in the skills of thinking as their equivalents today. I would encourage any of my readers who want to make such a claim, or who like to think that the inhabitants of our self-styled information society must inevitably be better at thinking than people of an earlier age, to take the time to read the Lincoln-Douglas debates in their entirety,[3] and then compare them to the 2012 presidential debates.

Lincoln and Douglas were not speaking to a roomful of PhDs. They were in a hotly contested congressional election, in front of audiences of farmers, millworkers, shopkeepers, and craftsmen, the ordinary voters of 1858 Illinois, few of whom had more than an eighth grade education and many of whom had much less. It does not speak well for the pretensions of today's America that its presidential candidates in 2012 pursued their debates on a level that a crowd of Chicago feedlot workers in 1858 would have found embarrassingly simplistic. Nor was this unique to 2012; it has been true of almost every American presidential debate since the 1960s.

That's among the many reasons why devising a framework for adult education outside the grip of the current American education industry is one of the most pressing needs of the decade or two right ahead of us. That huge topic, though, is going to require a book all to itself. What I want to stress here is that teaching the electorate to think is not the only challenge at hand; those of my readers who may be involved in trying to change the direction of contemporary American society on any scale, and for any reason, might find it useful to turn a cold and beady eye upon their own mental processes, and on those of the movements they happen to support.

As extraordinary amount of what passes for argument in today's activism, after all, is exactly the sort of linking of verbal noises with simple emotional reactions, warm and fuzzy or cold and prickly as needed. Some of this may be coldly cynical manipulation on the part of canny operators pushing the emotional buttons of their intended targets, to be sure, but a cold and cynical manipulator who sees his manipulations failing normally changes tack, and tries to find something that will work better. That's tolerably rare among activists, though. Consider the way that the climate change movement went from an apparently unstoppable juggernaut a decade ago to nearly total failure today. The strategy chosen by the great majority of climate change activists can be adequately described as the mass production of cold pricklies; when the other side in the debate figured out how to counteract that, the activists' sole response was to shout "Cold prickly! *Cold prickly!* COLD PRICKLY!!!" at ever-increasing volume, and then wonder why people weren't listening.

You can't craft an effective strategy if your mental processes are limited to linking up verbal noises, simple emotional reactions, and vague abstractions. It really is as simple as that. Until those who hope to have an influence on any level recognize this, they're not going to have the influence they seek, and America is going to continue stumbling on autopilot toward a wretched end. Once that hurdle is past, the remaining steps are a good deal easier.

Yet the recovery of reason has implications that go well past the obvious. Consider the inability of so many Americans with different beliefs to sit down and have a constructive conversation about their disagreements. Those of my readers who have tried to do this any time recently, unless they were very lucky, will have found stalemate the all but inevitable outcome. Each side trots out its favorite talking points, most of them sound bites culled from popular media of one kind or another. When these fail to have the expected effect on the other side, both sides try again, with similar results, until finally one or both sides withdraw into frustration and hostility.

Though it's unpopular these days to point this out, both sides in the current American culture wars follow this same wearily predictable pattern. The problem in each case is the debasement of thinking discussed above: the malign transformation of our inner discourse into a set of arbitrary linkages between verbal noises and simple emotional reactions. If a verbal noise produces warm fuzzy emotions in one person and cold prickly emotions in another, they are not going to be able to communicate unless both are able to get past that unthinking reaction—and getting past that unthinking reaction is something that very few Americans these days are able to do.

There's another useful way to speak of the confusion of language in today's America, and that's to point out that nearly all our collective discourse has been reduced to *phatic communication*. That seemingly exotic phrase describes a very familiar process: the use of verbal noises to signal belonging and readiness for social interaction. When two men sit down in a bar here in Cumberland, Maryland, and one says to the other, "So, how about them Ravens?"—we're halfway between Baltimore and Pittsburgh, so in football season it's either that or "How about them Steelers?"—the question needn't indicate any interest in the team in question. Rather, it's a formal way to acknowledge the other person's presence and claim membership in a community. In a different context, the question might be "Nice weather, isn't it?" or some other equally vacant utterance. The form varies but the content—or more precisely the lack of content—remains identical.

Much of today's political discourse serves exactly the same purpose: it signals readiness for social interaction and claims membership in a specific political subculture, and that's basically all it does. The verbal noises that get used for phatic communication in that context vary even with fairly small shifts across the political landscape, but if you sit in on a discussion among people who more or less agree with each other's politics, you can usually figure out pretty quickly what the relevant warm-fuzzy and cold-prickly phrases are, and once you've done that you can identify yourself either as a member of the community or as an outsider with a very few words. It's an experiment I recommend, partly for the entertainment value, and partly because there are few better ways to learn just how much of what passes for political thought these days is a set of essentially content-free signals meant to define the boundaries of a group.

It's really quite remarkable to watch the range of things that get turned into phatic labels for political subcultures these days. Not long ago, for example, "Merry Christmas" and "Happy Holidays" were equally content-free phatic utterances used from the middle of November to the end of the year across most of American society. These days, "Merry Christmas" has been turned into a phatic badge on the rightward end of the contemporary culture wars, and "Happy Holidays" is well on its way to becoming a phatic badge of equal force on the left. Myself, I have no problem wishing my Christian neighbors a merry Christmas—that is what they're celebrating, after all—and wishing a happy Hanukkah, a blessed solstice, or even a merry Krampustide to those who celebrate these other festivities; one of the benefits of being able to use language for purposes other than phatic communication is that, when a phatic noise is the right thing to use, you can choose your signals deliberately to get the results you want.

It thus probably needs to be said that there's nothing wrong with phatic communication. Human beings are social primates, with normal social primate instincts and reactions, and casual comments about football teams and the weather are no more objectionable in themselves than the grunts and postures baboons use to accomplish the same ends. The problem here is simply a function of the fact that human language has functions other than phatic communication, and when those other functions are of crucial importance, staying stuck in phatic communication doesn't help much.

There's an old word, dialectic, that may be worth introducing here. I should reassure my conservative readers that this doesn't have anything to do with Marxism; long before Hegel's time, it was used for exactly the kind of communication that's most lacking in American society these days, the kind in which two or more people sit down and say, in effect, "let us reason together." The ancient philosopher Plotinus described dialectic as the most precious part of philosophy,[4] and the point's a valid one; the ability to sit down with someone who disagrees with you about some important issue, discuss the matter, determine what common ground exists and where the differences of opinion lie, and either resolve the disagreement or sort out the questions of fact and value that have to be settled in order to resolve it, represents a high level of the practical wisdom that philosophy once upon a time was meant to cultivate.

Dialectic is a learned skill, and not a particularly difficult one, either. Anyone who can tell the difference between a fact and an opinion, recognize a dozen or so of the standard logical fallacies, follow an argument step by step from its premises to its conclusion, and forbear from dragging the discussion down to the level of personal slurs, can pick it up promptly given a competent teacher and a little practice. In the ancient world, dialectic was the way that philosophy was taught: a teacher would start a conversation with a couple of senior students on some specific theme, and go from there. If the dialogue that followed was any good, it wouldn't simply rehash existing knowledge, but turn into an adventure of the mind that broke new ground; those of my readers who are familiar with the dialogues of Plato, which were meant to imitate dialectic at work, will have some sense of how this worked.

Pass beyond the circle of students around a teacher, and dialectic merges into rhetoric. That's a word that gets plenty of use these days, nearly always with a heavy cargo of cold pricklies attached to it. Until quite recently, though, rhetoric was well understood as one of the essential skills of citizenship: the ability to stand up and explain, in clear, concise, and appealing terms, what you think about a given issue. Of all the skills essential to democracy, it's hard to think of one more thoroughly misplaced than this one. How many times, dear reader, have you heard people bemoaning the fact that people in America aren't willing to listen to one another? There's a reason for that, though it's rarely mentioned; it's that next to nobody in this country seems to be able to make a cogent, sensible comment on an issue—*any* issue—and then sit down, shut up, and let somebody else take the floor. It seems to have been completely forgotten nowadays that competent rhetoric makes the listener want to keep listening.

Rhetoric is another learned skill. There are plenty of good textbooks on the subject, ranging from ancient Greek texts to online tutorials packed with the latest buzzwords, and there's also a voluntary organization—Toastmasters International—that teaches rhetorical skills via a network of local clubs. It's not particularly difficult to learn, either. The great obstacle here is the terror of public speaking that's efficiently instilled in American schoolchildren by the culture of bullying that pervades our public schools, and that can be outgrown; I had a world-class case of it not all that many years ago, while today public speaking is a regular part of my work. The benefits to learning it are not small, and are far from limited to its crucial role in fostering democracy, but we'll stay focused on this latter for now.

When citizens can stand up in a meeting and present their points of view in concise, thoughtful, and convincing words, democracy becomes possible. When they can't—when the only thing that takes place in a meeting is a collection of verbal noises denoting "warm fuzzy!" and "cold prickly!" to those others present who happen to link noises and emotions in the same way the speaker does—democracy is not an option, because it's impossible to establish any shared basis for communication between those with different emotional reactions to any given set of verbal noises. Transform those noises into words with mutually agreed meanings and you can get past that barrier, but transforming verbal noises into words with mutually agreed meanings is a skill very few Americans know any more.

The ability to converse in a reasoned and reasonable fashion, and the ability to present a viewpoint in a clear, cogent, and convincing manner, are thus among the core skills of democratic process that have been lost by contemporary American society and need to be recovered. Add these to the basic capacity to reason and you've got all the foundations for democratic process. You don't yet have anything built on those foundations, but that's the next step. Democratic process itself comprises one more set of skills—the skills that allow a group of people to meet together, discuss controversial issues, and agree on a collective response to them.

Those skills are not to be found in the so-called consensus methods that have kept activists on the Left spinning their wheels uselessly for three decades now. I trust my readers remember the flood of self-congratulatory verbiage put forth by the Occupy movement in 2011; that movement vanished with scarcely a trace once the weather turned cold that fall, and despite loud claims that it would pop back up again in the spring, it did no such thing. There were a good many factors behind its failure, but among them was the insistence, on the part of activists, that all decisions had to be made—or, more precisely not made—by consensus methods.

After months of circular debate that never quite managed to result in meaningful action, the vast majority of the protesters were convinced that their concerns would not be addressed and their efforts were wasted, and simply went home. This would be significant enough if it was new; in point of fact, it's been the outcome of nearly every attempt at organized protest since the early 1980s, when the current suite of consensus methods were adopted across most of the activist Left. If you want to know why the Left accomplished next to nothing for thirty years, while activists of the Right were getting candidates into office and laws on the books, that's an important part of the reason.

This is all the more embarrassing in that the toolkit of democratic process has been sitting on the shelf the whole time, waiting for somebody to notice that liberal and radical groups in the past used to use methods of organization that, however unfashionable they have become, actually worked. There are a lot of details, and entire books in fine print have been written on the minutiae,[5] but the core elements of democratic process can be described in a paragraph.

This is how it works: Everyone has an equal voice and an equal vote, but the right to participate depends on willingness to follow the rules, and members can be ejected for abusive behavior. The chairperson of the meeting, and the handful of other people needed to make it work, are elected to be impartial referees of the process, and can be overruled or removed by vote if they abuse their positions. One person speaks at a time, and the chairperson determines who speaks next; an overly longwinded speaker can be told to shut up by the chairperson, or by vote of the members. Once a vote takes place on any issue, the issue can't be brought back up for debate again without a two-thirds majority, to keep a minority with an agenda from holding the meeting hostage. Finally, the goal of the meeting, and of every part of the process, is to come to a decision, act on it, and get home at a reasonable hour.

That's democratic process. It evolved organically over many centuries from its origins in the rough but functional practices of Anglo-Saxon tribal assemblies, and like other organic systems, it looks much sloppier but works much better than the idealized abstractions cooked up by radicals on either end of the spectrum. It's easy to compare it unfavorably to one or another of those idealized abstractions, but the proof of the pudding is in the eating; those who want to demonstrate that some other system is as effective as democratic process are welcome to use that other system on smaller scales, with voluntary organizations and local communities, and prove that it works. That was, after all, how democratic process emerged as the default option in the Western world: in actual practice, in an assortment of voluntary organizations, local communities, political parties and protest groups, it proved to be more effective than the alternatives.

I should say, finally, that even the liveliest revival of the core skills of democracy isn't likely to affect the political sphere much for a couple of decades at least. If nothing else, the sheer inertia of a political dialogue debased as far as America's will take at least a generation to pass off. The point in reviving these things now is to lay foundations for the future. Right now, in the fading years of an age of imperial abundance, it's fairly easy to learn the things I've discussed here; the intellectual resources needed for such a project can be found readily in libraries and on the internet, and a great many people have enough spare time to invest in such a project that much could be done. The further we proceed into resource depletion, infrastructure breakdown, environmental instability, and the rest of the bubbling witch's brew we've cooked up for ourselves in the cauldron of the near future, the less true that is likely to be. Thus any effort to make democratic process and the skills that make it possible available to the far future has to begin now.

REINVENTING SOCIETY

IT MIGHT SEEM THAT the logical response of a nation caught in
a predicament of the sort that faces the United States would be
to bite the bullet, back away from empire in a deliberate fashion,
and use the last bit of income from the tribute economy to pay for
the expenses of rebuilding a domestic economy of a more normal
kind. At the same time, there are compelling reasons why very
few empires in history have had the great good sense to manage
their decline in this manner. Imperial China did it in the fifteenth
century, scrapping a burgeoning maritime empire in the Indian
Ocean,[1] and of course Britain did it after 1945, though that was
largely because a 500-pound gorilla called the United States was
sitting on Britannia's prostrate body, informing her politely that
in future, the global empire would be American, thank you very
much; other than that, examples are few and far between.

The logic here is easy to follow. Any attempt to withdraw from
imperial commitments will face concerted resistance from those
who profit from the status quo, while those who claim to oppose
empire are rarely willing to keep supporting a policy of imperial
retreat once it turns out, as it inevitably does, that the costs of that
policy will include a direct impact on their own incomes or the

value of their investments. Thus politicians who back withdrawal from empire can count on being pilloried by their opponents as traitors to their country, and abandoned by erstwhile allies who dislike empire in the abstract but want to retain lifestyles that only an imperial tribute economy can support. Since politicians are, after all, in the business of getting into office and staying there, their enthusiasm for such self-sacrificing policies is understandably limited.

The usual result is a frantic effort to kick the can as far as possible down the road, so that somebody else has to deal with it. Most of what's going on in Washington, DC, these days can be described very exactly in those terms. Despite popular rhetoric, America's politicians are not unusually wicked or ignorant; they are, by and large, as ethical as their constituents, and rather better educated—though admittedly neither of these is saying much. What distinguishes them from the statesmen of an earlier era is that they are face to face with an insoluble dilemma that their predecessors in office spent the last few decades trying to ignore.

As the costs of empire rise, the profits of empire dwindle, the national economy circles the drain, the burden of deferred maintenance on the nation's infrastructure grows, and the impact of the limits to growth on industrial civilization worldwide becomes ever harder to evade, they face the unenviable choice between massive trouble now and even more massive trouble later; being human, they repeatedly choose the latter, and console themselves with the empty hope that something might turn up. It's a common hope these days. The current frenzy in the media about how shale gas is going to make the United States a net energy exporter gets a good share of its impetus from the same delusional hope—though admittedly the fact that a great many people have invested a great deal of money in companies in the fracking business, and are trying to justify their investments using the same sort of reasoning that boosted the late housing bubble, also has more than a little to do with it.

There's likely to be plenty more of the same thing in the decades ahead. Social psychologists have written at length about what James Howard Kunstler has usefully termed the psychology of previous investment,[2] the process by which people convince themselves to throw bad money after good, or to remain committed to a belief system even though all available evidence demonstrates that it isn't true and doesn't work. The critical factor in such cases is the emotional cost of admitting that the decision to buy the stock, adopt the belief system, or make whatever other mistake is at issue, was in fact a mistake. The more painful it is to make that admission, the more forcefully most people will turn away from the necessity to do so, and it's safe to assume that they'll embrace the most consummate malarkey if doing so allows them to insist to themselves that the mistake wasn't a mistake after all.

As America stumbles down from its imperial peak, in other words, the one growth industry this country will have left will consist of efforts to maintain the pretense that America doesn't have an empire, that the empire isn't falling, and that the fall doesn't matter anyway. (Yes, those statements are mutually contradictory. Get used to it; you'll be hearing plenty of statements in the years to come that are even more incoherent.) As the decline accelerates, anyone who offers Americans a narrative that allows them to pretend they'll get the shiny new future that our national mythology promises them will be able to count on a large and enthusiastic audience. The narratives being marketed for this purpose need not be convincing; they need not even be sane. So long as they make it possible for Americans to maintain the fiction of a brighter future in the teeth of the facts, they'll be popular.

The one bit of hope I can offer here is that such efforts at collective make-believe don't last forever. Sooner or later, the fact of decline will be admitted and, later still, accepted; sooner or later, our collective conversation will shift from how America can maintain perpetual growth to how America can hold onto what it has, then to how America can recover some of what it lost, and from there to figuring out how America—or whatever grab bag of successor societies occupies the territory currently held by the United States—can get by in the harsh new world that grew up around it while nobody was looking. It's a normal process in an age of decline, and can be traced in the literature of more than one civilization before ours.

It bears remembering, though, that individuals are going through the same process of redefinition all by themselves. This is primarily a matter of expectations, and of the most pragmatic sort of economic expectations at that. Consider a midlevel managerial employee in some corporation or other whose job, like so many other jobs these days, is about to go away forever. Before the rumors start flying, she's concerned mostly with clawing her way up the corporate ladder and increasing her share of the perks and privileges our society currently grants to its middle classes. Then the rumors of imminent layoffs start flying, and she abruptly has to shift her focus to staying employed. The pink slips come next, bearing bad news, and her focus shifts again, to getting a new job; when that doesn't happen and the reality of long term joblessness sinks in, a final shift of focus takes place, and she has to deal with a new and challenging world.

This has already happened to a great many people in America. It's going to happen, over the years ahead, to a great many more—probably, all things considered, to a large majority of people in the American middle class, just as it happened to a large majority of the industrial working class a few decades back. Not everyone, it has to be said, will survive the transition; alcoholism, drug abuse, mental and physical illness, and suicide are among the standard risks run by the downwardly mobile. A fair number of those who do survive will spend the rest of their lives clinging to the vain hope that something will happen and give them back what they lost.

It's a long, rough road down from empire, and the losses involved are not merely material in nature. Basing one's identity on the privileges and extravagances made possible by the current US global empire may seem like a silly thing to do, but it's very common. To lose whatever markers of status are respected in any given social class, whether we're talking about a private jet and a Long Island mansion, a fashionable purse and a chic condo in an upscale neighborhood, or a pickup and a six-pack, can be tantamount to losing one's identity if that identity has no more solid foundation— and a great many marketing firms have spent decades trying to ensure that most Americans never think of looking for more solid foundations.

This has sweeping implications for those who are trying to figure out how to live their lives in a world in which the conventional wisdom of the last three hundred years or so has suddenly been turned on its head. The first and, in many ways, the most crucial point is that you are going to have to walk the road down from empire yourself. Nobody else is going to do it for you, and you can't even assume that anybody else will make it easier for you. What you can do, to make it a little easier than it will otherwise be, is to start walking it before you have to.

That means, to return to a slogan I introduced in another book, using LESS—Less Energy, Stuff, and Stimulation.[3] The more energy you need to maintain your everyday lifestyle, the more vulnerable you'll be to sudden disruptions when the sprawling infrastructure that supplies you with that energy starts having running into serious trouble. Today, routine blackouts and brownouts of the electrical grid, and rationing or unpredictable availability of motor fuel, have become everyday facts of life in Third World nations that used to have relatively reliable access to energy. As America's global empire unravels and the blowback from a century of empire comes home to roost, we can expect the same thing here. Get ready for that in advance, and you won't face a crisis when it happens.

The same is true of the extravagant material inputs most Americans see as necessities, and of the constant stream of sensory stimulation that most Americans use to numb themselves to the unwelcome aspects of their surroundings and their lives. We will all be doing without those at some point. The sooner we learn how to get by in their absence, the better off we'll be—and the sooner we get out from under the torrent of media noise we've been taught to use to numb yourself, the sooner we can start assessing the world with a relatively clear head, and the sooner we'll notice just how far down the arc of America's descent we've already come.

Using LESS isn't the only thing that's worth doing in advance, of course. It's crucial to develop the skills needed to produce goods or provide services for other people, using relatively simple tools powered, if at all possible, by human muscles. As the imperial wealth pump winds down and the United States loses the ability to import cheap goods and cheap labor from abroad, people will still need goods and services, and will pay for them with whatever measure of value is available—even if that amounts to their own unskilled labor. There are plenty of other steps that can be taken to prepare for life in a post-imperial society, and the sooner those steps get taken, the less traumatic the transition to that society is likely to be.

That process is going to require the recovery or reinvention of many of the things this nation chucked into the dumpster with whoops of glee as it took off running in pursuit of its imperial ambitions. The basic skills of democratic process are among the things on that list, and so are the even more basic skills of learning and thinking that undergird the practice of democracy.

All that remains crucial. Still, it so happens that a remarkably large number of the other things that will need to be put back in place are all variations of a common theme. What's more, it's a straightforward theme—or, more precisely, it would be straightforward if so many people these days weren't busy trying to pretend that the concept at its center either doesn't exist or doesn't present the specific challenges that have made it so problematic in recent years. I am speaking of the mode of collective participation in the use of resources, extending from the most material to the most abstract, that goes most often these days by the name of "the commons."

The redoubtable green philosopher Garrett Hardin played a central role decades ago in drawing attention to the phenomenon in question with his essay "The Tragedy of the Commons."[4] It's a remarkable work, and it's been rendered even more remarkable by the range of contortions engaged in by thinkers across the economic and political spectrum in their efforts to evade its conclusions. Those maneuvers have been reasonably successful; there was, for example, a flurry of claims in the media a few years back that the late Nobel Prize-winning economist Elinor Ostrom had "disproved" Hardin with her work on the sustainable management of resources.

In point of fact, she did no such thing. Hardin demonstrated in his essay that an unmanaged commons faces the risk of a vicious spiral of mismanagement that ends in the common's destruction; Ostrom got her Nobel, and deservedly so, by detailed and incisive analysis of the kinds of management that prevent Hardin's tragedy of the commons from taking place.[5] A little later, we'll get to why those kinds of management are exactly what nobody in the mainstream of American public life wants to talk about just now; the first task at hand is to walk through the logic of Hardin's essay and understand exactly what he was saying and why it matters.

Hardin asks us to imagine a common pasture, of the sort that was standard in medieval villages across Europe. The pasture is owned by the village as a whole; each of the villagers has the right to put his cattle out to graze on the pasture. The village as a whole, however, has no claim on the milk the cows produce; that belongs to the villager who owns any given cow. The pasture is a collective resource, from which individuals are allowed to extract private profit; that's the basic definition of a commons.

In the Middle Ages, such arrangements worked well across Europe because they were managed by tradition, custom, and the immense pressure wielded by informal consensus in small and

tightly knit communities, backed up where necessary by local ma-
norial courts and a body of customary law that gave short shrift
to the pursuit of personal advantage at the expense of others. The
commons that Hardin asks us to envision, though, has no such
protections in place. Imagine, he says, that one villager buys additional cows and puts them out to graze on the common pasture.
Any given pasture can only support so many cows before it suffers
damage; to use the jargon of the ecologist, it has a fixed carrying
capacity for milk cows, and exceeding the carrying capacity will
degrade the resource and lower its future carrying capacity. Assume that the new cows raise the total number of cows past what
the pasture can support indefinitely, so once the new cows go onto
the pasture, the pasture starts to degrade.

Notice how the benefits and costs sort themselves out. The villager with the additional cows receives all the benefit of the additional milk his new cows provide, and he receives it right away. The
costs of his action, by contrast, are shared with everyone else in the
village, and their impact is delayed, since it takes time for pasture
to degrade. Thus, according to conventional economic theory, the
villager is doing the right thing. Since the milk he gets is worth
more right now than the fraction of the discounted future cost of
the degradation of the pasture he will eventually have to carry, he
is pursuing his own economic interest in a rational manner.

The other villagers, faced with this situation, have a choice of
their own to make. (We'll assume, again, that they don't have the
option of forcing the villager with the new cows to get rid of them
and return the total herd on the pasture to a level it can support
indefinitely.) They can do nothing, in which case they bear the
costs of the degradation of the pasture but gain nothing in return,
or they can buy more cows of their own, in which case they also
get more milk, but the pasture degrades even faster. According to
conventional economic theory, the latter choice is the right one,
since it allows them to maximize their own economic interest in
exactly the same way as the first villager. The result of the process,

though, is that a pasture that would have kept a certain number of cattle fed indefinitely is turned into a barren area of compacted subsoil that won't support any cattle at all. The rational pursuit of individual advantage thus results in permanent impoverishment for everybody.

This may seem like common sense. It *is* common sense, but when Hardin first published "The Tragedy of the Commons" in 1968, it went off like a bomb in the halls of academic economics. Since Adam Smith's time, one of the most passionately held beliefs of capitalist economics has claimed that individuals pursuing their own economic interest, without interference from government or anyone else, will reliably produce the best outcome for everybody. Defenders of free market economics still make that claim, as if nobody but the Communists ever brought it into question. That's why very few people like to talk about Hardin's work these days; it makes it all but impossible to uphold a certain bit of popular, appealing, but dangerous nonsense.

Does this mean that the rational pursuit of individual advantage always produces negative results for everyone? Not at all. The theorists of capitalism can point to equally cogent examples in which Adam Smith's invisible hand passes out benefits to everyone, and a case could probably be made that this happens more often than the opposite. The fact remains that the opposite does happen, not merely in theory but also in the real world, and that the consequences of the tragedy of the commons can reach far beyond the limits of a single village.

Hardin himself pointed to the destruction of the world's oceanic fisheries by overharvesting as an example. If current trends continue, many of my readers can look forward, over the next couple of decades, to tasting the last seafood they will ever eat. A food resource that could have been managed sustainably for millennia to come is being annihilated in our lifetimes, and the logic behind it is precisely that of the tragedy of the commons: participants in the world's fishing industries, from giant corporations to individual boat owners and their crews, are pursuing their own economic interests, and exterminating one fishery after another in the process.

Another example? The worldwide habit of treating the atmosphere as an aerial sewer into which wastes can be dumped with impunity. Every one of my readers who burns any fossil fuel, for any purpose, benefits directly from being able to vent the waste CO_2 directly into the atmosphere, rather than having to cover the costs of disposing of it in some other way. As a result of this rational pursuit of personal economic interest, there's a very real chance that most of the world's coastal cities will have to be abandoned to the rising oceans over the next century or so, imposing trillions of dollars of costs on the global economy.

Plenty of other examples of the same kind could be cited. At this point, though, I'd like to shift focus a bit to a different class of phenomena, and point to the Glass-Steagall Act, a piece of federal legislation that was passed by the US Congress in 1933 and repealed in 1999. The Glass-Steagall Act made it illegal for banks to engage in both consumer banking activities such as taking deposits and making loans, and investment banking activities such as issuing securities; banks had to choose one or the other. The firewall between consumer banking and investment banking was put in place because in its absence, in the years leading up to the 1929 crash, most of the banks in the country had gotten over their heads in dubious financial deals linked to stocks and securities, and the collapse of those schemes played a massive role in bringing the national economy to the brink of total collapse.

By the 1990s, such safeguards seemed unbearably dowdy to a new generation of bankers, and after a great deal of lobbying the provisions of the Glass-Steagall Act were eliminated. Those of my readers who didn't spend the last decade hiding under a rock know exactly what happened thereafter: banks went right back to the bad habits that got their predecessors into trouble in 1929, profited mightily in the short term, and proceeded to inflict major damage on the global economy when the inevitable crash came in 2008.

That is to say, actions performed by individuals (and those dubious "legal persons" called corporations) in the pursuit of their own private economic advantage garnered profits over the short term for those who engaged in them, but imposed long-term costs on everybody. If this sounds familiar, it should. When individuals or corporations profit from their involvement in an activity that imposes costs on society as a whole, that activity functions as a commons.

If that commons is unmanaged, the tragedy of the commons results. The American banking industry before 1933 and after 1999 functioned, and currently functions, as an unmanaged commons; between those years, it was a managed commons. While it was an unmanaged commons, it suffered from exactly the outcome Hardin's theory predicts; when it was a managed commons, by contrast, a major cause of banking failure was kept at bay, and the banking sector was more often a source of strength than a source of weakness to the national economy.

It's not hard to name other examples of what might be called "commons-like phenomena"—that is, activities in which the pursuit of private profit can impose serious costs on society as a whole—in contemporary America. One that bears watching these days is food safety. It is to the immediate financial advantage of businesses in the various industries that produce food for human consumption to cut costs as far as possible, even if this occasionally results in unsafe products that cause sickness and death to people who consume them; the benefits in increased profits are immediate and belong entirely to the business, while the costs of increased morbidity and mortality are borne by society as a whole, provided that your legal team is good enough to keep the inevitable lawsuits at bay. Once again, the asymmetry between benefits and costs produces a calculus that brings unwelcome outcomes.

The American political system, in its pre-imperial and early imperial stages, evolved a distinctive response to these challenges. The Declaration of Independence, one of the wellsprings of American political thought, defines the purpose of government as securing the rights to life, liberty, and the pursuit of happiness. There's more to that often-quoted phrase than meets the eye. In particular, it doesn't mean that governments are supposed to provide anybody with life, liberty, or happiness; their job is simply to secure for their citizens certain basic rights, which may be inalienable—that is, they can't be legally transferred to somebody else, as they could under feudal law—but are far from absolute. What citizens do with those rights is their own business, at least in theory, so long as their exercise of those rights does not interfere too severely with the ability of others to do the same thing. The assumption, then and later, was that citizens would use their rights to seek their own advantage, by means as rational or irrational as they chose, while the national community as a whole would cover the costs of securing those rights against anyone and anything that attempted to erase them.

That is to say, the core purpose of government in the American tradition is the maintenance of the national commons. It exists to manage the various commons and commons-like phenomena that are inseparable from life in a civilized society, and thus has the power to impose such limits on people (and corporate pseudopeople) as will prevent their pursuit of personal advantage from leading to a tragedy of the commons in one way or another. Restricting the capacity of banks to gamble with depositors' money is one such limit; restricting the freedom of manufacturers to sell unsafe food is another, and so on down the list of reasonable regulations. Beyond those necessary limits, government has no call to intervene. How people choose to live their lives, exercise their liberties, and pursue happiness is up to them, so long as it doesn't put the survival of any part of the national commons at risk.

As far as I know, you won't find that definition taught in any of the tiny handful of high schools that still offer civics classes to young Americans about to reach voting age. Still, it's a neat summary of generations of political thought in pre-imperial and early imperial America. These days, by contrast, it's rare to find this function of government even hinted at. Rather, the function of government in late imperial America is generally seen as a matter of handing out largesse of various kinds to any group organized or influential enough to elbow its way to a place at the feeding trough. Even those people who insist they are against all government entitlement programs can be counted on to scream like banshees if anything threatens those programs from which they themselves benefit; the famous placard reading "Government Hands Off My Medicare" is an embarrassingly good reflection of the attitude that most American conservatives adopt in practice, however loudly they decry government spending in theory.

A strong case can be made, though, for jettisoning the notion of government as national sugar daddy and returning to the older notion of government as guarantor of the national commons. The central argument in that case is simply that in the wake of empire, the torrents of imperial tribute that made the government largesse of the recent past possible in the first place will go away. As the United States loses the ability to command a quarter of the world's energy supplies and a third of its natural resources and industrial product, and has to make do with the much smaller share it can expect to produce within its own borders, the feeding trough in Washington, DC—not to mention its junior equivalents in the fifty state capitals, and so on down the pyramid of American government—is going to run short.

In point of fact, it's already running short. That's the usually-unmentioned factor behind the intractable gridlock in our national politics: there isn't enough largesse left to give every one of the pressure groups and veto blocs its accustomed share, and the pressure groups and veto blocs are responding to this unavoidable problem by jamming up the machinery of government with ever more frantic efforts to get whatever they can. That situation can only end in crisis, and probably in a crisis big enough to shatter the existing order of things in Washington, DC. After the rubble stops bouncing, the next order of business will be piecing together some less gaudily corrupt way of managing the nation's affairs.

That process of reconstruction might be furthered substantially if the pre-imperial concept of the role of government were to get a little more air time these days. At some point in the not too distant future, the political system of the United States of America is going to tip over into explosive crisis, and at that time ideas that are simply talking points today have at least a shot at being enacted into public policy. That's exactly what happened at the beginning of the three previous cycles of anacyclosis traced out earlier in this book. In 1776, 1860, and 1933, ideas that had been on the political fringes not that many years beforehand redefined the entire political dialogue, and in all three cases this was possible because those once-fringe ideas had already been widely circulated and widely discussed. It didn't matter that most of the people who circulated and discussed them never imagined that they would live to see those ideas put into practice.

There are plenty of ideas about politics and society in circulation on the fringes of today's American dialogue, to be sure. I'd like to suggest, though, that there's a point to reviving an older vision of what government can do, and ought to do, in the America of the future. The return to an older American concept of government as the guarantor of the national commons is one of the crucial steps that might just succeed in making a viable future for the post-imperial United States. A viable future, mind you, does not mean one in which any significant number of Americans retain any significant fraction of the material abundance we currently get from the wealth pump of our global empire.

The end of American empire, it deserves repeating, means the end of a system in which the five percent of humanity that live in the United States get to dispose of a quarter of the planet's energy and a third of its raw materials and industrial product. Even if the fossil fuels that undergird the industrial product weren't depleting out of existence—and of course they are—the rebalancing of global wealth driven by the decline of one empire and the rise of another will involve massive and often traumatic impacts, especially for those who have been living high on the hog under the current system and will have to get used to a much smaller portion of the world's wealth in the years immediately ahead. If you live in the United States or its inner circle of allies—Canada, Britain, Australia, Japan, and a few others—this means you.

I want to stress this point, because habits of thought already discussed make it remarkably difficult for most Americans to think about a future that isn't either all warm fuzzy or all cold prickly. If an imagined future is supposed to be better than the one we've got, according to these habits of thought, it has to be better in every imaginable way, and if it's worse, it has to be worse just as uniformly. Suggest that the United States might go hurtling down the far side of its imperial trajectory and come out of the process as a Third World nation, as I've done here, and you can count on blank incomprehension. Suggest further that the nation that comes out the other side of this project might still be able to provide a range of basic social goods to its citizens, and might even recover some of the values it lost a century ago in the course of its headlong rush to empire, and expect self-righteous anger.

Now in fact I do suggest this is possible, and I've already sketched out some of the steps that individuals might choose to take to lay the foundations for that project. Still, it's also worth noting that the same illogic shapes the other end of the spectrum of possible futures. These days, if you pick up a book offering a vision of a better future or a strategy to get there, it's usually a safe bet that you can read the thing from cover to cover no reference whatsoever to any downsides, drawbacks, or tradeoffs that might be involved in pursuing the vision or enacting the strategy. Since every action in the real world has downsides, drawbacks, and tradeoffs, this is not exactly a minor omission, nor does the blithe insistence on ignoring such little details offer any reason to feel confident that the visions and strategies will actually work as advertised.

Those of my readers who have been following conversations in the American alternative scene for any length of time, for example, will have encountered any number of enthusiastic discussions of relocalization:[7] the process, that is, of disconnecting from the vast and extravagant global networks of production, consumption, and control that define so much of industrial society, in order to restore or reinvent local systems that will be more resilient in the face of energy shortages and other disruptions, and provide more security and more autonomy to those who embrace them.

A very good case can be made for this strategy. The extreme centralization of the global economy has become a source of massive vulnerabilities straight across the spectrum from the most abstract realms of high finance right down to the sprawling corporate structures that put food on your table. Shortfalls of every kind, from grain and fuel to financial capital, are becoming a daily reality for many people around the world as soaring energy costs put a galaxy of direct and indirect pressures on brittle and overextended systems. That's only going to become worse as petroleum reserves and other vital resources continue to deplete. As this process continues, ways of getting access to necessities that are deliberately disconnected from the global economic system, and thus less subject to its vulnerabilities, are going to be well worth having in place.

At the same time, participation in the global economy brings with it vulnerabilities of another kind. For anyone who has to depend for their survival on the functioning of a vast industrial structure which is not answerable to the average citizen, any talk about personal autonomy is little more than a bad joke, and the ability of communities to make their own choices and seek their own futures in such a context is simply wishful thinking. Many people involved in efforts to relocalize have grasped this, and believe that deliberately standing aside from systems controlled by national governments and multinational corporations offers one of the few options for regaining personal and community autonomy in the face of an increasingly troubled future.

There are more points that can be made in favor of relocalization schemes, and you can find them on pro-relocalization websites all over the internet. For our present purposes, though, this fast tour of the upside will do, because each of these arguments comes with its own downside, which you most likely won't find mentioned anywhere on those same websites.

The downside to the first argument is plain: When you step out of the global economy, you cut yourself off from the imperial wealth pump that provides people in America with the kind of abundance they take for granted. The lifestyles that are available in the absence of that wealth pump are far more restricted, and far more impoverished, than most would-be relocalizers like to think. Peasant cultures around the world are by and large cultures of poverty, and for good reason: by the time you, your family, and the others in your village have provided food on the table, thatch on the roof, a few necessary possessions, and enough of the local equivalent of cash to cover payments to the powers that be, whether those are feudal magnates or the local property tax collector, you've just accounted for every minute of labor you can squeeze out of a day.

That's the rock on which the back-to-the-land movement of the Sixties broke. The life of a full-time peasant farmer scratching a living out of the soil is viable, and it may even be rewarding, but it's not the kind of life that the pampered youth of the Baby Boom era were willing to put up with for more than a fairly brief interval. It may well be that economic relocalization is still the best available option for dealing with the ongoing unraveling of the industrial economy—in fact, I'd agree that this is the case—but I wonder how many of its proponents have grappled with the fact that what they're proposing may amount to nothing more than a way to starve with dignity while many others are starving without it.

The downside to the second argument is subtler, but even more revealing. The best way to grasp it is to imagine two relocalization projects, one in Massachusetts and the other in South Carolina. The people in both groups are enthusiastic about the prospect of regaining their autonomy from the faceless institutions of a centralized society, and just as eager to bring back home to their own communities the power to make choices and pursue a better future. Now ask yourself this: what will these two groups do if they get that power? And what will the people in Massachusetts think about what the people in South Carolina will do once they get that power?

I've conducted a modest experiment of sorts along these lines, by reminding relocalization fans in blue states what people in red states are likely to do with the renewed local autonomy the people in the blue states want for themselves, and vice versa. Every so often, to be sure, I run across someone—more often on the red side of the line than the blue one—whose response amounts to "let 'em do what they want, so long as they let us do what we want." Far more often, though, people on either side are horrified to realize that those on the other side of America's cultural divide would use relocalization to enact their own ideals in their own communities.

More than once, in fact, the response has been a flurry of proposals to hedge relocalization about with restrictions so that it can only be used to support the speaker's own political and social agendas, with federal bureaucracies hovering over every relocalizing community, ready to pounce on any sign that a community might try to do something that would offend sensibilities in Boston and San Francisco, on the one hand, or the Bible Belt on the other. You might think that it would be obvious that this would be relocalization in name only; you might also think that it would be just as obvious that those same bureaucracies would fall promptly into the hands of the same economic and political interests that have made the current system as much of a mess as it is. Permit me to assure you that in my experience, among a certain segment of the people who like to talk about relocalization, these things are apparently not obvious at all.

Despite all this, however, relocalization is among the best options we have. The fact that it comes with significant downsides, drawbacks, and tradeoffs does not nullify that. Every possible strategy, again, has downsides, drawbacks, and tradeoffs; whatever we choose to do to face the end of America's age of empire, as individuals, as communities, or as a nation, problems are going to ensue and people are going to get hurt. Trying to find an option that has no downsides simply guarantees that we will do nothing at all—and in that case, equally, problems are going to ensue and people are going to get hurt. That's how things work in the real world.

Thus I'd like to suggest that a movement toward relocalization is another crucial ingredient of a viable post-imperial America. In point of fact, we've got the structures in place to do the thing already; the only thing that's lacking is a willingness to push back, hard, against certain dubious habits in the US political system that have rendered those structures inoperative.

Back in 1787, when the US constitution was written, the cultural differences between Massachusetts and South Carolina were very nearly as sweeping as they are today. That's one of the reasons why the constitution as written left most internal matters in the hands of the individual states, and assigned to the federal government only those functions that concerned the national commons as a whole: war, foreign policy, minting money, interstate trade, postal services, and a few other things. The list was expanded in a modest way before the rush to empire, so that public health and civil rights, for example, were brought under federal supervision over the course of the 19th century. Under the theory of government described earlier in this chapter, these were reasonable extensions, since they permitted the federal government to exercise its function of securing the national commons.

Everything else remained in the hands of the states and the people. In fact, the tenth amendment to the US constitution requires that any power not granted to the federal government in so many words be left to the states and the people—a principle which, perhaps not surprisingly, has been roundly ignored by everyone in Washington, DC, for most of a century now. Under the constitution and its first nineteen amendments, in fact, the states were very nearly separate countries which happened to have an army, navy, foreign policy, and postal system in common.

Did that system have problems? You bet. What rights you had and what benefits you could expect as a citizen depended to a huge extent on where you lived—not just which state, but very often which county and which township or city as well. Whole classes of citizens might be deprived of their rights or the protection of the laws by local politicians or the majorities that backed them, and abuses of power were pervasive. All of that sounds dreadful, until you remember that the centralization of power that came with America's pursuit of empire didn't abolish any of those things; it simply moved them to a national level. Nowadays, serving the interests of the rich and influential at the expense of the public good is the job of the federal government, rather than the local sheriff, and the denial of civil rights and due process that used to be restricted to specific ethnic and economic subgroups within American society now gets applied much more broadly.

Furthermore, one of the things that's rendered the US government all but incapable of taking any positive action at all in the face of a widening spiral of crises is precisely the insistence, by people in Massachusetts, South Carolina, and the other forty-eight states as well, that their local views and values ought to be the basis of national policy. The rhetoric that results, in tones variously angry and plaintive, amounts to "Why can't everyone else be reasonable and do it my way?"—which is not a good basis for the spirit of compromise necessary to the functioning of democracy, though it makes life easy for advocacy groups who want to shake down the citizenry for another round of donations to pay for the never-ending fight.

One of the few things that might succeed in unsticking the gridlock, so that the federal government could get back to doing the job it's supposed to do, would be to let the people in Massachusetts, South Carolina, and the other forty-eight states pursue the social policies they prefer on a state by state basis. Yes, that would mean that people in South Carolina would do things that outraged the people in Massachusetts, and people in Massachusetts would return the favor. Yes, it would also mean that abuses and injustices would take place. Of course abuses and injustices take place now, in both states and all the others as well, but the ones that would take place in the wake of a transfer of power over social issues back to the states would no doubt be at least a little different from the current ones.

Again, the point of relocalization schemes is not that they will solve every problem. They won't, and in fact they will certainly cause new problems we don't have yet. The point of relocalization schemes is that, all things considered, if they're pursued intelligently, the problems that they will probably solve are arguably at least a little worse than the problems that they will probably cause. Does that sound like faint praise? It's not; it's as much as can be expected for any policy this side of Neverland. In the real world, every solution brings problems of its own.

Now in fact, relocalization has at least two other benefits that tip the balance well into positive territory. The larger the area that has to be governed from a single political center, all things considered, the more energy and resources will be absorbed in the process of governing. This is why, before the coming of the industrial age, nations on the scale of the present United States of America rarely existed, and when they did come into being, they generally didn't last for more than a short time. In an age of declining energy availability and depleting resources, the maintenance costs of today's sprawling, centralized United States government won't be affordable for long. Devolving all nonessential functions of the central government to the individual states, as the US Constitution mandates, might just cut costs to the point that some semblance of civil peace and democratic governance can hang on for the long term.

That probably doesn't seem like much to those whose eyes are fixed on fantasies of a perfect world, and are convinced they can transform it from fantasy to reality as soon as everyone else stops being unreasonable and comes to agree with them. Still, it's better than most potential outcomes available to us in the real world— and again, we don't live in Neverland.

Furthermore, the political evolution of the United States over the last century has concentrated so many of the responsibilities of government in Washington, DC, that the entire American system is beginning to crack under the strain. I'd like, to pursue this point a little further, to offer two predictions about the future of American government.

The first is that the centralization of government has almost certainly reached its peak, and will be reversing in the decades ahead of us. The second is that, although there will inevitably be downsides to that reversal, it will turn out by and large to be an improvement over the system we have today. These predictions unfold from a common logic; both are consequences of the inevitable failure of overcentralized government.

It's easy to get caught up in abstractions here, and even easier to fall into circular arguments around the functions of political power that attract most of the attention these days—for example, the power to make war. It's more useful to start with a function of government slightly less vexed by misunderstandings. The one I have in mind is education.

In the United States, for a couple of centuries now, the provision of free public education for children has been one of the central functions of government. Until fairly recently, in most of the country, it operated in a distinctive way. Under legal frameworks established by each state, local school districts were organized by the local residents, who also voted to tax themselves to pay the costs of building and running schools. Each district was managed by a school board, elected by the local residents, and had extensive authority over the school district's operations.

In most parts of the country, school districts weren't subsets of city, township, or county governments, or answerable to them; they were single-purpose independent governments on a very small scale, loosely supervised by the state and much more closely watched by the local voters. On the state level, a superintendent of schools or a state board of education, elected by the state's voters, had a modest staff to carry out the very limited duties of oversight and enforcement assigned by the state legislature. On the federal level, a bureaucracy not much larger supervised the state boards of education, and conducted the even more limited duties assigned it by Congress.

Two results of that system deserve notice. First of all, since individual school districts were allowed to set standards, chose textbooks, and manage their own affairs, there was a great deal of diversity in American education. While reading, writing, and 'rithmetic formed the hard backbone of the school day, and such other standard subjects as history and geography inevitably got a look-in as well, what else a given school taught was as varied as local decisions could make them. What the local schools put in the curriculum was up to the school board and, ultimately, to the voters, who could always elect a reform slate to the school board if they didn't like what was on the local curriculum.

Second, the system as a whole gave America a level of public literacy and general education that was second to none in the industrial world, and far surpassed the poor performance of the far more lavishly funded education system the United States has today. Earlier in this book I encouraged readers to compare the Lincoln-Douglas debates of 1858 to the debates in our latest presidential contest, and to remember that most of the people who listened attentively to Lincoln and Douglas had what then counted as an eighth-grade education. The comparison has plenty to say about the degeneration of political thinking in modern America, but it has even more to say about the extent to which the decline in public education has left voters unprepared to get past the sound-bite level of thinking.

Those of my readers who want an even more cogent example should leaf through a high school textbook from before the Second World War. You'll find that the levels of reading comprehension, reasoning ability, and mathematical skill expected as a matter of course from ninth-graders in 1930 is hard to find among American college graduates today. If you have kids of high school age, spend half an hour comparing the old textbook with the one your children are using today. You might even consider taking the time to work through a few of the assignments in the old textbook yourself.

Plenty of factors have had a role in the dumbing-down process that gave us our current failed system of education, to be sure, but the centralization of control over the nation's educational system in a few federal bureaucracies played a crucial role. To see how this works, again, a specific example is useful. Let's imagine a child in an elementary school in Lincoln, Nebraska, who is learning how to read. Ask yourself this: of all the people concerned with her education, which ones are able to help that individual child tackle the daunting task of figuring out how to transform squiggles of ink into words in her mind?

The list is fairly small, and her teacher and her parents belong at the top of it. Below them are a few others: a teacher's aide if her classroom has one, an older sibling, and a friend who has already managed to learn the trick. Everyone else involved is limited to helping these people do their job. Their support can make that job somewhat easier—for example, by making sure that the child has books, by seeing to it that the classroom is safe and clean, and so on—but they can't teach reading. Each supporting role has supporting roles of its own; thus the district's purchasing staff, who keep the school stocked with textbooks, depend on textbook publishers and distributors, and so on. Still, the further you go from the child trying to figure out that C-A-T means "cat," the less effect any action has on her learning process.

Now let's zoom back twelve hundred miles or so to Washington, DC, and the federal Department of Education. It's a smallish federal bureaucracy, which means that in 2011, the latest year for which statistics have been published as of this writing, it spent around $71 billion. Like many other federal bureaucracies, its existence is illegal. I mean that quite literally; the US Constitution assigns the federal government a limited range of functions, and "those powers necessary and convenient" to exercise them. By no stretch of the imagination can managing the nation's public schools be squeezed into those limits. Only the Supreme Court's supine response to federal power grabs throughout the twentieth century allows the department to exist at all.

So we have a technically illegal bureaucracy running through $71 billion of the taxpayers' money in a year, which is arguably not a good start. The question I want to raise, though, is this: what can the staff of the Department of Education do that will have any positive impact on that child in the classroom in Lincoln, Nebraska? They can't teach the child themselves; they can't fill any of the supporting roles that make it possible for the child to be taught. They're more than a thousand miles away, enacting policies that apply to every child in every classroom, irrespective of local conditions, individual needs, or any of the other factors that make teaching a child to read different from stamping out identical zinc bushings.

There are a few—a very few—things that can usefully be done for education at the national level. One of them is to make sure that the child in Lincoln is not denied equal access to education because of her gender, her skin color, or the like. Another is to provide the sort of overall supervision to state boards of education that state boards of education traditionally provided to local school boards. There are a few other things that belong on the same list. All of them can be described as measures to maintain the commons.

Public education is a commons. The costs are borne by the community as a whole, while the benefits go to individuals: the children who get educated, the parents who don't have to carry all the costs of their children's education, the employers who don't have to carry all the costs of training employees, and so on. Like any other commons, this one is vulnerable to exploitation when it's not managed intelligently, and like most commons in today's America, this one has taken plenty of abuse lately, with the usual consequences. What makes this situation interesting, in the sense of the apocryphal Chinese proverb, is that the way the commons of public education is being managed has become the principal force wrecking the commons.

The problem here is precisely that of centralization. The research for which economist Elinor Ostrom won her Nobel Prize showed that, by and large, effective management of a commons is a grassroots affair; those who will be most directly affected by the way the commons is managed are also its best managers.[6] The more distance between the managers and the commons they manage, the more likely failure becomes, because two factors essential to successful management simply aren't there. The first is immediate access to information about how management policies are working, or not working, so that those policies can be changed if they go wrong; the second is a personal stake in the outcome, so that the managers have the motivation to recognize when a mistake has been made, rather than allowing the psychology of previous investment to seduce them into pursuing a failed policy right into the ground.

Those two factors don't function in an overcentralized system. Politicians and bureaucrats don't get to see the consequences of their failed decisions up close, and they don't have any motivation to admit that they were wrong and pursue new policies—quite the contrary, in fact. Consider, for example, the impact of the No Child Left Behind Act, pushed through Congress by bipartisan majorities and signed with much hoopla by George W. Bush in 2002. In the name of accountability—a term that in practice means "finding someone to punish"—the Act requires mandatory standardized testing at specific grade levels, and requires every year's scores to be higher than the previous year's, in every school in the nation. Teachers and schools that fail to accomplish this face draconian penalties.

My readers may be interested to know that in 2014, by law, every child in America must perform at or above grade level. It's reminiscent of the imaginary town of Lake Wobegon—"where all the children are above average"—except that this is no joke. What's left of America's public education system is being shredded by the efforts of teachers and administrators to save their jobs in a collapsing economy, by teaching to the tests and gaming the system, under the pressure of increasingly unrealistic mandates from Washington. Standardized test scores have risen slightly; meaningful measures of literacy, numeracy, and other real-world skills have continued to move raggedly downward. You can bet that the only response anybody in Washington is going to be willing to discuss is yet another round of federal mandates, most likely even more punitive and less effective than the current set.

Though I've used education as an example, nearly every part of American life is pervaded by the same failed logic of overcentralization. Consider the Obama administration's giddy pursuit of national security via drone attacks. As currently operated, Predator drones are the *ne plus ultra* in centralized warfare. The president himself must authorize each drone attack. The drone is piloted via satellite link from a base in Nevada, and you can apparently sit in the situation room in the White House and watch the whole thing live. Hundreds of people have been blown to kingdom come by these attacks so far, in the name of a war on terror that Obama's party used to denounce.

Now of course that habit only makes sense if you're willing to define young children and wedding party attendees as terrorists, which seems a little extreme to me. Leaving that aside, though, the key question is whether the program is working. Since none of the areas under attack are any less full of anti-American insurgents than they ever were, and the jihadi movement has been able to expand its war dramatically over the last few years into North Africa, the answer is pretty clearly no. However technically superlative the drones themselves are, the information that guides them comes via the notoriously static-filled channels of intelligence collection and analysis, and the decision to use them takes place in the even less certain realms of tactics and strategy. Nor is it exactly bright, if you want to dissuade people from seeking out Americans and killing them, to go around vaporizing people nearly at random in parts of the world where avenging the murder of a family member is a sacred duty.

In both cases, and others like them, we have alternatives, but they all require the recognition that the best response to a failed policy isn't a double helping of the same. That recognition is nowhere in our collective conversation at the moment. It would be useful if more of us were to make an effort to put it there, but there's another factor in play. One of the few good things about really bad policies is that they're self-limiting; sooner or later, a system that insists on embracing them is going to crash and burn. Once the smoke clears, it's not too hard for the people standing around the crater to recognize that something has gone very wrong. In that period of clarity, it's possible to make a great many changes, especially if there are clear alternatives available and people advocating for them.

In the great crises that ended each of America's three previous rounds of anacyclosis—in 1776, in 1861, and in 1933—a great many possibilities that had been unattainable due to the gridlocked politics of the previous generation suddenly came within reach. In those past crises, the United States was an expanding nation, geographically, economically, and in its ability to project power in the world; the crisis immediately ahead bids fair to arrive in the early stages of the ensuing contraction. That difference has important effects on the nature of the changes before us.

Centralized control is costly—in money, in energy, in every other kind of resource. Decentralized systems are much cheaper. In the days when the United States was mostly an agrarian society, and the extravagant abundance made possible by a global empire and reckless depletion of natural resources had not yet arrived, the profoundly localized educational system I sketched out earlier was popular because it was affordable. Even a poor community could count on being able to scrape together the political will and the money to establish a school district, even if it was only a one-room schoolhouse with one teacher taking twenty-odd children a day through grades one through eight. That the level of education that routinely came out of such one-room schoolhouses was measurably better than that provided by today's multimillion-dollar school budgets is just one more irony in the fire.

On the downside of America's trajectory, as we descend from empire toward whatever society we can manage to afford within the stringent limits of a troubled biosphere and a planet stripped of most of its nonrenewable resources, local systems of the one-room schoolhouse variety are much more likely to be an option than centralized systems of the sort we have today. That shift toward the affordably local will have many more consequences, and the next chapter will address some of the most important of those.

FACING A HARD FUTURE

THE OLD-FASHIONED SCHOOL DISTRICTS that provided a convenient example in the previous chapter represent a mode of politics that has vanished from public awareness in today's America. Across the whole landscape of our contemporary political life, with remarkably few exceptions, when people talk about the relationship between the political sphere and the rest of life, the political sphere they have in mind consists of centralized governmental systems of the kind that dominate American life today.

That's as true of those who denounce political interference in the lives of individuals and communities as it is of those who insist that such interference can be a very good thing. It's as though, in the American collective imagination, the political sphere consists only of the established institutions of government, and the established—and distinctly limited—ways that individual citizens can have an influence on those institutions. The idea that citizens might create local political structures, for purposes they themselves choose, and run them themselves, using the tools of democratic process, has been erased from our national conversation.

Less than a lifetime ago, however, this was a standard way of making constructive change in America. Local school districts were only one example, though they were probably the most pervasive. Most of the time, when people in a community wanted to create some public amenity or solve some community problem, they did it by creating a local, single-purpose governmental body with an elected board and strictly limited powers of taxation to pay the bills. Sewer districts, streetcar lines, public hospitals, you name it, that's usually how they were funded, constructed, and operated. The state government had supervision over all these bodies, usually provided by state boards whose members were, once again, elected by the voters of the state.

Was it a perfect system? Of course not. The interlocking checks and balances of board supervision and elections were no more foolproof than any other mode of democratic governance, and a certain fraction of these single-purpose local governmental bodies failed due to corruption or mismanagement. Still, a substantial majority of them do seem to have worked tolerably well, and they had a crucial advantage not shared by today's more centralized ways of doing things: if something went wrong, the people who had the power to change things were also the people most directly affected.

If the management of your local sewer district turned out to be hopelessly incompetent, for example, you didn't have to try to get a distant and uninterested state or federal bureaucracy to stir out of its accustomed slumber and do its job, nor did you have to try to find some way to convince tens of thousands of unaffected voters in distant parts of the state to cast their votes to throw somebody out of office for reasons that didn't matter to them in the least. The right to vote in the next sewer board election was limited to those people who were actually served by the sewer district, who paid the bills of the district with their monthly assessments; who'd had to deal with balky sewers for the last two years, and were thus qualified to judge whether a "Throw the Rascals Out" campaign was justified. Keeping control of the system in the hands of the people most directly affected by it thus served as a preventive to the serene indifference to failure that pervades so much of American government today.

It might be worth proposing as a general rule, in fact, that democratic governance works best when the people directly affected by any function of government elect the people who run that function of government, subject to appropriate oversight by those responsible for maintaining the public commons. In the case of our imaginary sewer district, that means giving those who live within the district the sole power to choose members of the board, while placing the local board under the supervision of a state board tasked with making sure local decisions don't violate state public health standards and the like. In the case of school districts, it means giving the local school boards broad powers to set policy for the schools they administer, giving citizens who live within the school district the sole right to vote in school elections, and placing the school boards under the supervision of a state board of education charged with enforcing a few very broad educational standards, health and safety regulations, and so on.

This system was quite effective in the past. As long as the roles of state and federal governments remained that of policing the commons, it worked quite well—better, by most measures, than the failed equivalents we have today. What put paid to it was the explosive spread of government centralization after the Second World War, and this in turn was driven by the imperial tribute economy described earlier.

The linchpin of local control, as it turned out, was local funding. Sewer districts, school districts, and all the other little local governmental bodies received all their funding directly from the people they served, by whatever arrangements the voters in the district had accepted when the district was founded. When federal and state governments gained the power to dangle lavish grants in front of the various local governments, most if not all of them took the bait, and only later discovered that the power to give or withhold funding trumps every other form of political power in our society. That was how the local single-purpose governments were stripped of their autonomy and turned into instruments of centralized government, subject to micromanagement by state and federal bureaucracies.

That process of centralization was justified in many cases by claims of efficiency. Now of course when somebody starts prattling about efficiency, the question that needs to be asked is "efficient at what?" A screwdriver is highly efficient at turning screws but very inefficient at pounding nails; the modern corporate economy, in much the same sense, is highly efficient at concentrating paper wealth in the hands of the already rich, and very inefficient at many other tasks, such as producing goods and services. It's interesting to speculate about just what it is that centralized bureaucracies can do more efficiently than local single-purpose governmental bodies, but in retrospect, we can be certain that running schools, sewer districts, and other public goods do not belong in that category.

Today's massively centralized American education system, to return to a previous example, is much less effective at teaching children to read, write, calculate, and exercise the other basic skills essential to life in a modern society than were the old-fashioned, locally managed, locally funded school districts of the not so distant past. It takes only a glance at the old McGuffey's Readers, the standard reading textbooks in those one-room schoolhouses, to show that levels of reading comprehension, grammar, and vocabulary that were considered normal at every elementary school grade level in the late 19th century were vastly greater than those achieved in today's schools; in fact, the reading ability assumed by the first pages of the 8th grade McGuffey's is by no means common in American college classes today.

The collapse of educational standards that can be observed here, and in a hundred similar examples, has had many causes. A similar collapse has taken place in many other areas in which the old system of independent local governmental bodies has been replaced by micromanagement by state or federal bureaucracies.

That collapse has been discussed nearly as widely in the media as the implosion of American education, and it's ironic to note that, just as media discussions of public education's breakdown have gone out of their way to avoid considering the role of over-centralization in driving that collapse, the media coverage of the parallel breakdown I have in mind has been just as careful to avoid touching on this same issue.

The collapse in question? The disintegration of America's infra-structure in recent decades.

A great many factors, to be sure, have had a part in creating the crisis in our national infrastructure, just as a great many fac-tors have contributed to the parallel crisis in our national public education system. In both cases, though, I'd like to suggest that overcentralization has played a crucial role. There are at least three reasons why, all other things being equal, a centralized government bureaucracy will by and large be less able to provide good schools, working sewers, and other public goods than a local governmental body of the type we've been discussing.

First, centralized government bureaucracies aren't accountable for their failures. To borrow a bit of gambler's slang, they have no skin in the game. No matter how disastrous the consequences of an administrative decision made in the state or national capital, the bureaucrats who made the decision will still draw their pay, exercise their authority, and pursue whatever fashionable agendas they picked up in college or elsewhere, even if their actions turn out to be hopelessly counterproductive in terms of the goals their bureaucracy ostensibly exists to serve. Local single-purpose gov-ernmental bodies by and large don't have that freedom; if the local sewer board pursues policies that fail to provide adequate sewer service to the people in the sewer district, the members of the board had better look for other jobs come the next local election.

Second, centralized government bureaucracies provide many more places for money to get lost. As it stands, there are three separate bureaucracies involved in education. You have the federal

Department of Education; each state has its own agency to oversee its own school systems; and then there are the local school districts, many of which have hundreds of employees filling administrative positions these days. All of these are doing a job that used to be done by a handful of employees working for each school board. This all adds up to a whale of a lot of money that might otherwise go to improve schools instead being siphoned off into administrative salaries and expenses. The same thing is true of the money that might go to repair bridges and sewer pipes; how much of that goes instead to pay for administrative staff in the federal Department of Transportation and the equivalent state and county bureaucracies? All this is aside from corruption, which is also an issue; it's a good general rule that the more hands money must pass through on its way to a project, the higher the likelihood that some of those hands will have sticky fingers.

The third reason is subtler, and ties back into the proposal that the proper role of government is that of preserving the public commons. To make a commons work, there needs to be some system in place to monitor the state of the commons, assess how changes will impact it, and prohibit those things that will cause harm to it. On a purely local level, as Elinor Ostrom showed, a self-regulating commons is easy to establish and easy to maintain, since it's in the direct self-interest of everyone who benefits from the commons to prevent anyone else from abusing it. The local single-purpose governmental bodies we've been discussing rely on that logic: if you depend on the local sewer board to provide you with sewage service, to return to our example, you have a very strong incentive not to permit the board to ignore its duties.

Still, for a variety of reasons, the mechanisms of local government don't always function as they should. It's for this reason that the American political tradition long ago evolved the useful habit, already referred to, of making the decisions of local government subject to review at the state level, by way of the supervisory boards discussed earlier. The state boards, like the local boards they supervised, were elected by the voters, so they remained accountable for their failures. More importantly, though, was the simple fact that the officials tasked with assessing the legality and appropriateness of policies were not the same officials that were making the policies.

This is a basic principle of cybernetics, by the way.[1] If you've got one system carrying out a function, and another system monitoring how well the first system carries out its function, you need to make sure that the only input the second system receives from the first system is the input that allows the second system to perform that monitoring function. Otherwise you get feedback loops that prevent the second system from doing what it's supposed to do. That's exactly the problem we have now. When public schools are being micromanaged by regulations drafted by federal bureaucrats, who is assessing the legality and appropriateness of those regulations? The same federal bureaucrats—and whether you analyze this by way of cybernetics, politics, or plain common sense, this is a recipe for disaster.

These three factors—the lack of accountability endemic to centralized professional bureaucracies; the tendency for money to get lost as it works its way down through the myriad layers of a centralized system; and the unhelpful feedback loops that spring up when the policy-making and monitoring functions of government are confounded—go a long way to explain the cascading failure of many of the basic systems that an older, more localized, and less centralized approach to government used to maintain in relatively good order. The accelerating decline of American public education and the disintegration of the national infrastructure are only two examples of this effect in practice. There are plenty of others—a great deal of what's wrong with America's health care system, for example, can be traced to the same process of overcentralization.

I'm pleased to say, though, that help is on the way. On second thought, "pleased" is probably not the right word, since the help in question will almost certainly bring about the wholesale implosion of a great many of the basic systems that provide public goods to Americans, and its arrival will have to be followed by the slow, costly, and potentially painful rebuilding of those systems from the ground up. The source of that unwelcome assistance, of course, is the twilight of America's global empire. In the absence of the torrents of unearned wealth American society currently receives from the imperial wealth pump, many of the centralized systems in place today—governmental, corporate, and nonprofit—will likely stop functioning altogether. Those who think they will cheer this development are invited to imagine how they will feel when their sewers stop working and nobody, anywhere, is willing or able to do anything about that fact.

As the impact of America's imperial decline echoes through the fabric of the nation, a great many of the basic systems of everyday life will need to be repaired and replaced. One of the very few tools that might enable that to be done effectively is the system of local single-purpose governmental bodies that I've discussed in these pages. As municipal services become intermittent or stop altogether, schools shut down, and infrastructure collapses, people with skin in the game—local residents, that is, who want basic services enough to tax themselves at a modest rate to pay for them—could readily use the old system to pick up the pieces from imploding government bureaucracies.

Equally, the same process can be used to pursue any number of public goods not currently served at all by existing governmental systems. All that's needed is for systems that used to be an integral part of American community life to be rediscovered and put back to work, before the imperial structures that replaced them finish coming apart. Mind you, the system of local single-purpose government bodies is far from the only element of an older way of community that could use being rediscovered and restored.

When the French nobleman Alexis de Tocqueville toured the newly founded American republic in the early years of the nineteenth century, he encountered plenty of things that left him scratching his head. The national obsession with making money, the atrocious food, and the weird way that high culture found its way into the most isolated backwoods settings—"There is hardly a pioneer's hut which does not contain a few odd volumes of Shakespeare," he wrote. "I remember reading the feudal drama of Henry V for the first time in a log cabin"[2]—all intrigued him, and found their way into the pages of his remarkable book *Democracy in America*.

Still, one of the things de Tocqueville found most astonishing bears directly on the theme of this chapter. The Americans of his time, when they wanted to make something happen, didn't march around with placards or write their legislators demanding that the government do it. Instead, far more often than not, they simply put together a private association for the purpose, and did it themselves.

De Tocqueville wrote: "The Americans make associations to give entertainments, to found institutions for education, to build inns, to construct churches, to diffuse books, and to send missionaries to the antipodes; and in this manner they found hospitals, prisons, and schools. If it be proposed to advance some truth or to foster some feeling by the encouragement of a great example, they found a society. Whenever, at the head of some new undertaking, you find the government in France, or a man of rank in England, in the United States you are sure to find an association. I met with several kinds of association in America of which I confess I had no previous notion; and I have often admired the extreme skill with which the inhabitants of the United States succeed in proposing a common object to the exertions of a great many men, and getting them voluntarily to pursue it."[3]

The types of associations de Tocqueville encountered used an assortment of ingenious legal structures borrowed, for the most part, from English common law. Those of my readers who dislike the role of corporations in contemporary American life may be interested to know that the distant and much less toxic ancestor of today's corporate structure was one of them. A corporation, back in those days, was not a privileged legal pseudoperson with more rights and fewer responsibilities than a human being. It was simply a group of people who set out to accomplish some purpose, and got a charter from the state government allowing them to raise money for that purpose by selling shares of stock. Most had single purposes—building a hospital, say, or a canal—and limited lifespans, defined either as a fixed number of years or until the purpose of the corporation was completed.

Making money was sometimes an object in such exercises, but by no means always. Members of a local religious community who wanted to build a new church, for example, would very often do that by organizing a corporation to raise money for the construction costs. Each member would buy as many shares as he or she could afford, and fellow believers in neighboring towns who wanted to support the project might also buy shares to chip in. When the church was finished, the corporation would be wound up, and thereafter a portion of the income from tithes and donations might be set apart to buy back the shares a few at a time; on the other hand, the members of the congregation might consider themselves well repaid when they filed into a new building on Sunday mornings. It was a remarkably effective means of local microfinance, and it paid for a huge number of civic improvements and public amenities in the young republic.

Not all associations that directed their efforts toward the public good in this way were corporations, and I hope I may be allowed a personal reminiscence about one of the others. I think many of my readers know that I'm a Freemason. Yes, I'm quite aware that this makes me an object of vilification across most of the further reaches of contemporary American political life; no, I don't particularly care, though it tickles my sense of absurdity to be accused to my face now and then of being one of the evil space lizards David Icke rants about in his books.[4] In the town where I live, the various Masonic bodies meet in a large and lovely century-old building—which was, by the way, constructed by the sort of building corporation described earlier in this chapter—and share certain projects in common. In 2013, I was appointed secretary to one of those, the Masonic Endowment Fund. Half a century ago, it had a different and more revealing name: the Masonic Relief Fund.

Here's how it functioned back in the day. Donations from living members, bequests from dead ones, and a variety of fundraising activities kept the Fund supplied with money, which it invested, and the interest from those investments went to help Masonic brothers and their families who fell onto hard times. The members of the Relief Board, who were appointed by each lodge or other Masonic body, investigated each case and then started writing checks.

Elderly brethren still recall the days when a long hard winter meant that the poorer families in town would run out of money for coal well before spring, and those who had a family member in the Masons could count on the truck from the local coal provider making a delivery anyway. Groceries, visiting nurse services, school expenses, funeral costs—the Relief Fund covered all those and much more. Everyone in the local Masonic scene supported the project to whatever extent their means allowed. Partly that was because that's what you do when you're a Freemason, and partly it was because everyone knew that, however well off they were at the moment, some unexpected turn of events might leave them in a situation where they had to rely on the Fund for their own survival.

The Fund no longer buys truckloads of coal for poor Masonic families in the winter, and the reason for that is a microcosm of the impact of empire on American communities. In the wake of Lyndon Johnson's "Great Society" programs of the 1960s, government welfare programs took the place of the Masonic Relief Fund and its many equivalents in the lives of the local poor. Requests for help slowed and then stopped, and the Relief Board found itself sitting on an increasing pile of money that no one seemed to need any more. After much discussion, by vote of the Masonic bodies that funded the Board, its name was changed to the Masonic Endowment Fund and its income was put to work paying for improvements on an aging Masonic building.

The same thing, often in much more drastic terms, happened to many other voluntary organizations that once occupied the roles currently more or less filled by government social welfare programs. In 1920, for example, something like 3,500 different fraternal orders existed in the United States, and around 50 percent of the country's adult population—counting both genders and all ethnic groups, by the way—belonged to at least one of them.[5] Reasons for belonging ranged across the whole spectrum of human social phenomena, but there were hard pragmatic reasons to put in a petition for membership at your local lodge of the Odd Fellows, Knights of Pythias, or what have you: at a time when employers generally didn't provide sick pay and other benefits for employees, most fraternal orders did.

If you belonged to the Odd Fellows, for example, you went to lodge one evening a week and paid your weekly dues, which were generally around twenty-five cents—that is, about the equivalent of a twenty-dollar bill today. In exchange, if you became too sick to work, the lodge would give you sick pay, and if you died, the lodge would cover the costs of your funeral and guarantee that your family would be taken care of. If, as often happened, the husband belonged to the Odd Fellows and the wife to the Rebekahs, the women's branch of the same organization, the family had a double claim on the order's help.

Here again, I can call on something more personal than the abstract facts found in old history books. My paternal grandfather's father was a city police officer in the wide-open port town of Aberdeen, Washington, and an Odd Fellow. In 1920 he was shot to death in the line of duty, leaving a wife and thirteen children. The Aberdeen Odd Fellows lodge paid for his funeral and then took care of his family—his children until they reached adulthood, his widow for the rest of her life. It's not an accident that my grandfather, when he was in his twenties, became a founding member of another community service organization, Active 20-30 International.

In 1920, Odd Fellowship was at the peak of its size and influence, and ranked as the largest fraternal organization in North America. Today, it's a faint flickering shadow of its former self. When welfare programs and employer-paid pensions came in, the core function of the Odd Fellows and many organizations like it went out by the same door. So, in due time, did most of the organizations. We once had a thriving Odd Fellows lodge here in Cumberland; the building is still there, with the letters IOOF in mosaic work on the front step, but the lodge is long gone.

Now it's only fair to point out that the shift from private relief funds to government welfare programs had certain definite advantages. The voluntary associations that handled relief in the pre-welfare era—fraternal orders such as the Freemasons and Odd Fellows, religious bodies such as churches and synagogues, and the like—had limited resources, and usually conserved them by limiting their relief payments to their members, or to other narrowly defined populations. To return to a point made earlier, the relief organizations of an earlier day had to treat their resources as a commons that could be destroyed by abuse, and so they put a variety of limits on access to those resources to make sure that the people who got help actually needed it, and weren't simply trying to game the system.

The deep pockets of government in an era of imperial expansion made it possible, for a while, to ignore such factors. The new social welfare programs could reach out to everyone who needed them, or at least to everyone whose claim to need them advanced the agenda of one political faction or another. The resulting largesse was distributed all over the class spectrum—welfare for the poor, a dizzying array of direct and indirect federal subsidies for the middle class, ample tax loopholes and corporate handouts to benefit the rich—and did a great deal to fund the lavish lifestyles

Americans by and large enjoyed during their nation's imperial zenith.

That's the kind of thing a society can do when it can draw on half a billion years of stored sunlight to prop up its economy, not to mention a global empire that gives it privileged access to the energy, raw materials, and products of industry that a half a billion years of stored sunlight made possible. Whether or not it was a good idea isn't really at this point. It's far more important to recognize that the welfare states of the late twentieth century were the product of a vast but temporary abundance of energy and the products of energy; they did not exist before that glut of energy arrived, and it's thus a safe bet that they won't exist after the glut is gone.

It's at least as safe a bet, mind you, that nobody in America will be willing to face that fact until long after the abundance of the recent past is a fading memory. The last decade or so of bickering in the nation's capital is more than adequate evidence of the way the winds are blowing. Republicans talk about jobs, Democrats talk about justice, but in both cases what's going on is best described as a bare-knuckle brawl over which party's voting blocs get to keep their accustomed access to the federal feeding trough. Choose any point on the convoluted political landscape of modern America, and the people at that position eagerly criticize those handouts that don't benefit them, but scream like irate wildcats if anything threatens their own access to government largesse.

It would be pleasant to suppose, as the United States slides down the trajectory of imperial decline and the number of Americans in serious trouble increases, that middle-class voters would recognize the severity of the situation and support, say, means tests on middle-class welfare programs, so that those who don't actually need help can be asked to step aside in favor of those who do. I hope none of my readers plan on holding their breath and waiting for this to happen, though. Quite the contrary: as economic contraction accelerates and energy and resource shortages bite harder, the fight around the feeding trough will just get worse. I doubt many of the combatants will take enough time from the struggle to notice that, in the long run, it's a fight with no winners.

In the time of limits ahead of us, no country on earth will be able to afford a welfare state of the kind that was common in industrial societies over the last century or so. That's one of the harsh realities of our predicament. National economies powered by diffuse renewable energy sources, bound by strict ecological limits, and coping with the instabilities of a damaged planetary biosphere, simply won't be able to produce the surplus wealth needed to make that a possibility. Methods of providing for urgent social needs that worked in the days before the economy of abundance are another matter, and for this reason it makes sense to suggest a revival of the old American custom of forming voluntary associations to fund and manage public amenities.

There are at least two important advantages to such a project, and both of them take the form of lessons that Americans once knew and are going to have to learn again in a hurry. The first is that a private association doesn't have the luxury of pretending that it has limitless resources. Currently some 60 percent of Americans receive more in the way of financial benefits from government than they pay in taxes. Conservative pundits like to insist that this means the well-to-do are getting robbed by taxation, but the facts of the matter are considerably more troubling: the gap in question is being covered with borrowed money—which means, in an era of quantitative easing, that it's being paid for by printing money. That's a recipe for massive economic trouble in the short term. A private association, by contrast, can't print its own money, and if its members vote themselves more benefits than the treasury can pay for, they will discover promptly enough why this isn't a good idea.

That's the first advantage. The second is closely related to it. The benefit funds of the old fraternal orders, and their equivalents across the spectrum of voluntary associations, learned two crucial lessons very early on. The first was that some people are solely interested in gaming the system for whatever they can get out of it, and are unwilling to contribute anything in return. The second is that allowing such people to get their way, and drain the fund of its resources, is a fast road to failure. The standard response was to limit access to the benefit fund to those who had contributed to it, or to the organization that sponsored it, at least to the extent of joining the organization and keeping current on their dues.

That's why the Masonic Relief Fund here in Cumberland bought coal only for those poor families who had a family member in Freemasonry, and why so many programs operated by other lodges, by churches, and by a range of other social institutions in the pre-welfare days had similar rules. The reasoning involved in this custom is the same logic of the commons we've discussed several times already in the course of this book. A relief fund is a commons; like any other commons it can be destroyed if those who have access to it are allowed to abuse it for their own benefit; to prevent that from happening, limits on access to the commons are essential.

There were also organizations that existed to provide help to people other than their own members, and in fact most of the old lodges directed some part of their efforts to helping people in the community at large—as indeed most of them still do. Here again, though, access to the limited resources that were available was controlled, so that those resources could be directed where, in the best judgment of the sponsoring organization, they would do the most good. Nineteenth-century talk about "the deserving poor"—that is, those whose poverty was not primarily the result of their own choices and habits, and who thus might well be able to better their conditions given some initial help—is deeply offensive to many people in our present culture of entitlement, but it reflects a hard reality.

Whether the habit of throwing money at the poor en masse is a useful response to poverty or not, the fact remains that a post-imperial America on the downslope of the age of cheap energy won't have the resources to maintain that habit even with the poor it's already got, much less the vastly increased numbers of the newly poor we'll have as what's left of our economy winds down. Those who worry about ending up destitute as that process unfolds need to be aware that they won't be able to turn to the government for help, and those whose sense of compassion leads them to want to do something helpful for the poor might want to consider some response that will be less futile than trying to pry loose government funds for that purpose.

In both cases, the proven approaches of a less extravagant time might be worth adopting, or at least considering. It's fair to admit that the voluntary associations central to those approaches won't be able to solve all the problems of a post-imperial society in a deindustrializing world, but then neither will anything else. They can, however, accomplish some good. In a time of limits, that may well be the best that can be done.

More generally, at a time when the United States is spending hundreds of billions of dollars a year it doesn't happen to have, and making up the difference by spinning the printing presses at ever-increasing speeds, a strong case can be made that rolling back spending increases and giving up tax breaks are measures that deserve serious consideration. Any such notion, though, is anathema to most Americans these days, at least to the extent that it might affect them. Straight across the convoluted landscape of contemporary American political opinion, to be sure, you can count on an enthusiastic hearing if you propose that budget cuts ought to be limited to whatever government payouts don't happen to benefit your audience. Make even the most timid suggestion that your audience might demand a little bit less for itself, though, and your chances of being tarred, feathered, and ridden out of town on a rail are by no means small.

The only consensus to be found about budget cuts in today's America, in other words, is the belief that someone else ought to take the hit.[6] As politicians in Washington, DC, try to sort out how many federal dollars to give to each of the many groups clamoring for handouts, that consensus isn't exactly providing them useful guidance. It will be interesting to see how long it takes before Congress runs out of gimmicks and has to admit to the crowd of needy, greedy pressure groups crowding close around the feeding trough that the gravy train has come to an end.

That latter detail is the one piece of news you won't hear anywhere in the current uproar. It's also the one piece of news that has to be understood in order to make sense of the American politics in the present and the near future. When the economics of empire start running in reverse, as they do in the latter years of every empire, familiar habits of extravagance that emerged during the glory days of the empire turn into massive liabilities, and one of the most crucial tasks of every empire in decline is to find some way to cut its expenses down to size. There are always plenty of people who insist that this isn't necessary, and plenty more who are fine with cutting all expenditures but those that put cash in their own pocket; the inertia such people generate is a potent force, but eventually it gives way, either to the demands of national survival, or to the even more unanswerable realities of political, economic, and military collapse.

Between the point when a nation moves into the penumbra of crisis, and the point when that crisis becomes an immediate threat to national survival, there's normally an interval when pretense trumps pragmatism and everyone in the political sphere goes around insisting that everything's all right, even though everything clearly is *not* all right. Each of the previous cycles of anacyclosis in American history has featured such an interval: the years leading up to the Revolutionary War, when leaders in the American colonies insisted that they were loyal subjects of good King George and the little disagreements they had with London could certainly be worked out; the bitter decade of the 1850s, when one legislative compromise after another tried to bandage over the widening gulf between slave states and free states, and succeeded only in making America's bloodiest war inevitable; the opening years of the Great Depression, when the American economy crashed and burned as politicians and pundits insisted that everything would fix itself shortly.

We're in America's fourth such interval. Like the ones that preceded it, it's a time when the only issues that really matter are the ones that nobody in the nation's public life is willing to talk about, and when increasingly desperate attempts to postpone the inevitable crisis have taken over the place of any less futile pursuit. How long the interval will last is a good question. The first such interval ran from the end of the Seven Years War in 1763 to the first shots at Lexington in 1775; the second, from the Compromise of 1850 to the bombardment of Fort Sumter in 1861; the third, the shortest to date, from the stock market crash of 1929 to the onset of the New Deal in 1933. How long this fourth interval will last is anyone's guess at present; my sense, for what it's worth, is that historians in the future will probably consider the crash of 2008 as its beginning, and I would be surprised to see it last out the present decade before crisis hits.

During the interval before the explosion, if history is any guide, the one thing nobody will be able to get out of the federal government is constructive action on any of the widening spiral of problems and predicaments facing the nation. That's the cost of trying to evade a looming crisis: the effort that's required to keep postponing the inevitable, and the increasing difficulty of patching together a coalition between ever more divergent and fractious power centers, puts any attempt to deal with anything else out of reach.

The decade before the Civil War is as good an example as any. From 1850 until the final explosion, on any topic you care to name, there was a Northern agenda and a Southern agenda, and any attempt to get anything done in Washington ran headlong into ever more tautly polarized sectional rivalry. Replace the geographical labels with today's political parties, and the scenery is all too familiar.

If there's going to be a meaningful response to the massive political, economic, and social impacts of the end of America's age of empire, in other words, it's not going to come from the federal government. It probably won't come from state governments, either. There's a chance that a state here and there may be able to buck the trend and do something helpful, but most state governments are as beholden to pressure groups as the federal government, and are desperately short of funds as a result. That leaves local governments, local community groups, families and individuals as the most likely sources of constructive change—if, that is, enough people are willing to make "acting locally" something more than a comforting slogan.

This is where the dysfunctional but highly popular form of protest politics critiqued earlier becomes a major obstacle to meaningful change, rather than a vehicle for achieving it. As that critique showed, protest is an effective political tool when it's backed up by an independent grassroots organization, one that can effectively threaten elected officials—even those of the party its members normally support—with removal from office if said elected officials don't pay attention to the protest. When that threat isn't there, protest is toothless, and can be ignored.

That distinction remains relevant, since very few of the groups gearing up to protest these days have taken the time and invested the resources to build the kind of grassroots support that gives a protest teeth. Yet there's another way that protest politics can become hopelessly dysfunctional, and that's when what the protesters demand is something that neither the officials they hope to influence, nor anyone else in the world, can possibly give them.

If current attitudes are anything to judge by, we're going to see a lot of that in the years immediately ahead. The vast majority of Americans are committed to the belief that the lavish wealth they enjoyed in the last half dozen decades is normal, that they ought to be able to continue to enjoy that wealth and all the perks and privileges it made possible, and that if the future looming up ahead of them doesn't happen to contain those things, somebody's to blame. Try to tell them that they grew up during a period of absurd imperial extravagance, and that this and everything connected with it is going to go away forever in the near future, and you can count on getting a response somewhere on the spectrum that links blank incomprehension and blind rage.

The incomprehension and the rage will doubtless drive any number of large and vocal protest movements in the years immediately ahead, and it's probably not safe to assume that those movements will limit themselves to the sort of ineffectual posturing that featured so largely in the Occupy protests a couple of years back. It's all too easy, in fact, to imagine the steps by which armed insurgents, roadside bombs, military checkpoints, and martial law could become ordinary features of daily life here in America, and the easy insistence that everything that's wrong with the country must be the fault of some currently fashionable scapegoat or other is to my mind one of the most important forces pushing in that direction.

Right now, the US government is one of those fashionable scapegoats. The pornography of political fear that plays so large a role in American public discourse these days feeds into this habit. Those people who spent the eight years of the second Bush administration eagerly reading and circulating those meretricious claims that Bush was about to impose martial law and military tyranny on the United States, and their exact equivalents on the other end of the political spectrum who are making equally dishonest claims about Obama as I write these words, are helping to feed the crisis of legitimacy that I discussed in detail earlier in this book. The habit that Carl Jung described as "projecting the shadow"—insisting, that is, that all your own least pleasant traits actually belong to whoever you hate most—has a great deal to do with the spread of that mood. I've wondered more than once if there might be more to it than that, though.

It's hard to think of anything that would give more delight to America's rivals on the world stage, or play out more to their advantage, than a popular insurgency against the US government on American soil. Even if it was crushed, as it likely would be, such a rising would shred what's left of the American economy, cripple the ability of the United States to intervene outside its borders, and yield a world-class propaganda coup to any nation tired of the US government's repeated posturing over issues of human rights. Funding antigovernment propaganda here in the United States without getting caught would be easy enough to do, and plenty of hostile governments might find it a gamble worth taking. I find myself suspecting at times that this might be what's behind the remarkable way that American public life has become saturated with propaganda insisting that the current US system of government is evil incarnate, and that any replacement whatsoever would necessarily be an improvement.

Now of course that latter is a common opinion in revolutionary eras; equally common, of course, is the discovery that as bad as the status quo might happen to be, its replacement can be much, much worse. Those who witnessed the French and Russian revolutions, to name only two examples, got to find that out the hard way. It would be helpful, to use no stronger word, to avoid a repeat of that same unpleasant object lesson in the post-imperial United States. As long as Americans keep on trying to convince themselves that the limits to growth don't matter, the profits of empire never came their way, and the reckless extravagance that American popular culture considers basic to an ordinary lifestyle is no more than their due, steering clear of some such outcome is going to be a very tricky proposition indeed.

It would be helpful, in other words, if more Americans were to come to terms with the fact that deciding what kind of future they want, and then insisting at the top of their lungs that they ought to have it, is not a useful response. Instead, it's going to be necessary to start by thinking, hard, about the kind of futures a post-imperial, post-petroleum America might be able to afford, and then trying to make the best possible choice among the available options. Making such a choice, in turn, will be made much easier once we have some practical experience of the way the various options work out in the real world—and this brings us back again to the question of local action.

Nobody knows what political, economic, and cultural forms will be best suited to thrive in the wake of America's failed empire, or to deal with the broader consequences as the industrial world stumbles down the long, ragged slope toward the deindustrial world of the future. Plenty of people think they know; there's no shortage of abstract ideologies proclaiming the one true path to a supposedly better future; but betting the future on an untested theory or, worse, on a theory that's failed every time it was put to the test, is not exactly a useful habit.

What's needed instead, as the United States stumbles toward its fourth great existential crisis, is the broadest possible selection of options that have been shown to work. This is where local communities and community groups can play a critical role, for it's precisely on the local scale that options can be tested, problems identified and fixed, and possibilities explored most easily. Furthermore, since the whole country isn't committed to any one response, options tested in different places can be compared with one another, and the gaudy rhetoric of triumphalism that so often fills so much space online and off—how many projects, dear reader, have you seen hailed as the one and only definitive answer to the crisis of our time, without the least bit of evidence to show that it actually works?—can be set aside in favor of straightforward demonstrations that a given option can do what it's supposed to do.

In an earlier chapter, for example, I discussed some of the possibilities that might come out of a revival of traditional democratic process. The simplest and most effective way to launch such a revival would be by way of existing community groups, which very often retain the remnants of democratic process in their organizational structure, or in newly founded groups using democratic principles. These groups would then become training grounds from which people who had learned the necessary skills could proceed to such other venues as local government, the organization of new political parties, or what have you, and put those skills to good use.

The same principle applies to almost any other aspect of our collective predicament you care to name. Whether the issue that needs a meaningful response is the impending shortage of energy and other resources, the increasingly unstable climate, the disintegration of an economy in which accounting fraud is nearly the only growth industry left, and so on down the list, the scale of the problem is clear but the details are murky, and the best way to deal with it remains shrouded in blackest night. For that matter, there's no way to be sure that the response that works best in one place will be suited to conditions elsewhere. Tackle the issues locally, trying out various options and seeing how well they work, and the chances of hitting on something useful go up sharply.

It will doubtless be objected that we don't have time for any such program of trial and error. Quite the contrary, we no longer have time for anything else. Spinning grand theoretical programs, waiting for the improbable circumstances that might possibly lead to their being adopted on a national or global scale, and hoping that they work as advertised if they ever do get put to the test, is a luxury best suited to those eras when crisis is still comfortably far off in the future. We don't live in such an era, in case you haven't noticed.

Over the decades ahead, the people of the United States and the rest of the industrial world are going to have to deal with the unraveling of an already declining American global empire, the end of a global economic order dominated by the dollar and thus by America's version of the imperial wealth pump, the accelerating depletion of a long list of nonrenewable resources, and the shattering impact of rapid climate change, just for starters. If history is any guide, the impact of those crises will likely be compounded by wars, revolutions, economic crises, and all the other discontinuities that tend to crop up when one global order gives way to another. It's going to be a very rough road—quite probably at least as rough as the road the world had to travel between 1914 and 1954, when the end of Britain's global empire brought the long peace of 19th century Europe to a messy end and unleashed a tidal wave of radical change and human blood.

Equally, the hard road ahead will likely be comparable in its scope and impacts to the harrowing times brought by America's first three rounds of anacyclosis. To live through the Revolutionary War, the Civil War, or the Great Depression was not an easy thing; those of my readers who are curious about what might be ahead could do worse than to read a good history of one or more of those, or one of the many firsthand accounts penned by those who experienced them and lived to tell about it. The records of such times do not give any noticeable support to the claim that we can have whatever kind of future we want. The hope they offer instead is simply that change is possible—that the stalemate that ends the cycle will not last forever. What lies beyond the inevitable crisis is a more complex matter, and requires at least a brief discussion.

AFTERWORD:
A CHOICE OF TOMORROWS

I T'S ONLY IN THE IMAGINARY WORLDS erected by madmen and politicians that the world is limited to one crisis at a time. In the real world, by contrast, multiple crises piling atop one another are the rule rather than the exception, and it is often the pressure of immediate troubles that puts a solution to the major crises of an age out of reach. Here in America, at least, that's the situation we face today. The end of the industrial age, and the long descent toward the ecotechnic societies of the far future, defines the gravest of the predicaments of our time,[1] but any action the United States might pursue to deal with that huge issue also has to cope with the less gargantuan but more immediate effects of the end of America's age of empire.

This latter issue has a great deal to say about what responses to the former predicament are and aren't possible for us. Among the minority of Americans who have awakened to the imminent twilight of the age of cheap energy, for example, far and away the most popular response is to hope that some grand technological project or other can be deployed in time to replace fossil fuels and keep what James Howard Kunstler calls "the paradise of happy motoring"[2] rolling on into the foreseeable future. It's an understandable hope, drawing on folk memories of the Manhattan Project and the Apollo program. There are solid reasons why no such project could replace fossil fuels, but let's set that aside for the moment, because there's a more immediate issue here: can a post-imperial America still afford any project on that scale?

History is a far more useful guide here than the wishful thinking and cheerleader rhetoric so often used to measure such possibilities. What history shows, to sum up thousands of years of examples in a few words, is that empires accomplish their biggest projects early on, when the flow of wealth in from the periphery to the imperial center—the output of those complex processes I've termed the imperial wealth pump—is at its height, before the periphery is stripped of its movable wealth and the center has slipped too far into the inflation that besets every imperial system sooner or later. The longer an empire lasts and the more lavish the burden it imposes on its periphery, the harder it is to free up large sums of money (or the equivalent in nonfinancial resources) for grand projects, until finally the government has to scramble to afford even the most urgent expenditures.

We're well along that curve in today's America. The ongoing disintegration of our built infrastructure is only one of the many warning lights flashing bright red, signaling that the wealth pump is breaking down and the profits of empire are no longer propping up a disintegrating domestic economy. Most Americans, for that matter, have seen their effective standard of living decline steadily for decades. Fifty years ago, for example, many American families supported by one person earning a full-time, working-class income owned their own homes and lived relatively comfortable lives. Nowadays, in many parts of the country, a single full-time, working-class income won't even keep a family off the street.

The US government's ongoing response to the breakdown of the imperial wealth pump has drawn a bumper crop of criticism, much of it well founded. Under most circumstances, after all, an economic policy that focuses on the mass production of imaginary wealth via the deliberate encouragement of speculative excess is not a good idea. Still, it's only fair to point out that there really isn't much else any US administration could do—not and survive the next election, at least. In the abstract, most Americans believe in fiscal prudence, but when any move toward fiscal prudence risks setting off an era of economic contraction that would put an end to the extravagant lifestyles most Americans see as normal, abstract considerations quickly give way.

Thus it's a safe bet that the federal government will keep following its present course, pumping the economy full of imaginary wealth by way of the Fed's printing presses, through artificially low rates of interest and a dizzying array of similar gimmicks, in order to maintain the illusion of abundance a little longer, and keep the pressure groups that crowd around the government feeding trough from becoming too unruly. In the long run, it's a fool's game, but nobody in Washington, DC, can afford to think in the long run, not when their political survival depends on what happens right now.

That's the stumbling block in the way of the grand projects that still take up so much space in the peak oil blogosphere: the solar satellites, the massive buildout of thorium reactors, the projects to turn some substantial portion of Nevada into algal biodiesel farms, or what have you. Any such project that was commercially viable would already be under construction—with crude oil hovering around $100 a barrel on world markets, remember, there's plenty of incentive for entrepreneurs to invest in new energy technologies. Lacking commercial viability, in turn, such a project would have to find ample funding from the federal government, and any such proposal runs into the hard fact that every dollar that rolls off the Fed's printing presses has a pack of hungry pressure groups baying for it already.

It's easy to insist that solar satellites are more important than, say, jet fighters, the Department of Education, or some other federal program, and in a good many cases, this insistence is probably true. On the other hand, jet fighters, the Department of Education, and other existing federal programs have large and politically savvy constituencies backing them, which are funded by people whose livelihoods depend on those programs, and which have plenty of experience putting pressure on Congress and the presidency if their pet programs are threatened. It's easy to insist, in turn, that politicians ought to ignore such pressures, but those who want to survive the next election don't have that luxury—and if they did make it a habit to ignore pressure from their constituents, where would that leave the people who want to lobby for solar satellites, thorium reactors, or the like?

Meanwhile the broader economic basis that could make a buildout of alternative energy technologies possible has mostly finished trickling away. The United States is a prosperous country on paper, because the imaginary wealth manufactured by government and the financial industry alike still finds buyers who are willing to gamble that business as usual will continue for a while longer. Mind you, the government's paper wealth is finding a dwindling supply of takers these days. Most treasury bills are currently being bought by the Fed, and while any number of reasons have been cited for this policy, I've come to suspect that most of what's behind it is the simple fact that other potential buyers aren't interested.

If the law of supply and demand were to come into play, interest rates on treasury bills would have to rise as the pool of buyers shrank. That's not something any US government can afford—the double whammy of a major recession and a sharp rise in the cost of financing the national debt would almost certainly trigger the massive economic and political crisis both parties are desperately trying to avoid. Instead, the torrent of paper liquidity allows the same thing to happen more slowly and less visibly, as creditor nations take their shares of that torrent and use it to outbid the United States in the increasingly unruly global scramble for what's left of the planet's fossil fuels and other nonrenewable resources.

A great many people are wondering these days when the result-ing bubble in US paper wealth—for that's what it is, of course—is going to pop. That might still happen, especially as a side effect of a sufficiently sharp political or military crisis, but it's also possible that the trillions of dollars in imaginary wealth that currently prop up America's domestic economy could trickle away more gradu-ally, by way of stagflation or any of the other common forms of prolonged economic dysfunction. We could, in other words, get the kind of massive crisis that throws millions of people out of work and erases the value of trillions of dollars of paper wealth in a matter of months; we could equally well get the more lengthy and less visible kind of crisis, in which every year that passes sees an ever larger fraction of the population driven out of the work force, an ever larger fraction of the nation's wealth reduced to pa-per that would be worth plenty if only anybody were willing and able to buy it, and an ever larger part of the nation itself turning visibly into one more impoverished and misgoverned Third World country.

Either way, the economic unraveling is bound to end in politi-cal crisis. Take a culture that assumes an endlessly rising curve of prosperity and place it in a historical setting that puts that curve forever out of reach, and sooner or later an explosion is going to happen. A glance back at the history of Communism makes a good reminder of what happens in the political sphere when rhetoric and reality drift too far apart, and the expectations cultivated by a political system are contradicted daily by the realities its citi-zens have to face. As the American dream sinks into an American nightmare of metastatic poverty, disintegrating infrastructure, and spreading hopelessness, presided over by a baroque and dysfunc-tional bureaucratic state that prattles about freedom while loudly insisting on its alleged constitutional right to commit war crimes against its own citizens, scenes like the ones witnessed in a dozen eastern European capitals in the late 20th century are by no means unthinkable here.

Whether or not the final crisis takes that particular form or some other, it's a safe bet that it will mark the end of what, for the last sixty years or so, has counted as business as usual here in the United States. As discussed earlier, this process of anacyclosis has happened many times before. The three previous versions of the United States—Colonial America, Federal America, and Gilded Age America—followed the same trajectory toward a crisis all too familiar from today's perspective. Too much political power diffusing into the hands of pressure groups with incompatible agendas, resulting in gridlock, political failure, and a collapse of legitimacy that in two cases out of three had to be reestablished the hard way, on the battlefield: we're most of the way there this time around, too, as Imperial America follows its predecessors toward the recycle bin of history.

Our fourth trip around the track of anacyclosis may turn out to be considerably more challenging than the first three, though, partly for reasons already explored, and partly due to another factor entirely. I've already discussed at length the twilight of America's global empire and the end of the age of cheap abundant energy, both of which guarantee that whatever comes out of this round of anacyclosis will have to get by on much less real wealth than either of its two most recent predecessors. The reason I haven't yet covered is a subtler thing, but in some ways even more potent.

The crises that ended Colonial America, Federal America, and Gilded Age America all came in part because a particular vision of what America was, or could be, was fatally out of step with the times, and had to be replaced. In two of the three cases, there was another vision already in waiting: in 1776, a vision of an independent republic embodying the ideals of the Enlightenment; in 1933, a vision of a powerful central government using its abundant resources to dominate the world while, back at home, embodying the promises of social democracy. (Not, please note, socialism. Socialism is collective ownership of the means of production, while social democracy is the extension of democratic ideals into the social sphere by means of government social welfare programs. The two are not the same, and it's one of the more embarrassing intellectual lapses of today's American conservatism that it so often tries to pretend otherwise.)

In the third, in 1860, there were not one but two competing visions in waiting: one that drew most of its support from the states north of the Mason-Dixon line, and one that drew most of its support from those south of it. What made the conflicts leading up to Fort Sumter so intractable was precisely that the question wasn't simply a matter of replacing a failed ideal with one that might work, but deciding which of two new ideals would take its place. Would the United States become an aristocratic, agrarian society fully integrated with the 19th century's global economy and culture, like the nations further south between the Rio Grande and Tierra del Fuego, or would it go its own way, isolating itself economically from Europe to protect its emerging industrial sector and decisively rejecting the trappings of European aristocratic culture? The competing appeal of the two visions was such that it took four years of war to determine that one of them would triumph across a united nation.

Our situation in the twilight years of Imperial America is different still, because a vision that might replace the imperial foreign policy and domestic social democracy of 1933 has yet to take shape. The image of America welded into place by Franklin Roosevelt during the traumatic years of the Great Depression and the Second World War still guides both major parties—the Republicans, for all their eagerness to criticize Roosevelt's legacy, have proven themselves as quick to use federal funds to pursue social agendas as any Democrat, while the Democrats, for all their lip service to the ideals of world peace and national self-determination, have proven themselves as eager to throw America's military might around the globe as any Republican.

Both sides of the vision for Imperial America depended utterly on access to the extravagant wealth that America could get in 1933, partly from its already substantial economic empire in Latin America, partly from the even more substantial "empire of time" defined by Appalachia's coal mines and the oilfields of Pennsylvania and Texas. Both those empires are going away now, and everything that depends on them is going away with equal inevitability—and yet next to nobody in American public life has begun to grapple with the realities of a post-imperial and post-industrial America, in which debates over the fair distribution of wealth and the extension of national power overseas will have to give way to debates over the fair distribution of poverty and the retreat of national power to the borders of the United States and to those few responsibilities the constitution assigns to the federal government.

We don't yet have the vision that could guide that process. I sometimes think that such a vision began to emerge, however awkwardly and incompletely, in the aftermath of the social convulsions of the 1960s. During the decade of the 1970s, between the impact of the energy crisis, the blatant failure of the previous decade's imperial agendas in Vietnam and elsewhere, and the act of collective memory that surrounded the nation's bicentennial, it became possible for a while to talk publicly about the values of simplicity and self-sufficiency, the strengths of local tradition and memory, and the worthwhile things that were lost in the course of America's headlong rush to empire.

I've talked elsewhere about the way that this nascent vision helped guide the first promising steps toward technologies and lifestyles that could have bridged the gap between the age of cheap abundant energy and a sustainable future of relative comfort and prosperity.[3] Still, as we know, that's not what happened; the hopes of those years were stomped to a bloody pulp by the Reagan counterrevolution, Imperial America returned with a vengeance, and stealing from the future became the centerpiece of a bipartisan consensus that remains welded into place today.

Thus one of the central tasks before Americans today, as our nation's imperial age stumbles blindly toward its end, is that of reinventing America: of finding new ideals that can provide a sense of collective purpose and meaning in an age of deindustrialization and of economic and technological decline. We need, if you will, a new American dream, one that doesn't require promises of limitless material abundance, one that doesn't depend on the profits of empire or the temporary rush of affluence we got by stripping a continent of its irreplaceable natural resources in a few short centuries.

I think it can be done, if only because it's been done three times already. For that matter, the United States is far from the only nation that's had to find a new meaning for itself in the midst of crisis, and a fair number of other nations have had to do it, as we will, in the face of decline and the failure of some extravagant dream. Nor will the United States be the only nation facing such a challenge in the years immediately ahead. Between the tectonic shifts in geopolitics that will inevitably follow the fall of America's empire, and the far greater transformations already being set in motion by the imminent end of the industrial age, many of the world's nations will have to deal with a similar work of revisioning.

That said, nothing guarantees that America will find the new vision it needs, just because it happens to need one, and it's already very late in the day. Those of us who see the potential, and hope to help fill it, have to get a move on.

Notes

Prologue: Understanding Empire

1. Hayakawa 1949, p. 44.
2. Ferguson 2002.
3. Ferguson, op. cit., p. 29.
4. Hochschild 1998.
5. Kipling 1899.
6. Ricardo 1963.
7. Spengler 1928, Toynbee 1954a.
8. Greer 2008, pp. 225–240.
9. See Tainter 1988 on the Roman imperial economy.

Chapter One: Origins of American Empire

1. See Mann 2006.
2. Mann, op. cit., and Grann 2009.
3. Dent 1995.
4. Hornborg 2001.
5. Catton 1961 is a readable summary.

Chapter Two: The Struggle Over Empire

1. Ferguson 2002.
2. O'Connor 1971.
3. McCabe 1874, despite its partisan biases, remains the only thorough study.
4. See, for example, Rothbard 2001.
5. The classic source is Smith 1952.
6. Tuchman 1966, 117–167, provides a readable account of the debate over American imperialism.

Chapter Three: America at Zenith

1. Fay 1975.
2. Spies 1977
3. Tuchman 1966, pp. 136–140.

4. Doyle 1892.
5. Lobell 2006.
6. Catton 1965 is a good narrative overview.
7. Middlebrook and Mahoney 1979.
8. See, for example, Dorpalen 1942 and Mackinder 1919.
9. Mackinder 1904, p. 436.
10. Mackinder 1919, p. 106.
11. Kennan 1947.

Chapter Four: The Failure of Politics
1. Polybius, Book VI.
2. Spengler 1928, vol. 2, pp. 431–435.
3. Kay 2011.
4. Domhoff 2013,
5. For example, Sprey & Wheeler 2009.
6. Machiavelli 1952, p.3.
7. Urbina 2011.
8. Nichols 1967.
9. Compare recent party conventions in the United States with those chronicled in, e.g., White 1961.
10. The classic study is Putnam 2000.
11. Mao 1966.
12. Schama 1989.

Chapter Five: The Economic Unraveling
1. Hubbert 1956.
2. See Zehner 2012 for a good survey of the problems.
3. Galbraith 1954, p. 69.
4. See, for example, Heinberg 2003 and Greer 2008.
5. shadowstats.com tracks unemployment and other official US economic statistics using unchanged methodologies; the results are eye-opening.
6. https://en.wikipedia.org/wiki/Petroleum_in_the_United_States, accessed 20 June 2013.
7. Meadows et al. 1972.
8. Heinberg 2007.
9. Daly 2011.
10. Prigogine and Stengers, 1984.
11. Parkinson 1958.
12. Korowicz 2012.

Chapter Six: The Specter of Defeat

1. I have relied in Drews 1995 for the following.
2. Massie 1992.
3. Clarke 1951.
4. "Malaclypse" 1970.
5. See, for example, United States Joint Forces Command 2007.
6. See especially Bloch 1968.
7. Gongora and von Riekhoff 2000.

Chapter Seven: The Consequences of Collapse

1. Estimates are based on Glasstone and Dolan 1977.
2. Harris and Paxman 1982.
3. United States Air Force 2009.
4. Runciman 1954.
5. Sharp 2013.
6. Greenberg 2012.
7. See, for example, Goble 2006.
8. Toynbee 1939.
9. Toynbee 1954b, pp. 1–72.

Chapter Eight: The Future of Democracy

1. Bureau of Justice Statistics 2012.
2. Korzybski 1994.
3. These are available in countless print and online editions; see nps. gov/liho/historyculture/debates.htm for a convenient online copy.
4. Plotinus 1992, p. 45.
5. The standard text is Robert 2011; Jennings 2008 is a good introduction.

Chapter Nine: Reinventing Society

1. Lavathes 1994.
2. Kunstler 2005.
3. Greer 2013.
4. Hardin 1968.
5. Ostrom 1990.
6. Ibid.
7. See, for example, Hopkins 2008.

Chapter Ten: Facing a Hard Future

1. This can be traced all the way back to Weiner 1948.

2. de Tocqueville 1840, p. 57.

3. Ibid, pp. 114–115.

4. See, for example, Icke 2001.

5. Ferguson 1979.

6. See, for example, Appelbaum and Gebeloff 2012.

Afterword: A Choice of Tomorrows

1. Greer 2008.

2. Kunstler 2005.

3. Greer 2013.

Bibliography

Appelbaum, Binyamin, and Robert Gebeloff, "Even Critics of Safety Net Increasingly Depend on It," New York Times, 11 February 2012, nytimes.com/2102/02/12/us/even-critics-of-safety-net-increasingly-depend-on-it.html?_r=0

Bloch, Marc, *Strange Defeat*, Norton, 1968.

Bureau of Justice Statistics, "Correctional Populations in the United States, 2011," United States Department of Justice, 2012.

Catton, Bruce, *The Coming Fury*, Doubleday, 1961.

———, *Never Call Retreat*, Doubleday, 1965.

Clancy, Tom, *Carrier: A Guided Tour of an Aircraft Carrier*, Berkley, 1999.

Clarke, Arthur C., "Superiority," Magazine of Fantasy and Science Fiction, August 1951.

Daly, Herman, "Growth, Debt and the World Bank," steadystate.org /growth-debt-and-the-world-bank/, accessed 26 June 2013.

Dent, Richard J., *Chesapeake Prehistory: Old Traditions, New Directions*, Springer, 1995.

Domhoff, G. William, "Wealth, Income, and Power," http://www2.ucsc .edu/whorulesamerica/power/wealth.html, accessed 20 May 2013.

Dorpalen, Andreas, *The World of General Haushofer: Geopolitics in Action*, Farrar & Rinehart, 1942.

Doyle, Arthur Conan, "The Adventure of the Noble Bachelor," The Strand Magazine, April 1892.

Drews, Robert, *The End of the Bronze Age: Changes in Warfare and the Catastrophe of c. 1200 BC*, Princeton University Press, 1995.

Fay, Peter Ward, *The Opium War 1840–1842*, University of North Carolina Press, 1975.

Ferguson, Charles Wright, *Fifty Million Brothers: A Panoply of American Lodges and Clubs*, Greenwood, 1979.

Ferguson, Niall, *Empire: The Rise and Demise of the British World Order and the Lessons for Global Power*, Basic Books, 2002.

Galbraith, John Kenneth, *The Great Crash 1929*, Houghton Mifflin, 1954.

Glasstone, Samuel, and Philip J. Dolan, *The Effects of Nuclear Weapons*, US Department of Defense, 1977.

Goble, Paul, "Chinese Come to Russia," Terra Daily, 10 February 2006; terradaily.com/reports/Chinese_Come_To_Russia.html; accessed 26 June 2013.

Gongora, Thierry, and Harold von Riekhoff, (eds.), *Toward a Revolution in Military Affairs? Defense and Security at the Dawn of the Twenty-First Century*, Greenwood, 2000.

Grann, David, *The Lost City of Z: A Tale of Deadly Obsession in the Amazon*, Random House, 2009.

Greenberg, Amy, *A Wicked War: Polk, Clay, Lincoln, and the 1846 U.S. Invasion of Mexico*, Knopf 2012.

Greer, John Michael, *Green Wizardry*, New Society Publishers, 2013.

———, *The Long Descent: A User's Guide to the End of the Industrial Age*, New Society Publishers, 2008.

———, *The Wealth of Nature: Economics As If Survival Mattered*, New Society, 2011.

Hardin, Garrett, "The Tragedy of the Commons," Science Vol. 162 no. 3859 (1968), pp. 1243–1248.

Harris, Richard, and Jeremy Paxman, *A Higher Form of Killing: The Secret History of Gas and Germ Warfare*, Hill and Wang, 1982.

Hayakawa, S. I., *Language in Thought and Action*, Harcourt Brace, 1949.

Heinberg, Richard, *The Party's Over: Oil, War, and the Fate of Industrial Societies*, New Society Publishers, 2003.

———, *Peak Everything: Waking Up to the Century of Declines*, New Society Publishers, 2007.

Hochschild, Adam, *King Leopold's Ghost*, Houghton Mifflin, 1998.

Hopkins, Rob, *The Transition Handbook*, Chelsea Green, 2008.

Hornborg, Alf, *The Power of the Machine: Global Inequalities of Economy, Technology, and Environment*, Alta Mira Press, 2001.

Hubbert, M. King, *Nuclear Energy and the Fossil Fuels*, Shell Development Company, 1956.

Icke, David, *Children of the Matrix*, Bridge of Love Publications, 2001.

Jennings, C. Alan, *Robert's Rules for Dummies*, For Dummies Press, 2008

Kay, Jonathan, *Among the Truthers: A Journey Through America's Growing Conspiracist Underground*, Harper, 2011.

Kennan, George F. (as "X"), "The Sources of Soviet Conduct," Foreign Affairs 24 (4), 1947.

Kipling, Rudyard, "The White Man's Burden," McClure's Magazine 12, 1899.

Korowicz, David, "Trade-Off: Financial system supply chain cross-contagion—a study in global systemic collapse," feasta.org/wp

-content/uploads/2012/10/Trade_Off_Korowicz.pdf; accessed 26 June 2013.

Korzybski, Alfred, *Science and Sanity: An Introduction to Non-Aristotelian Systems and General Semantics*, Institute of General Semantics, 1994.

Kunstler, James Howard, *The Long Emergency*, Atlantic Monthly Press, 2005.

Laszlo, Ervin, *Introduction to Systems Philosophy: Toward a New Paradigm of Contemporary Thought*, Gordon and Breach, 1972.

Lavathes, Louise, *When China Ruled the Seas*, Oxford University Press, 1994.

Lobell, Steven, "The Political Economy of War Mobilization," International Politics 43 (3), 2006.

Machiavelli, Nicolò, *The Prince*, trans. W.K. Marriott, William Benton, 1952.

Mackinder, Halford, *Democratic Ideals and Reality*, Holt,1919.

———, "The Geographical Pivot of History," The Geographical Journal 23 (4), 1904.

"Malaclypse the Younger," Principia Discordia, Rip Off Press, 1970.

Mann, Charles, *1491: New Revelations of the Americas Before Columbus*, Vintage, 2006.

Mao Tse-Tung, *Quotations from Chairman Mao Tse-Tung*, Peking Foreign Languages Press, 1966.

Massie, Robert K.,*Dreadnought: Britain, Germany, and the Coming of the Great War*, Ballantine, 1992.

McCabe, James D., *History of the Grange Movement, or, the Farmers' War against Monopolies*, National Book Co., 1874.

Meadows, Donnella, Dennis Meadows, Jorgen Randers, and William W. Behrens, III, *The Limits to Growth*, Universe, 1972.

Middlebrook, Martin, and Patrick Mahoney, *Battleship: The Loss of the Prince of Wales and Repulse*, Penguin, 1979.

Nichols, Roy Franklin, *The Invention of the American Political Parties*, Macmillan, 1967.

O'Connor, Richard, *The Cactus Throne*, Putnam, 1971.

Ostrom, Elinor, *Governing the Commons: The Evolution of Institutions for Collective Action*, Cambridge University Press, 1990.

Parkinson, C. Northcote, *Parkinson's Law: The Pursuit of Progress*, John Murray, 1958.

Plotinus, *The Enneads*, tr. Stephen MacKenna, Larson Publications, 1992.

Polybius, *The Histories*, tr. Evelyn Schuckburgh, Macmillan, 1889.

Prigogine, Ilya, and Isabelle Stengers, *Order Out Of Chaos*, Bantam, 1984.

Putnam, Robert D., *Bowling Alone: The Collapse and Revival of American Community*, Simon & Schuster, 2000.

Ricardo, David, *The Principles of Political Economy and Taxation*, repr. Richard D. Irwin, 1963.

Robert, General Henry M., *Robert's Rules of Order Newly Revised*, Da Capo Press, 2011.

Rothbard, Murray, *The Case for a 100 Percent Gold Dollar*, Mises Institute, 2001.

Runciman, Stephen, *A History of the Crusades, Vol. 3*, Cambridge University Press, 1954.

Schama, Simon, *Citizens: A Chronicle of the French Revolution*, Knopf, 1989.

Sharp, Jeremy M., *U.S. Foreign Aid to Israel*, Congressional Research Service, 2013.

Smith, Adam, *The Wealth of Nations*, William Benton, 1952.

Spengler, Oswald, *The Decline of the West*, tr. Charles Francis Atkinson, Alfred A. Knopf, 1928.

Spies, S.B., *Methods of Barbarism*, Human & Rousseau, 1977.

Sprey, Pierre M., and Winslow T. Wheeler, "Glossing over the F-35 JSF aircraft project," Jane's Defence Weekly, 6 May 2009.

Tainter, Joseph A., *The Collapse of Complex Societies*, Cambridge University Press, 1988.

de Tocqueville, Alexis, *Democracy in America*, tr. Henry Reeve, Weeks, Jordan & Co., 1840.

Toynbee, Arnold, *A Study of History, Vol. 5: The Disintegrations of Civilizations*, Oxford University Press, 1939.

———, *A Study of History, Vol. 7: Universal States*, Oxford University Press, 1954; cited as Toynbee 1954a.

———, *A Study of History, Vol. 8: Heroic Ages*, Oxford University Press, 1954; cited as Toynbee 1954b.

Tuchman, Barbara, *The Proud Tower*, Macmillan, 1966.

United States Air Force, Publication AFI21-204, Nuclear Weapons Maintenance Procedures, Department of Defense, 2009.

United States Joint Forces Command, Joint Operating Environment, *Trends and Challenges for the Future Joint Force through 2030*, Department of Defense, 2007.

Urbina, Ian, "Insiders Sound an Alarm amid Natural Gas Rush," The New York Times, 25 June 2011, nytimes.com/2011/06/26/26gas.html ?_r=3&; accessed 26 June 2013.

Ward-Perkins, Brian, *The Fall of Rome and the End of Civilization*, Oxford University Press, 2005.

Weiner, Norbert, *Cybernetics: Communication and Control in the Animal and the Machine*, MIT Press, 1948.

White, Theodore, *The Making of the President 1960*, Atheneum, 1961.

Zehner, Ozzie, *Green Illusions*, University of Nebraska Press, 2012.

Index

About the Author

JOHN MICHAEL GREER — Archdruid, historian, and
one of the most influential figures in the peak oil
movement, writes the widely cited weekly blog "The
Archdruid Report" and has published more than
twenty books on nature, spirituality and the future of
industrial society. His involvement in sustainability

issues dates back to the early 1980s, when he was active in the Ap-
propriate Technology movement and became certified as a Master
Conserver. He is the author of numerous titles, including *The Long
Descent*, *The Ecotechnic Future* and *The Wealth of Nature*. He lives
in Cumberland, MD, an old mill town in the Appalachians, with
his wife Sara.

If you have enjoyed *Decline and Fall,* you might also enjoy other

BOOKS TO BUILD A NEW SOCIETY

Our books provide positive solutions for people who want to
make a difference. We specialize in:

**Sustainable Living • Green Building • Peak Oil
Renewable Energy • Environment & Economy
Natural Building & Appropriate Technology
Progressive Leadership • Resistance and Community
Educational & Parenting Resources**